Finally It's Friday

Finally It's Friday

School and Work in Mid-America, 1921–1933

Loren Reid

University of Missouri Press
Columbia & London
1981

Copyright © 1981 by
The Curators of the University of Missouri
University of Missouri Press, Columbia, Missouri 65211
Library of Congress Catalog Card Number 80-27453
Printed and bound in the United States of America

Library of Congress Cataloging in Publication Data

Reid, Loren Dudley, 1905–
    Finally It's Friday.

    1. Reid, Loren Dudley, 1905–   2. Teachers—United
States—Biography.   3. Oral communication—Study and
teaching—United States.   4. Journalists—United States
—Biography.   I. Title.
PN4094.R44A33   070'.92'4 [B]   80-27453
ISBN 0-8262-0330-2

Dedication

Father and Mother, without whom this book could hardly have been written

Don, beloved kid brother, who really amounted to something, despite my early doubts

Ottmar Mergenthaler, German machinist-inventor, whose ingenious linecasting machine financed many years of our higher education

Undergraduate and graduate professors, formerly students at Johns Hopkins, Columbia, Cornell, Chicago, McGill, Toronto, Berlin, Paris, Leipzig, and even Podunk, who opened doors that could never again be closed

Publishers, printers, operators, schoolmates, roommates, and students, in Osceola, Grinnell, Vermillion, Chicago, Iowa City, and Washington, D.C.

Numerous adorable and indomitable folk who thrived on the steam locomotive, fussed over the internal combustion engine, patronized the first tourist camps, thrilled at newly paved roads, remember their first airplane, flew on the first commercial aircraft, heard the first radio and talking picture, explored the new field of speech, and so witnessed the incredible development of transportation and communication

All who survived the Great Depression—and also Prohibition, The Great Experiment

Gus—a party date, a dance date, and the world was never again the same

Preface

Every book should have a preface. As a schoolboy in Gilman City, Missouri, population 600, I took each mint-new textbook, turned to the opening page, and, above the line, opposite the corresponding letter, wrote *Peter Rabbit Eats Fish Alligators Catch Eels*. That took care of PREFACE. Below the line, starting at the right, the reverse: *Eels Catch Alligators Fish Eat Raw Pertaters*. That disposed of ECAFERP. I turned to the next blank page and wrote my name, along with a warning such as: *Death to All Who Borrow This Book and Don't Return It*. With these incantations, the book was safe to take to school. Sometimes I wish I had kept up the practice.

My forebears did not grow up in alligator country but they struggled against other natural enemies. Grandfather Tarwater owned a farm alongside Grand River, in northwest Missouri. A heavy spring rain made the river overflow and drowned out acres of young corn. Once, when I was fourteen, I walked with him across a soggy field and saw the destruction. He could replant, but the flooding could recur. It was Grandfather against the river. If he lost too many replantings, the shortened season would not let the corn mature. But each year he took the gamble, sometimes winning, sometimes losing.

What we know as the Roaring Twenties and the Depressed Thirties were like that. When the news was good, we flourished. When the news was bad, we suffered. We prospered during the booms and went under during the busts. If a bank failed, we lost our deposits. If a business collapsed, we got laid off. If the bottom dropped out of the corn market or the cattle market, it was even worse than being flooded.

In *Hurry Home Wednesday* (University of Missouri Press, 1978), I mused about what it was like to grow up in a small town, in a newspaper family that also ran the post office. Our lives were intensified on Wednesday, when my younger brother, Don, and I had to hurry home from school to help Father and Mother get out the paper. We were at the center of the action. Wednesday after Wednesday we printed the doings of the merchants, the doctors, the school, the coming of the auto, the effect of World War I, and the railroad, the Quincy, Omaha, & Kansas City, that nourished everything. When the news became bad, because of the unforgiving forces that defeated small towns everywhere, families had to move away. The revenues of our newspaper steadily declined, and Father lost the post office, so he sold out and moved to a larger town, with a larger newspaper, in Iowa.

During the boom-bust years, when I was a high-school, college, and university student, I continued to be a linotype operator in order to finance all that education. In the daytime I studied the ancient scholastic disciplines and in the evening set current local and national news. The details that filled my daytime hours and that clattered off the linotype keyboard at night reflected the background that has shaped the lives of all of us, even to today. In a single decade I helped to record the rise of the automobile, the peak years of the railroad, the dawn of commercial aviation. I saw radio develop from a feeble crystal set to a coast-to-coast network. I heard an experimental film that demonstrated simple acts like a banjo playing and a quartet singing, and moved on to Al Jolson and Rudolph Valentino. I was around when communication by radio, by public speaking, and by theater became significant enough so that a handful of university departments began to offer a Ph.D. in those areas. Though communication through newspapers and other forms of the written word more than held its own, communication through the spoken word exploded. Along the way I made the shift myself, from a career in newspaper publishing to one in teaching the art of the spoken word. The peak day of the week also shifted, from Wednesday to Friday.

These interchanges have led me not only to recount a personal narrative but also to reflect on some of the underlying events.

L. R.
Columbia, Missouri
October 1980

Contents

I. The Battle of the Boolge

1

What Mother and I really did that August day in 1921 was to make an eighty-five-mile trip in space and a forty-year trip in time. Well, anyway, twenty years.

I'll describe the eighty-five-mile trip first. Father had sold the *Guide*, published in Gilman City, population 600, and had bought the *Tribune*, published in Osceola, population 2,250. He had resigned his postmastership and had got Mother appointed acting postmaster, in charge of the town mail and three rural routes. He and my younger brother, Don, had gone to Iowa several weeks previously; Mother and I had remained in Missouri—to help the government keep the mail going, to advise the new editor and his wife, to collect overdue bills, and to auction off most of our household stuff and ship the rest. Now we were ready for the trip north.

I had spent the day before getting our 1914 Overland touring car in shape for the journey. One didn't just climb in and go. Before any venture those days we had to check oil and gas, tires, radiator, and battery. Old Betsy was more temperamental than most cars; if we neglected any of her necessities, she would give us trouble on the road. In her way she was the most distinctive car in town: steering wheel on the right, dull black body with white wooden-spoke wheels, upright two-piece windshield to which the top was firmly tied down with stovepipe wire, extra casings strapped on at the rear. Now she had settled herself on the dry, brittle grass of our front yard. Neighbors gawked as we brought out bundles and suitcases.

Old Betsy had never been driven as far as eighty-five miles; her life had been spent inside a twenty-five-mile circle. So, for that matter, had most automobiles of her acquaintance. "Do you think you can make it as far as Osceoly?" our neighbor, who ran the poultry house, asked, only half-jokingly. "Oh, sure," I replied confidently, "we'll be there in four hours."

Mother finally announced that she was ready to go. She stood just off Old Betsy's flank, dressed in her new, long, dark-blue dress, wearing a floppy straw hat, firmly anchored by a wide ribbon that passed over the hat and was tied under her chin, so her hat would not blow off during the ride. As usual, she refused to get in the car until I got it started, reflecting, I thought, a slight personal doubt. I flipped the ignition switch, adjusted spark and gas levers from the driver's seat, got out and gave the crank a few sharp, upward pulls. Spinning the engine was something to be deferred as long as possible; if it backfired on the upward pull the crank would be jerked harmlessly from your grasp, but if it backfired when you were pushing down, you might leave the scene with a broken arm. Yet even after many reckless revolutions of the crank, Old Betsy refused to start. Our small audience drifted away. Mother cranked, and I cranked again. "Go get Heinie," she said. We called on Heinie in times of stress.

Heinie, the most powerfully built man in town, with tattoos from elbow to shoulder, gave the crank such a spinning as was seldom seen, but when the engine failed to start, he unbolted the carburetor and carried it back to his shop, the Auto Livery. I trailed along, of course; my natural curiosity would not let me stay home and just wait. I watched him take the carburetor apart, remove the cork float, and shellac it to make it impervious to gasoline and thus float better. The shellac dried so rapidly that before long the float could be put back in the carburetor and the carburetor bolted to the engine. Old Betsy started immediately. Heinie would accept no pay for so slight a service; perhaps he considered it a good-bye present. And I learned a great truth; when a car won't start, remove the cork float from the carburetor and shellac it. Alas, I haven't seen a cork float since that August morning.

We drove up Broadway and down Main Street in low, taking a last look at the town where Mother had come as a bride, where I had been born sixteen years ago, and where both of us learned almost all that needs to be known about running a country weekly. After three or four blocks, we reached the city limits; I opened the cutout, gradually eased into high, and soon we were spinning along at twenty-five miles an hour. Old Betsy performed beautifully at twenty-five; but it you pushed her to thirty-five, the vibration made you feel that she was about to fly apart. We had no map, but we knew we would go through four different towns; at each stop we could inquire the best route to the next, though the road, now known as the Jefferson Highway, should be at least partly marked.

The trip in time was more subtle. I noticed one difference as soon as I passed the sign, "Missouri State Line." We had been driving over dusty roads just barely wide enough for passing; slowing down frequently for bridges to avoid being shaken up by the rough approach; watching for places made even narrower by erosion or by overhanging limbs; keeping alert for chuckholes that might break a wheel. Suddenly the road became wider; the yellow clay was freshly crowned and ditched; the hills had been tamed by heavy grading. When we suddenly overtook a steam-powered grader, with blade and big rollers, so different from the horse-drawn road drag that we were used to, we knew why the roads were better. We had never seen such opulence in road construction; we felt we were entering a new era.

Two hours later we saw the first advertising signs of Osceola merchants. At the edge of town we drove onto its brick pavement, passed the courthouse square, and arrived at the *Tribune*. Father and Don, who had been eyeballing the street all afternoon, rushed out to help us unload, took us inside to meet the staff, and then to the three-room apartment in a front corner of the building. Don had his own surprises to show us; he punched a button on the wall and the lights turned on, though it was still daylight. Electricity is available twenty-four hours a day, even Sunday, he explained, a novelty to a family that was used to service only from sunset until ten at night. Then in the back room he showed us a cooking facility: he lit a

match, turned a valve, and instantly we saw a low flame. "Gas," he announced. "It's not much of a flame," I noted. "It's hot enough," he declared. "And you don't need a tank, you don't need wicks, you don't have to pump up the pressure."

That seemed like enough technology to confront me with in one day, but he led me to the back of the *Tribune* office, and pointed to a sink with a faucet: "The city water isn't fit to drink, but you can wash in it," he commented, and then showed me, in a tiny closet nearby, a toilet with a high, overhead tank; he pulled a chain, and the water cascaded with an awesome rumble.

So in just a few minutes I saw these innovations that updated me by twenty years. In the weeks that followed I noticed still other differences. The milk was cold, having come from a market with refrigeration, and was in glass bottles, each capped with a circular, paraffin-coated, cardboard disk. You could see the cream line, which ran well below the neck of the bottle; if you did not shake it too hard, you could get a rich drink as well as a cool one. Gilman City milk had been delivered every afternoon in a small, red wagon; the milk came in tin buckets and was warm or cool according to the day's temperature. Its richness varied with the season; people said, unkindly, that when a cow went dry the dairyman added enough water to make up the difference. As for meat, well, Iowa has always been a great hog state, and the cold, boiled ham, fresh out of a big, walk-in refrigerator, cut on a mechanical slicer, made wonderful sandwiches with thick slices of bread haggled from a fresh loaf. Of course we were at the age when we believed store-bought food was better than homemade, anyway. We also noticed that flies were less numerous. Paved streets, regularly sprinkled and occasionally swept, plus the dwindling number of horses and privies, kept the fly population down.

We had been proud of the Rex Theatre in Gilman City, offering a movie three nights a week. The Lyric, however, had two shows every night but Sunday. And since it had two projectors, the operator did not have to interrupt the show after every other reel to change the film, though an experienced moviegoer could tell by the short blur that the pictures were coming from the other projector. Since the Rex had had only one, when these interruptions came at an exciting place, the audience let out yells of protest. As with the

Guide, the *Tribune* exchanged a weekly 2-column 4-inch ad for free admission to the movies for the whole family. Mother, a devoted fan, loved them all—Bill Hart, Tom Mix, Mary Pickford, Lillian Gish—and often after she had finished her long day at the office, she caught the second show.

Gilman City was served by the single-track Quincy, Omaha, & Kansas City Railway; everybody called it the O.K. And let me say at the outset that wild horses can't drag out of me a single critical statement about the railway I grew up with, which helped to develop the most productive land in northwest Missouri. Still, I have to record that Osceola had east-west, mainline, double track, Chicago-to-Denver service on the Burlington. Its long trains were equipped with Pullmans, parlor cars, and diners, as well as with the ordinary coaches and mail and express cars that I was accustomed to. And they stopped at the depot only two blocks from the *Tribune*.

As a child of the Great Train Era, I regularly feasted on the sight of the Burlington's big trains. To me they were as thrilling as ships in port, great planes rising into the sky, and rockets disappearing behind a fiery tail. Every day I passed the station on the way to school, sometimes finding my way blocked by the classy Chicago-Denver Limited. The long guardrails had been dropped down from either side of the street, and the bells started their dinging and the lights their flashing. As I had never seen Pullmans, though they had been around as long as Father, which is to say, forever, I gave them my full attention. I would walk past three or four of them, note their fancy names such as "City of Denver" or "Cortez," see the millionaires eating at the dining-car tables set with spotless linens, gleaming silver, and long-stemmed roses in vases. Eventually the guardrails would be lifted, the bells would stop ringing and the lights flashing, and the train would slowly pull out. As we watched the observation car recede into the hills, we would suddenly realize that this display of opulence was over, and that we still had physics and French ahead of us.

Osceola was also on a north-south Burlington spur, connecting us with Des Moines, sixty-five miles north. We were, therefore, a junction point. Just to live in a town that was a junction point added excitement to life. Eighteen passenger trains a day served our 2,250 people, plus numerous freight trains, with their mix of coal cars, boxcars, and odorous, slatted, stockcars. Considering the thousands of passengers and the thousands of tons of freight that moved through just this one town, I have to wonder at the colossal folly that made us neglect, and finally almost abandon, our nationwide mass transportation system.

No one then viewed Osceola's highways as a competitor to the Burlington. Anybody could see that the automobile was displacing the horse, but none would have dreamed that the change would affect the Denver Limited. Who would ride a horse to Denver? Since the big idea those days was to pamper the roads connecting county-seat towns, Osceola was well favored. Gilman City, not being a county seat, had had to be satisfied with secondary roads leading to the bigger towns; even these roads were often re-routed in a way that bypassed the small places altogether or stranded them at the end of a spur. Osceola was not only on an east-west route that linked it with Burlington and Omaha but also on a north-south highway that connected it with Minneapolis and Kansas City. These roads were to become federal highways 6 and 69, and later one of them an interstate freeway. This possibility was beyond imagining except, possibly, by editors and chambers of commerce secretaries who had their heads in the clouds, since roads then were dirt or clay, barely passable in bad weather. A driver on a slick road who slithers into a ditch spends little time dreaming about whether the road is on its way to becoming a federal highway or is doomed to become a county spur identified only by a letter like "A" or "KK."

Another notable difference in our relocation was that we had gone from a one-newspaper town to a two-newspaper town. The editor of the only newspaper in town can be fairly casual about it; in fact, Father often called the *Guide*, "The Great Moral and Religious Weekly." But here, we immediately saw that the other paper, the *Osceola Sentinel*, would throw up such persistent competition that newspaper publication would be a relentless struggle for survival. We had suddenly jumped into the twentieth-century style of pace and pressure. Father's writing lost some of its relaxed quality; if he poked fun at his own paper, people would take him seriously.

The differences didn't come from moving to a new state but from moving from a small town to a large town. After only a few days I had seen many ways in which we had also moved from Yesterday to Today, with Tomorrow right on our heels. I would become aware of other developments, more subtle but more revolutionary, in the months ahead.

2

To make a go of the *Tribune* was a supreme challenge to the whole family. The *Sentinel,* a Republican paper in a Republican county, was solidly entrenched under able, continuous management. We had poured our entire wealth into the *Tribune's* $18,000 price tag; we had to meet two $500 payments a year, plus 5 percent interest. The payroll was an enormous $90 a week—$30 each for the printer and the operator, $20 for the reporter-ad salesman, and $10 for the receptionist, who also did reporting. For $18,000 you could buy almost any business around the square, or equip half a dozen doctors' or dentists' offices. You could buy twenty Buicks, loaded with self-starters, demountable rims, and Klaxon horns. You could send ten boys to college and keep them there, two, maybe three years.

The twenties and thirties were peak years for the newspaper profession. Big cities had three or four *dailies;* smaller cities like nearby Creston had at least one. Nearly every town had a weekly. Iowa, in fact, had more than five hundred, two hundred of which eventually disappeared. Competition for news, ads, and subscriptions was hot, but the struggle stopped at the front office. On mechanical details, papers cooperated. If one paper had a power failure, a breakdown, or was hit by fire or flood, its competitors did everything possible—worked all night if necessary—to help get that paper printed and in the mail on time.

Don, now a high-school freshman, became the principal press feeder, presiding over the big Huber's two tons of rollers and cylinders with the skill of a journeyman. Typesetting for the office was done on a Linograph, a brand less expensive than the Linotype or Intertype, but also less rugged. It was on the market only a few years. Ours, being an early model, needed constant adjusting. We replaced it with a new Linotype that was equipped to set different sizes of type. As about that time the operator left us, Mother took over the job of typesetting, or, as we put it, she ran The Machine. Father assumed the ad selling and much of the newswriting. Our foreman was Ledru Barstow, himself the son of a printer. Everybody worked a fifty-three-hour week, from 8:00 A.M. to 6:00 P.M. with an hour off for lunch. A nine-hour day is a long day. On Saturday, however, we quit at 5:00, and over the years I still remember how sweet it was to quit an hour early on Saturdays.

The owner and editor of the *Sentinel* was Frank Abbott, whom we called "Uncle Frank." He had the advantage of long residence and continuity; we were out-of-state newcomers. His Republican politics were in harmony with the majority of the county's voters. The *Sentinel* had the larger circulation and wore the image of the "established" newspaper. Even the name, *Tribune*, was new; the paper had started as the *Osceola Democrat*, but the previous owner had changed it because the Democratic party carried so little clout either in Clarke County or the State of Iowa. Since the turn of the century, Iowa had not had a Republican governor, and in national elections had gone Republican except when Woodrow Wilson had carried it. In those days, since political parties were blood cousins to religion, most papers had to be identified politically. Few things in the business world are as difficult as for Number Two to overtake Number One, whether the commodity is newspapers or rent-a-cars.

Our situation, however, did have a solid floor under it. Neither Father nor Uncle Frank wanted to start a price-cutting war. Though they competed bitterly for every ad and sale bill, they did have an arrangement that if a stranger came in off the street in an obvious bartering mood, sought a price on, for example, five hundred bills, got a bid of $4 and walked away without ordering, that editor would call the other and say, "I just gave a fellow a price of $4 on five hundred bills." When the stranger showed up at the other office, the price for the same job would be $4.15 or more—any sum over $4—and as likely as not he would pay the extra 15 cents rather than walk all the way back. On other jobs, though, bidding was competitive; each editor sought a fair profit, so that no price war got under way. In general the *Sentinel*'s customers were loyal to them and ours to us, though we thought our better equipment and newer typefaces gave us an edge in the quality of work turned out.

The two papers also had a cooperative policy of "picking up" ads. If Ettinger's department store gave the *Tribune* a 3-column 10-inch ad and later told the *Sentinel* to "use the same ad as the *Tribune*," the *Sentinel* was free to pick up the ad we had already set up—a saving in manpower. Or if we heard that the *Sentinel* had sold a 2 x

10 ad to the Blackbird Cafe, we would ask the proprietor if we could print the same ad—"you won't have to write new copy for us"—and often were given permission to use it. The policy had to be implemented with caution, however; when the printer from one office came to make the pickup he could observe a hurried covering of already-printed sheets and partly made-up pages to keep him from gleaning information about what the opposition had in store in the way of news and ads. Covering up was doubly necessary because any printer can read print or type as easily upsidedown as rightsideup. Sometimes I keep in practice by holding the hymnal upsidedown in church; this behavior confuses my neighbor and has been known to make him lose his place in his own book.

One never knows when a dormant talent will be useful. Years later when we were in Cambodia, seeking a plane to Bangkok, we suspected there would be far too few seats on the incoming Vietnamese Airline plane to accommodate the crowd at the airport, but were able to get our names on the waiting list along with a few others who shared this premonition. So undependable was the available information that the French-speaking official at the airline counter did not actually know how many seats would be available until the plane arrived and he could make a count. I stood at the counter and saw, at his elbow, the waiting list, with my name toward the bottom. Handwriting is more difficult to read upside-down than print, but I was able to spot our names. As he ticked off the names ahead of ours I saw we were getting closer and closer to seats. At that juncture an American couple, talking volubly, tried to talk him out of two spaces, and seemed about to succeed. I leaned over the counter, pointed to our names, and said quietly, "Regardez les priorités, monsieur, s'il vous plaît." The effect was immediate; he abandoned them, turned to me, smiled, handed over two boarding passes, came around to the front of the counter, personally tagged our luggage, and escorted us to the gate. Mr. and Mrs. Pushy, left behind, couldn't imagine what had happened to them. They probably thought we were the French prime minister and his lady.

3

Though the hours were as long, Wednesday's press day did not have the same buildup of tension in Iowa that it had had in Missouri, because the work was shared by more people. Don and I still had to hurry home after school but our absence was not so conspicuous if we were delayed. Yet we had little hope of being finished before midnight, and often 2:00 A.M. came before the last paper was printed, addressed, and bundled.

There were exceptions. One incredible Wednesday I showed up at the office right after school and the final pages were *already* on the press, being printed. At 4:30 the press was silenced, at 5:00 the folder, and at 5:30 the job of printing two thousand papers was completely finished. We stood and stared at each other.

As quitting time was not until 6:00, Mother and Don, somewhat dazedly, began to pick up the torn and wrinkled sheets that littered the floor, sheets that had been misprinted or misfolded. Father gathered scattered sheets of copy and proof. I picked up mats under the Linotype and did the next morning's job of graphiting spacebands. (Don't go away—this is no more complicated than polishing your silver.) Edna Beaman, our receptionist and reporter, rinsed the paste pot and put away the roll of binder twine, the leftover sheets of yellow paper, and the mailing machine, a hand-operated Wing Horton. Foreman Barstow turned to the stones—the marble surfaces of a print-shop worktable—and returned scattered types, slugs, and spacing materials to their proper places. Normally these were Thursday morning chores.

For once, everyone left at 6:00. We went to our apartment and munched sandwiches with glasses of cold milk. Mother's announcement that she was going to the Lyric sounded like a prime idea, so we scanned the newly printed *Tribune* to see what the film was—not that it ever mattered. At 7:00 we were there, each with a big nickel sack of buttered popcorn. That first press day on which we finished before quitting time still looms in my mind as vividly as a first date with a nice girl, and with a similar, all-pervasive magic.

Facing the Thursday cleanup was like facing the kitchen the morning after a late party. The ritual began by comparing the new *Sentinel* with the new *Tribune*, the two issues side by side on one of the big tables. The first step was to check the number of pages; if We had eight and They had eight, the week was a standoff. If They had ten and We had only eight, we felt that we had each taken a personal beating. Obviously They had picked up some advertising that We had not. If We had ten and They only eight, we cheered like spectators at a finish line. In general the odds were so over-whelmingly against us that we magnified any margin of victory, however slight. Win or lose, we checked advertiser by advertiser to see where the margin, either of defeat or victory, was. We also reviewed news stories, to see if We had covered the week without overlooking anything vital, and if our write-ups were more complete or more accurate. We were pleased if We had dug deeper into sources than They had. Any newspaper loves a scoop, especially on a big story, but these are hard to come by; in a small town news travels fast.

Father developed the philosophy that the opposition must not be allowed to get the bulge on you. Led accepted this point of view wholeheartedly; the *Sentinel* is "a great nuispaper," he declared, in his own inimitable pronunciation, and if it got the "boolge" on you, you would never catch up. So we worried about the "boolge." They outbid us on a job; We got a new subscriber and They didn't; one of Their subscribers came over to us; one of ours went over to Them. If They started getting ahead, They would work all the harder. Never let the competition get the edge, the advantage, the momentum; in short, don't let them get the boolge.

After this soul-searching ritual, Don and I scurried to school while others began the cleanup. First came the weekly sweeping of the floor with sweeping compound, an odorous mix of oily sawdust, with a whiff of formalin or other disinfectant to give the premises a sani-tary smell. Next came the cleanup of pages of type. Following a marked copy that indicated what was to be saved and what was not, Led lifted fistfuls of linotype slugs and put them in galleys—shallow metal trays—eventually to be dumped into the big refining pot with its gas burner and remelted into three-pound chunks called "pigs." Ads scheduled to be run again were saved. Even doubtful ads were saved in case the advertiser decided to rerun them; a printer's heartiest dislike was to have to reset an ad that he could have saved. Hand-set lines had to be distributed, character by character, into the typecases.

I mention these ancient procedures because half a century later cleanup time had shrunk to minutes if not seconds. In our day we relished the deep-seated satisfaction of cleaning up eight pages in two or three hours, because we could recall when the paper was set by hand and cleanup took a day and a half. A housewife who has

soaked her week's wash overnight in a copper boiler, using a powerful solution of Fels-Naphtha or lye soap shavings, boiling the clothes
the next morning while stirring with a length of broom handle, then
rubbing each piece over a washboard, with extra strokes to collars
and cuffs, and then, after running everything through a hand-
operated wringer, has hung each piece on a line, with starching and
ironing still to come, shudders over these memories as today she
sets the dials of her washer-dryer. She and her contemporary, the
printer, are among the last practitioners of vanished skills.

All sorts of things could go wrong. In times of stress Father could
swear as elegantly as George Washington and Mark Twain com-
bined. So could any printer. Despite this environment, I never
heard Mother swear at all. Well, maybe once. On a cleanup morning when she needed to replace the standby supply of metal for the
Linotype, she started down the rickety basement stairs to get a
double handful of pigs, slipped, missed her footing, and tumbled to
the bottom. I heard the noise from the back of the shop, ran to the
head of the stairway, and stood aghast at the heap of arms, legs,
ruffled skirts, and mussed hairdo that represented my one and only,
ever-loving mother. She was, after all, a woman of solid and substantial proportions. I rushed down the stairs to survey the wreckage closer, not quite knowing what part to take hold of first. I
needn't have troubled. She waved off all help, gradually sorted
herself out, rose to a semi-sitting position, shook herself to see if
anything flew off, gave a pat to her hair, and exclaimed: "Gosh
almighty darn!" It was her mightiest oath.

I exploded into laughter, helping her to her feet. She climbed the
stairs under her own full, ample power, shunning further assistance.
She was entirely unhurt—hardly even bruised. The Lord had decided He would let her off easy, at least this once. Later I carried up
enough pigs to supply her machine for days.

4

Father could not completely woo away established *Sentinel* customers like the Spurgeon or Ettinger department stores. An Ettinger clerk once said that if the firm advertised a Saturday potato
special in the *Sentinel* he would bring in fifty sacks of potatoes from
the warehouse, whereas if the ad appeared in the *Tribune* he would

bring in only thirty-five. This hard reading of the market was difficult to overcome.

Father did have a few favorites among the advertisers, mostly proprietors of lesser establishments, but their small 2-column and occasionally 3-column ads helped swell the total. Among his friends was Paul Beecham, owner of a family-operated tailor shop, who was one of the *Tribune*'s most faithful customers. Naturally he had a kindred sympathy for the total involvement of the Reids in the newspaper business. "Your father should be real proud of you," he once told me. Before I could break out a full grin, he added: "You're good, cheap help." These words became a family expression.

Father also had a steady patronage from Osceola's two butcher shops. They looked pretty much alike: counter along the side with large scales that had dials front and back; two hard maple chopping blocks, each bearing hundreds of marks left by cleaver or saw; quarter or half beef or hog carcasses hanging from hooks just behind the blocks; occasionally part of a sheep carcass; several chickens and a turkey or two, feathers plucked but still equipped with head, feet, and insides. Toward the back was the large, walk-in refrigerator: ice-cooled in the South Side Market, electrically refrigerated in the East Side.

If you wanted a couple of round steaks, the butcher brought a leg of beef from the refrigerator, patted it to get the proper contour for cutting, gave his knife a couple of passes on the steel, asked how thick you desired your steak to be, and cut it to order, pausing halfway through the slicing to saw the bone. Next he tore a piece of waxed paper from its roll, put the steaks on it, and weighed the packet, making a mental calculation and then announcing the cost, awaiting your nod before he wrapped your meat in the paper and tied it with a string. Or he would put slices of freshly carved liver in a paper boat, or scoop a pound of lard from a tub, or bring out a long string of wienies, tearing off fifteen inches or so to meet your exact personal needs. Butchers had a keen eye for weights, knowing just how many pork chops to saw if you wanted precisely two pounds. And they could produce anything from that giant refrigerator; I often requested cold boiled ham, sliced to order on a hand-cranked circular slicing machine that could be adjusted to make the cuts as thick or thin as I liked. For years now, butchers have hidden in the back ends of supermarkets or at central distributing points. You can see their cellophaned wares but never the artistry of their craft. The arrangement is more sanitary but the fascination has gone forever.

Although neither of our butchers cared to write ads, Father was delighted to assume this duty. For the South Side Market he extolled the advantages of cold, pure ice as the choice way to keep meat fresh. For the East Side Market he described the superiority of controlled, low-temperature, electric refrigeration. Both proprietors knew that he was composing the script for both sides of the argument, but each had a strong feeling about his own way of doing, and happily accepted Father's advocacy of his cause. This rivalry gradually deepened into the Great Osceola Meat Market War, with boiling beef, fancy grade, going as low as four cents a pound, picnic hams at nineteen cents, and premium bacon at twenty-five cents.

F. W. Paul, proprietor of the implement store on the West Side, adored big ads with big type. As Father never saw any sound reason for selling a customer who preferred a half-page display ad a mere 3 x 10, he provided layouts with large type, ample illustrations, and lots of white space. The Paul ads offered such notable items as a John Deere spreader for only $165, or an iron-clad wagon, complete with triple box-spring seat, and the best scoop available, a steal at $135. Farming then did not call for the massive investments of capital that it did later. Mrs. Paul, the store's bookkeeper, saw little reason for spending money on advertising, so Father discovered that he could almost always sell an ad if he talked to Mr. Paul, and almost never if he talked to Mrs. Paul. Tidy bits of technique like this are seldom found in the books taught in schools.

If Father had had even a halfway clear crystal ball, he would not have selected 1921 as the time to quadruple his debts. He had been in Osceola only a few months when he, along with the merchants, noted that the economy was dwindling. I can see him now, bent over his desk, green celluloid shade over his eyes, black sleeve protectors pulled over his cuffs to his elbows, penciling two columns of figures; the short one, with large sums headed by the mortgage payments, representing amounts owed, and the long one, made up of small sums like $2 and $5, representing amounts due the office. He was operating on such a slender margin that I learned not to ask for spending money when he was adding columns.

The spring of 1922 was such a demoralizing time for Iowa farmers that many sold out altogether. For a few weeks the influx of sale bills and sale ads was a prime source of revenue, helping to compensate for reduced advertising by the merchants around the courthouse square. Father was unbeatable as a salesman. He knew the auctioneers well—the leading crier, Col. Clell Collier, was, in fact, a staunch Democrat—and the bank officials who acted as clerks; from them he often got advanced notice of who was planning a sale. He and I made many a trip in Old Betsy over country roads, struggling with steep hills, sharp turns, potholes and mudholes, to locate a farmer, get copy for his sale bill, and then, as an added clincher, persuade him to run the whole bill in the *Tribune*—a 4-column 15-inch ad. "Just one extra bidder," Father argued, "will more than repay the cost of the ad."

Father's rearing on a farm meant that he could talk the language. Each success created its own small ripple effect; the farmer's neighbors, seeing the *Tribune* ad, would likely advertise with us when they held their own sales. A few extra 4 x 15's more than offset a lost Red Ball Store ad and meant that the *Tribune* could occasionally come out with ten pages to the *Sentinel*'s eight, enough to make Uncle Frank in his turn worry about the boolge.

Advertising is the major source of newspaper revenue; subscriptions are a drop in the bucket. If the competition with the *Sentinel* were to be met, it had to be met on the advertising front. Our opposing the *Sentinel* was much like the *Des Moines Capital*, which today nobody remembers, bucking the *Des Moines Register*. Often the Thursday morning huddles revealed that we had the boolge on the news but the *Sentinel* had the boolge on the advertising. Once in a while, however, the *Tribune* scooped it on both counts. We could see that those happy Thursdays, while rare, were coming along more frequently. Those slender rays of cheer kept the family going.

5

When I was not in school or running the machine, I helped with reportorial duties. One of my assignments was to visit the hospitals.

Medical and dental services were not only years ahead of those in my small Missouri town, but superior to those in many other Iowa count-seat towns. Dr. Sells, Dr. Harken, and the Drs. Shively not only had a general practice but each had an attached hospital, doing many kinds of surgery: tonsils, adenoids, appendixes, gall bladders, fractures. Vaccination and inoculation, rare in small towns, were a common occurrence in Osceola. X-rays were available. Blood transfusions, however, or sulfa drugs and antibiotics, were still unknown. For general anesthesia, physicians used ether and veterinarians used chloroform. Patients went to Mount Vernon for "consumption," and to Des Moines and the Mayo Clinic for advanced and dangerous operations, but Osceola physicians could manage most ailments that came along. Osceola dentists were also good; they used drills powered by electric motors, not foot treadles; they gave shots for extractions; they straightened teeth and did minor surgery.

I realized I was in a new medical world when one day I went to see Dr. Harken for a stomach ailment. He located the sensitive spots, examined my nose and ears, peered in my mouth, took my temperature, listened with his stethoscope to my breathing, asked several questions in a cheerful tone of voice, and finally announced that I had probably eaten something that I shouldn't, and that I would certainly be all right in a couple of days.

Suddenly I realized that the examination had come to an end and that I was not given any medicine: no castor oil, no calomel and salts, no pills of any kind. I could not believe what was happening. "Do I need to take any medicine?" I asked, thinking he might have overlooked this vital step. "No," he replied, "you'll be all right without it. Take things easy and don't eat a lot of junk. Call me, though, if you don't improve in a day or so."

I left in a daze; I could not see how you could get well if you did not take any medicine. Nothing like this had ever happened before. By week's end I had fully recovered. As the years went on and served up other encounters of this sort, I realized that doctors were learning to rely more on nature's own healing abilities and less on medicines. The doctor's main concern became to discover what was wrong and not to reach routinely for some drug but to determine whether the ailment would go away in the natural course of events. Once he was reasonably sure of that outcome, he did not interfere with the process. So in still another way I crossed a time line.

Two of our hospitals were white-frame, three-story structures; the third, just across the alley from the *Tribune*, consisted of two floors above a business establishment. The growing practice of each hospital was reflected in continual remodeling and expanding. Despite their internal rivalry, they collectively gave Osceola the reputation of having good regional medical facilities. Osceola achieved this notoriety perhaps because of its network of railroads and highways and its location in a prosperous area. Or maybe the reason was that our physicians got the boolge over those in neighboring communities and never yielded the lead.

As a reporter, I knew the physicians at close range. The hospital people were glad to see me, since news of prominent people making splendid recoveries from serious illness or operations was fine publicity at no cost. Because of the keen rivalry, each physician was eager to make the news columns. Although, in fact, it might have been wiser not to mention the names of hospitals at all, generally we did, trying to be evenhanded about it. Father had always liked to boost the business and professional fraternity; that policy occasionally had got him in hot water even in Missouri and he quickly saw that it was disastrous in Iowa. What was printed had to be lean, unadorned, and factual.

I became accustomed to the odor—ether and carbolic acid predominating—that told me as soon as I walked through the door that I was among sick people. Basically a hospital consisted of an office and waiting room, a treatment room, an X-ray room, and a cluster of private rooms. These latter were simple affairs—a white-enameled iron bed and stand with a pitcher of water and a tumbler, a white cabinet with a bedpan in it, a scrubbed linoleum floor—all surrounded by white walls and ceilings. Anybody could enjoy this cleanliness for a dollar or two a day. A woman could have an appendix or a baby removed, enjoy full care for the two weeks that either of these situations usually demanded, and the total bill for both hospital and physician would not be far beyond fifty dollars.

One day a nurse had an exciting story to tell of two baby boys that had been born, one at midnight and the other at dawn, each weighing eight and a half pounds. In the confusion the babies got mixed, so that no one knew which boy belonged to which mother. As the mothers had not seen their babies, they were of no help. When the hospital staff embarrassingly revealed the predicament, the mothers were upset and the angry fathers threatened to sue. Here were two unidentifiable babies, each in his own way adorable, each dearly hoping to be fed and loved, and here were two sets of parents, eager to supply a lifetime of care and affection to the proper baby.

In desperation, the nurses summoned the physician who had presided over both deliveries. Fortunately he had made a mental note of a detail that enabled him to associate each baby with its own mother—so all was solved to the satisfaction of the parents and, for that matter, to mine. The incident so appealed to my imagination that, after interviewing the physician, I gave it full front-page treatment. I compared this mixup to the one in Mark Twain's *Pudd'nhead Wilson*, of two babies that had been switched in the crib and had therefore grown up in vastly different environments. Nothing that had happened in Osceola had ever received such nationwide publicity, and I suspect the record still stands. What especially became discomfiting to the local hospital was that most of the editors who reprinted my account added a paragraph boasting that *this* mishap could never happen in *their* hospitals, because of name tags, bracelets, or footprints. Our hospital, which had expected commendation for solving a puzzle, was mortified to read the kind of publicity that actually followed and promptly issued a denial, claiming that the second boy had been labeled at birth with a white ribbon around its ankle, along with other notations duly recorded. So my love affair with that hospital came to an abrupt end; the staff continued to give me news items but with less ardor. Father and Mother, however, thought it was a good story. I was delighted to see it reprinted in the newspapers that came to our desk the next two or three weeks.

And there were other assignments. One Monday afternoon Father said: "Son, a missionary is speaking tonight at the Methodist Protestant Church. His name is Hilary Marshall. He's here from Africa. Will you write a short squib about the meeting?"

I said I would, but when press day rolled around and he asked me where my story was, I had to admit that I had forgotten the meeting and, therefore, wasn't able to write anything.

Father was annoyed. "I didn't ask you to go to the meeting; I just asked you to write it up. You don't have to hear a dadburn missionary speak to know what he's going to say."

He sat down at his typewriter and in minutes had produced a page of copy. The Reverend Mr. Hilary Marshall met with a small but enthusiastic group at the Methodist Protestant Church Monday evening. The Reverend gave a vivid description of his experiences among the African tribes, commenting not only on the medical help the church was bringing to the natives but also on the growing attendance at religious services. He mentioned that at first the mission had met stubborn resistance, but he persuaded the tribal chief to the way of the cross, and that afterwards, one by one, others followed. Right now the enterprise was desperately short of funds, but he hoped Osceola people would contribute what they could. If everybody gave only a small sum, the mission would be able to carry on its work. The Reverend was gratified by the reception that he had received at meetings throughout the country, but was especially impressed by the interest of Osceola church people.

Father concluded this masterpiece of bogus eyewitness, on-the-spot reporting with: "The talk was much enjoyed by those present and it is believed that new ideas were developed in the minds of listeners as to the importance of the missionary branch of church work."

I took the sheet to the machine and left it on the copy tray. Anyone could tell, I reflected, that Father had set down transparent generalities. Since I was a regular patron of the Methodist Protestant Sunday school, I was beginning to regret that I had not attended the meeting and written the story myself. Still, there was nothing to do but print it as Father wrote it.

The morning after press day I was in the front office when a distinguished-looking stranger entered and asked to buy a copy of the *Tribune*. Something in his resonant voice instantly told me: "This is the Reverend Mr. Marshall. He is going to read Father's story, recognize it for the fraud it is, and since I am the only one here, he will give me the dickens." I tendered him a copy and shamelessly took his nickel. He stood there, scanned the columns, and settled down to read. I awaited the blast.

"Did you write the news story about the missionary meeting at the Methodist Protestant Church?" he asked.

I had to be truthful. "No, I didn't. The editor wrote it personally."

"Well, tell him I have traveled over the Midwest and this is the finest write-up we have had." I replied lamely that at the *Tribune* we liked to do things right. When he left, I felt greatly relieved, as I was not fully prepared to answer detailed questions.

I also filed away the thought, for future reference, that the world is not overrun with originality and that after an editor has heard a few dozen political or religious speeches he can make a fair guess as to what the next one that comes down the pike will be like. In fact, I

Part of the *Tribune* staff in 1927: Gene McFarland (advertising), Edna Beaman (receptionist and reporter), Dudley Reid (proprietor), and Oran Ames (foreman). In the left foreground is a lever-operated paper cutter; rear left, barely visible, the Huber cylinder press; along the right side, work surfaces and typecases.

have myself heard an overload of just such speeches. Specific detail is a priceless, rare, commodity.

To set the record straight, I need to say that Father, or other good newspaper men of my acquaintance, would walk the second mile or make a dozen telephone calls to get an important fact straight. And I have seen him write and rewrite paragraphs so that when printed they reflected not only actual circumstances but also movement and mood. When I told him the epic climax of his missionary story, he grinned and said: "Most of us get so few compliments that it's flattering to hear one even if we don't entirely deserve it."

6

The Clarke County Courthouse was the scene of another of my news beats; its park was also a popular playground for the town boys.

The red brick building sat at a hub with eight spokes—four

sidewalks that ran to the surrounding streets plus four others that angled to the corners. The park, deeply shaded with maples and elms, had massive benches where shoppers could rest, and a bandstand for summer evening concerts or occasional patriotic ceremonies. Just past the west side of the square was the tall water tower. Near one crosswalk was a twenty-foot Alaska totem pole, two feet in diameter, with three great heads, one atop the other—a strange sight for a midwestern prairie town. A resident, seeing it on one of his travels, had decided it should be displayed in Osceola and had arranged for the shipment; the city fathers took it from there. Along two sides of the park, hitching chains were strung for the convenience of rural shoppers. As the years went on, however, more cars were parked around the square and fewer teams and buggies. Even during my stay I saw a few of the chains come down.

One Saturday afternoon we were playing baseball in the park, our outfield backing up against a row of teams. Now and then a batted ball rolled under the chain and we had to retrieve it from around the horses' hooves. Any adult could have predicted what was bound to happen. Before long, some one knocked a fly ball into the ribs of a horse; he and his companion reared, broke their reins, backed the buggy into the street, and ran away at full speed. In earlier days I had set many a story about what had happened when a runaway team panicked. I suddenly remembered I had an errand to run— and I was not the first to have such a thought.

Monday morning the prosecuting attorney called on Father at the *Tribune* office. As soon as I learned the purpose of his visit I drifted into the back room but kept within hearing distance; one never knows when he can pick up information that will prove revealing and useful. The attorney explained that the buggy had been smashed, the total damage being $48. So far, so good; nobody had been maimed or killed. Eyewitnesses, however, tattlers and gossips of the most odious sort, had given him the names of six young baseball players. Regrettably the list was astonishingly accurate, even including me. The attorney was entirely good-natured about the incident; I recall his saying, "We know, Dudley, that boys will be boys." The owner had agreed that if he could sell six shares in the demolished buggy at $8 each, he would drop charges; Father was offered a share at the going rate. He got his checkbook and, pleasantly enough, wrote a check for $8. He probably contemplated putting his own young player out on waivers—$8 would buy a ton or two of newsprint. When the attorney left I strolled into the front office to participate in a little plea bargaining, but Father simply quizzed me about what had happened and then observed that it was time for me to go to school.

Later I learned that one boy's father, a poor man, did not have $8 to cough up and saw no reason why he should have to pay merely on somebody's say-so that his son was involved. What followed was not a cheerful "boys will be boys," but jawboning and angry threats. So I learned at an early age that justice wore a pleasant face for the boy whose father could write an $8 check and a stern face for the boy whose father couldn't.

In later years I noted also that boys and girls who came from average or better homes enjoyed a certain protection by the community and were probably entirely unaware of it. In fact, I myself once wrote an $8 check for a boy who eventually reached admirable manhood. Boys and girls, however, who come from poverty-stricken homes—the American phrase, "the wrong side of the tracks" was once literally true—have a rougher time of it. Public defenders, consumer advocates, and small-claims courts are a recent adaptation in the law's evolution.

On the courthouse lawn I heard my first radio. One of the boys had constructed a cat's whisker, crystal radio, and he and two others were tinkering with it when I happened by. We clustered around the set in great expectation and, finally, heard faint musical sounds—from where, we never knew. It was pure, unbelievable magic. Pulled out of the obviously empty air around me, the sounds were my first inkling of other dimensions. I was vastly impressed.

Soon afterwards on my hospital rounds I dropped in to visit Dr. Sells. I found him at a relaxed moment, and in the course of our conversation I mentioned that I had heard my first radio. "Come with me, son," he said and led the way to a small cubbyhole, containing a table and chair. On the table was a set, a tall horn, and a huge amplifier with three dials, powered by what we called a "storage" battery. He also showed me his logbook, a list of stations with the proper setting for each dial. Since each set had its own idiosyncrasies, each owner had to twiddle the dials randomly until he located a station, making fine adjustments for the best effect, and then recording the settings so that next time he could find that station. In short order Dr. Sells tuned in a station, and despite howls, squeals, and buzzes, he brought talk and music from faraway Des Moines right into the room. He had paid $700 for the set—twice what a Ford then cost. The thought of this immense wealth staggered me; not many families could ever afford a full-size, battery-powered radio. My memory of radio begins with these two sets; months passed before I saw a third. Most people sensibly concluded that radio was a gadget they could get along without.

Mainly, though, I remember the courthouse itself, since I visited it every week in search of news. I can close my eyes and call back its pervasive odor: a mix of sweeping compound, spittoon effluent, ancient cigar smoke, stale air, and disinfectant from the public rest rooms in the basement. If you were blindfolded and led at random into a depot, grade school, livery stable, or courthouse, even in a strange town, you could identify each one. Some odors never change.

I regularly called on N. S. Wiley, justice of the peace. He was red-faced, broad-bodied, and so badly crippled with rheumatism he could hardly climb the stairs to his small office, yet he carried on, day after day. He was agreeable to talk to, and, seldom being overly busy, was willing to visit. As his conversation was punctuated with asthmatic wheezes, a news story took a while to emerge. Once I commented on his sticking to the job when he was not in good health. "Son (wheeze)," he declared, "I may wear out (wheeze) but I'm not going to (wheeze) rust out (more wheezes and a coughing spell)." How could I ever forget this tincture of wisdom? If Dickens had known Wiley, he would have written a book about him.

Sometimes Wiley gave me information about a marriage or a hen house burglary, and sometimes a tip on a major crime that sent me bounding to the sheriff's office. As the sheriff was usually surrounded by cronies who had dropped in to chew tobacco and gab, I often found it difficult to hold his attention long enough to get the details I needed. As a consequence, the *Sentinel* got longer and better stories on any given still-raiding or hog-stealing than I got. Often I had to ask three questions when one should have done. I sharpened a host of reportorial and conversational skills while standing at the corner of the desk of a Republican county official. The sheriff apparently did not think that what appeared in "the other paper" was important, until Father, realizing that I was having to do a lot of wheel-spinning, marched to his office one day and reminded him that the duty of an elected official was to serve all citizens, even Democrats, and to supply legitimate information to both papers, even the Democratic one. As Father described the interview later, "I touched him up a little." Father could talk straight, even saltily, when the occasion warranted, and I had better luck at the court-house after word of his visit got around.

As the early twenties were peak years of the great Prohibition adventure, the sheriff's office had prime information about raids on homemade wineries, breweries, and distilleries. One man was arrested for manufacturing peach brandy and selling it for $7.75 a quart—truly a double offense. Another was caught with a hoard of forty gallons of homemade brew, plus a barrel of fruit mash. Des Moines authorities who had analyzed it declared that it had already foamed its way to a 4 percent alcoholic content. Another raid located $20,000 worth of liquor; our sheriff made news when he refused to turn this prize over to the United States marshal. A hot jurisdictional fight ensued, but Clarke County's lawman refused to give it up. We rejoiced in this legal victory but history is dark about what happened to all that splendid booze. When other local operators were caught with supplies of rye mash, red-eye, or white mule, the sheriff hauled the accused persons before the justice of the peace, to face the choice of making a $500 bond or going to the county clink.

The vast fortunes, however, were made in the big cities. An enterprising Des Moines citizen transformed distilled water, alcohol, and flavoring ingredients into fifteen-year-old rye, Scotch, or bourbon, in fifteen minutes. By only slightly different formulas he produced sparkling burgundy and champagne. Using bottles adorned with lithographed labels and authentic-looking seals, corks, and caps, he took the merchandise he manufactured for $14 a case and sold it to selected customers at $140. The lush years of bootleg-gers and speakeasy operators lasted until the first year of the Roosevelt administration, when the Twenty-first Amendment repealed the Eighteenth. Iowa's talent did not achieve the notoriety of Chicago's or New York's but in later years it could narrate its own adventures, both in and out of court. Our bootleggers were as gifted as anybody's bootleggers.

Other offenses passed through the courthouse. One poor devil was caught stealing watermelons in the nighttime. If he had hooked a couple by daylight he might have gone free, but the law draws a distinction between day crimes and crimes at night when people are sleepy and more easily terrified. The defendant was fined $10 plus $3.15 in costs, but when it appeared that he could not raise these sums, he was released on his promise to pay later. I doubt if the fine was ever paid and I doubt even more that Wiley sent him any reminders.

One day the sheriff got a report that four suspicious characters driving a battered Hudson had been seen near Murray, ten miles west. Accompanied by three deputies, the sheriff charged westward, reached the car, and ordered the men out of it. Instead, the men started shooting, got the drop on the lawmen, and forced them to lie on the ground; then they drove away in the sheriff's car, but had a puncture and returned to their Hudson. Once more they started to leave, and when a farmer who was dragging the road seemed to threaten their escape, they shot him; later he died of his wounds. One of the gang members, Fintelman, was captured soon thereafter and brought to Osceola on a charge of first-degree murder.

The trial was the most exciting event in years. Both papers had reporters on hand as the jury was selected and witnesses called. Each evening our reporter typed pages of copy that I set on the Linotype. Each day I relieved him at court for a brief time so he could organize his notes; when he resumed his post in the courtroom, I transformed my own notes into copy. We hoped that the verdict would be in on Wednesday, so we could come out with live news on Thursday, but the trial dragged. Not until late Saturday did the case finally go to the jury.

At the *Tribune* we held a council on strategy. As we had the story in type, we decided to publish an extra when the jury brought in its verdict. We wrote headlines to cover every possible outcome, so we could be sure to hit the streets before the opposition.

At 5:00 in the morning the verdict came in: first-degree murder, with imprisonment for life at hard labor. In less than an hour Don and I were out hawking copies, selling to early risers on the streets or to those who came to their doors when we went past shouting the headlines. We were elated by our achievement. The *Sunday Register* arrived in Osceola on the morning train but with no mention of the verdict, and the *Sentinel* did not give its readers a full account until the following Thursday. So we won handily this phase of the battle of the boolge.

I also called regularly at the county clerk's office. My curiosity led me to scan all sorts of public documents; some led to news stories and some didn't. Reading divorce petitions was my first exposure to the unhappy side of domestic life. Here was Anna, praying for divorce from Robert and the other relief requested in such cases, giving the names and ages of their children, and alleging inhuman treatment. Here was Nancy, with three minor children, seeking divorce from Mark, praying that he be restrained from coming to her premises, charging cruel and inhuman treatment and lack of support, seeking judgment for attorney's fees and maintenance for their daughter. Here was Cecilia, having problems with George; they had lived together as man and wife for seven years; now she was seeking the care and custody of their child. We printed only a few of these items, the *Sentinel* printed only a few; divorce then was rare, difficult to understand, embarrassing to talk about. A divorced woman was a little suspect; if not actually classed as a "fast" woman, she was associated with a failure of respectability. There was a taint, a tarnish, that no doubt contributed to the rarity of divorce, not to mention the total economic vulnerability that must have haunted thousands of never-made decisions.

For months my courthouse interviews exposed me to what is usually called the dignity and majesty of the law. But to me the law is not Blackstone, writing its principles, nor Madison and Hamilton, debating the Constitution, nor John Marshall, interpreting its broader aspects. It is not Daniel Webster, who made more appearances before the Supreme Court than anybody, nor J. Edgar Hoover, who broke the stranglehold of a tenacious band of criminals. The law is justice of the peace Nathan Wiley and circuit-court judge Homer Fuller, who presided over the Fintelman trial and a hundred others. It is the sheriff, mostly serving subpoenas and overseeing foreclosures, but at times bringing in robbers, and, at least once, murderers. It is the county clerk, filing documents and preparing the court calendar. It is Mabel seeking a divorce from James, and Reuben, watching the lawmen carry away his peach brandy. It is a brick building in a park, with benches, a bandstand, and a length of hitching rack. It is a runaway team, a demolished buggy, and an $8 check. And in this mix of images is a twenty-foot Alaskan totem pole, bearing three heroic faces, steadfastly gazing, in one sense at everybody, and, in another, at nobody at all.

7

Osceola had a separate building for its high school; younger kids had their own buildings elsewhere in town. It seemed strange to Don and me to see a school that had a grassy front yard, not a cluster of swings and teeter-totters on a trampled dirt surface. Moreover, the student body was five times larger than the one we had left behind in Gilman City. Don was in a freshman class not of 20 but of 105. My senior class had 41; the Missouri class I left behind had 11. Most of our Iowa schoolmates had traveled together through eight years of the town's grade schools; Don and I were total strangers.

As I have always had a sentimental feeling about doing something for the first time, I can readily visualize the small group that first Monday morning just outside the front door, which would not be unlocked until classes were to convene. I listened to the easy football talk of the others, all of whom seemed poised and confident. I was wearing long trousers, feeling uneasy even though I knew no one there realized they were my first pair. Back in Gilman City I would have had to endure the usual kidding that a boy needed to face when he abandoned knee britches and appeared in long pants. This ordeal was one of the rites of manhood, like starting to shave, or hearing your voice suddenly break from its newly acquired tenor or baritone into its previous childish cackle, or going on your first solo date. In a small town everybody, yes everybody, notes these landmarks and everybody, yes everybody, has a comment.

Someone asked if I were the new boy from Missouri and I said I was. "How come you're wearing shoes?" he demanded, in an unneighborly fashion. "They do feel strange," I grinned. "In Missouri we go barefooted until the snow falls. . . . Even the girls," I added, warming to the discussion. He was not prepared for that kind of reply, so he turned to his friends and resumed the football talk. I listened intently. I had never seen a football.

Soon my attacker resumed the skirmish. "Is it true that Missourians suck eggs?" I had an answer for that hoary gag: "Just the Republicans." For the moment the laugh was on him. "Do you know one reason I'm proud to be a Missourian?" He did not especially care to be informed, but I went on: "Missouri has produced so many great men. Name a great Iowan."

This question was a poser, but he made a quick and creative shift: "Well, you name a great Missourian." "Mark Twain and Jesse James, to start with," I offered. Just then the bell rang; I was as relieved as he was.

As I had not yet even registered, I was sent to the main office, and found myself sitting across the desk from the superintendent himself, Daniel Boone Heller. Heller, short, chunky, powerfully built, with a full, lopsided face that usually crinkled into a full lopsided smile, immediately made me feel at home, asking what courses I had already had.

Then came another eye-opener: there were not just four classes available (the situation I had been accustomed to), but four different *courses* of study: normal training, leading to a certificate to teach in grade school; English, which led to anything and everything; commercial, which included typing, shorthand, and bookkeeping; and Latin, which was college preparatory. I had no intention of going to college, but since my previous three years of courses best fit the Latin curriculum, he put me there.

I signed for something called civics, which Heller taught himself; English literature, physics, Latin, and, as an extra, typing. But just imagine—I could have taken chemistry, French, art, or manual training. The building had a gym, though it was one of those inept facilities that doubled as an auditorium, and everybody took a gym class; there was a music hour in which everybody participated; anyone could try out for sports, school plays, speech contests, debates.

From the superintendent's office I went next door to his classroom, where students were already assembling. When he entered and called the class to order, I saw he would be fully in charge. He began by reading the headlines from the *Register*, inviting our comments on the day's news. He was well informed and knew how to spark a discussion.

Heller, a controversial figure, had been hired to improve discipline. The previous year he had captained such a tight ship that students had rebelled, but he put down the rebellion, demanded good order, gave teachers powerful support when problems arose, and now had complete control. The management of classes by individual teachers is always easier when the general atmosphere is businesslike. Moreover, most students would really rather be learning than wasting time. Heller also took a keen interest in extracurricular activities, which helped that mystical asset called school spirit.

Gradually I formed impressions of the rest of the faculty. My English teacher, whom I will call Mrs. Z, as in zero, was not merely the worst teacher I ever had; she was no teacher at all. She spent each hour asking simple questions from the text. With the book immediately in front of us, we gave simple answers. What year was Wordsworth born? 1770. What was his first important work? The *Lyrical Ballads*. What year did it appear? 1798. How old was he then? 28. Since then I have had other mediocre teachers whose names I have forgotten, but Mrs. Z I cannot shake out of my mind. Perhaps one reason I later became a teacher was the secret assurance that at least I could do better than Mrs. Z, though in the years that followed I had bad days when I equaled her worst performances. Heller, sympathetic to her as a person, knew she eventually had to go. On her part she must have been happy to abandon a situation that was over her depth and at times even intimidating.

Physics with Mrs. Bailey, the principal, was intriguing because of the laboratory sessions. We studied wheels, levers, gases, and magnets, in connection with heat, light, and sound, now dismissed irreverently as "classical physics." A typesetting machine, for example, is chock full of classical physics, with its springs, slides, levers, temperatures, air cushions, gravity pulls, wheels, gears, and bolts. Mrs. Bailey would have been astonished to know that she had a practising physicist in her midst, but I never told her.

One day I read in the text that if you set an alarm clock ringing, put it under a tightly sealed glass dome, and then pumped out the air, the sound of the alarm would grow fainter and fainter. When the air was exhausted, you would not be able to hear the bell at all. I looked forward to having this nonsense exposed. On the appointed day, Mrs. Bailey set up the experiment and explained what would happen. She wound the clock, started the alarm, positioned it under the dome, clamped the dome down tight, and began to operate the vacuum pump. Though she pumped vigorously, the bell sounded as loud as ever, just as I had expected all along. Finally she stopped, explaining, lamely I thought, that the pump was not working properly. I escaped with my common-sense notions intact.

An important adjunct of Osceola High School was the City Library, a few blocks south, something lacking in Gilman City and also in many county-seat towns. When Andrew Carnegie gave away millions to endow libraries, he included a few thousand for Osceola. One morning when I was browsing I read that he had made $24 million at the turn of the century, $48 million the next year, and $96 million the next. Not everybody can double his income three years in a row. I was aghast that one person could earn so much, but grateful that Osceola got at least a chunk of his wealth.

Then there was my first football game, approached with excitement and anticipation; only big schools can have a football team. The game was not at all what I had imagined. As the field had no bleachers, the spectators moved along the sidelines, following the ball. The contest was monotonous. Our team advanced the ball a few yards and then kicked it to the visitors; in turn they moved it a few yards and kicked it back to us. During the first half nobody scored at all. I did not see much point in standing and shivering when so little was happening. If this was football, I wanted no part of it.

Yet I did learn one priceless lesson that cold afternoon. No activity, whether football or tennis, grips your attention unless you know what is going on in the players' heads: what they are trying to do, and what skills are demonstrated in doing it. In fact you can't become interested in anything at all—music, art, going to school, running a newspaper—unless you get involved in it.

8

When I was twelve and Don was nine, I could have cheerfully traded him for a Ranger bicycle. By nature he was a slow mover, whereas I was quick; the very moment I sought someone to play chess with or go along on an errand was exactly the moment he wanted to reread the funnies. Moreover, as he was reluctant to learn various bits and pieces of the printing craft, the elders in the family found it simpler to assign these tasks to me than to teach him. Hardly a day went by without a squabble.

I could recite times when he was just plain stupid. He himself recalls our being in Bethany and visiting an indoor toilet, a luxury he had never seen before, and the moment of my pulling the chain; when he saw the sudden gush of water, he thought I had broken the tank. I should have demonstrated the old trick of standing him in the bowl, bidding him good-bye and holding him firmly in place while the water rushed past his feet.

Sometimes he watched me, just for kicks, pour raw gasoline on the cement floor, and, after lighting the Linotype burner, set the puddle on fire, just to see it burn harmlessly away. Once when I was seated at the machine,he decided on his own to touch a match to half a cup full of gasoline; the sudden flare made him toss the blazing cup away, unfortunately in my direction, so I was enveloped in flame. As he saw me slowly turn incandescent, he yelled: "Should I go tell Father?" "No, no," I shouted, "not that—see, it's burning itself out." I danced around maniacally, slapping at wisps of flame. Though my overalls were smoking in places, I happily had no burns. I shudder to think of the penalities if I had let him go running to Father.

In short, when I was twelve and Don was nine, he was a bother, a nuisance, and at times a hazard. But when I was sixteen and he was thirteen, he had become alert, willing to manage his share of the chores, and on occasion even to volunteer to do something he wasn't required to. He became bright, even brilliant. Do all kid brothers undergo such a transformation?

I began to enjoy having Don around and also to associate with his friends as well as with my own. His group included two spirited, venturesome boys, Sport Stansell and Scappy Squier. Occasionally I went to the movies with this trio, later taking part in their nighttime exploits, such as going swimming in the city reservoir. Though city water was not drinkable, swimming in the reservoir was strictly forbidden. Don and I were naturally law-abiding, but Don was determined his friends would not outdo him, so when they suggested swimming, he went along. And as I was three years older, I could not, in pride and honor, back out, so I accompanied them. Since no one would drink the water anyway, I thought it ridiculous not to allow us to swim in it. We stripped at the edge of the lake and splashed around, keeping an alert eye for the watchman. Once we had a close call, but saw him in time to scoop up our clothes and scamper away before he realized what was going on.

After the movie one night, the Fearless Trio proposed to climb the city water tower, which was five stories high but seemed like fifteen. My heart froze when I heard the suggestion, but though I had the responsibility as the older person to veto such a foolhardy notion, I had an even greater responsibility to believe in my own spirit and courage. Since none of them hooted the idea down, we moved silently to the base of the tower, as committed to the climb as if we had taken an oath and had written our names in blood. We had passed the point of no return.

I looked at the narrow iron ladder that snaked along one of the tall, steel legs stretching up into the black sky—lighted only partly by the feeble aura from the streetlights. At the point where the massive cylindrical tank protruded over its four legs, the ladder turned outward for a couple of rungs, then went straight up along the side of the tank itself, then over the top to the summit. Those two rungs were the most hazardous part of the climb since one would have to depend almost entirely on the strength of his arms. I recalled that twice Don had fallen from trees, and once he had been unconscious all night; and that as a result Father had sternly forbidden him to climb any more trees. Nothing, however, had been said about water towers.

In seconds we were scampering up the ladder, Don first, I last. The boys did follow my urging to space themselves several rungs apart, in case a rung was weak. I kept saying, "Take one rung at a time. Don't let go of one rung until you have tried the next." As I climbed I felt myself getting closer to the top—even without looking down I could see I was getting higher than the neighboring trees and buildings—and began to wonder if I could make it. Then I realized that somebody else might not make it. A rung, partly rusted, might give way. Who knows when anybody last climbed this ladder? Why hadn't I vetoed the enterprise, with the scorn that an older boy can command?

Higher and higher we climbed the leg, then out under the projecting bottom of the tank, up its side, and then to the conical top. We gathered around the ornamental knob at the apex and caught our breath. We had no flag to plant, but at least we could stand on our heads on the knob. We stretched out on the roof, shared our feelings, looked over the city spread out below, identifiable mostly by a scattering of streetlights. Sensible people had long since gone to bed. But the top of anything can be a boresome place if all you wanted was to get there, so eventually we started down the ladder. Not until we were on the ground did I overhear a chance remark that indicated that the boys had frequently climbed the tower. "We've gone up and down it like a yo-yo," was the way Don put it. My stream of cautions had been entirely wasted.

Times come when every parent has to decide what a boy or girl can or cannot be allowed to do. When should son or daughter be allowed to ride a bicycle, shoot a gun, drive a car, own a motorcycle, go to a party unaccompanied? The child seems so young, and the venture so hazardous. Inevitably parents ask themselves: What are other boys and girls, this age, doing? And especially: What did I do at this age? Only then can they find the courage to give assent. But for things parents never did do as youngsters, like flying a plane, or hiking around Europe, there are no remembrances in which to find comfort.

Usually, of course, children reach an age of readiness before their parents realize it. The year before we had come to Osceola I had said to Don, "You ought to learn to drive the car. You will need to some day." Father could not drive. We were wise enough not to ask for permission. I drove Don to the edge of town and explained brake, clutch, accelerator pedal, and gearshift. I showed the correct position of ignition and gas levers for cranking the engine, and he practiced it. He took the wheel and we went roaring, jerking, and over-correcting, down the road. In the days that followed, we had other lessons.

In those years, of course, people were utterly casual about learning to drive. A man would visit a dealer, buy his first car, take a brief lesson on the street in front of the agency, and proudly drive the car home. Traffic was light—one car every ten miles—and speeds were slow—ten to twenty miles an hour—so the road was a safe place to practice. Months later, when Father needed to go to Osceola and suddenly realized that only Don would be available to drive, we took Don on an instruction trip. He, of course, listened patiently once more to the advice I had given him weeks previously. After the trip to Osceola, Father reported that Don had learned to drive "mighty quick." That was such a handsome compliment that we decided it should be accepted in the same handsome spirit, without any explanation.

Next time you walk down Main Street and see a well-coifed lady, seventy or eighty or whatever, obviously a picture of refinement, you can be sure that as a teen-age girl she had wild escapades never reported at the supper table. And if you see a gentleman shuffling along, perhaps with a cane, perhaps without, white-haired, bleary-eyed, arthritic, you can, if you look carefully, see in him the boy that once climbed a water tower and stood on his head on the top, and lived to be seventy or eighty, or whatever.

9

I do not know the mingled feelings of doubt and assurance that flood the mind of a boy who for the first time joins a football or basketball squad, but I do know what it means to try out for a speech event in a brand new school. Everybody else seems poised and confident; you can only hope and tremble.

I did know that in Iowa, as in many mid-American states, speech was highly competitive. Audiences of respectable size heard the local events and at times traveled to out-of-town meetings along with the contestants. Interscholastic events supervised by the Iowa High School Debating League and the University of Iowa were supplemented, in Osceola, with triangular and quadrangular competitions with nearby county-seat towns. Those who won interscholastic speech events received a letter, just as did those who participated in football or basketball. And at the end of the row were medals and even scholarships.

The season opened with an announcement by Superintendent Heller that those who wanted to join the debate squad should sign the posted tryout sheet. When Don and I hurried to sign at the end of the school day, we saw that the sheet already was filled with signatures written in large, intimidating scrawls. We added our names in small letters, hoping that nobody had seen us. A week later each person would give a short argument on the topic: compulsory arbitration of labor disputes.

On the afternoon of the tryout, twenty students appeared. Heller asked us to draw for speaking positions. Don's number was toward the beginning, mine toward the end.

I listened so intently to the speeches that I almost forgot my number was coming up. I heard two or three poor ones, and two or three good ones, Don's being in that group. As a team consisted of three debaters, all that was necessary was to be one of the three. When I finished I thought I had done only fairly well; every speaker worries about his flaws and discounts his virtues. After the last speech, Heller said that the results would be posted the next morning. Don and I walked home in an uncertain frame of mind. I thought he had made the team and he thought I had. Next day we saw that both of us, along with Gerald Wadsworth, a tall, good-looking senior, had been selected.

In the days that followed we spent hours at the City Library, but Heller, who doubled as our coach, did not think much of our debate speeches and ended up by dictating new ones, producing streams of artful prose that we more or less memorized. Although we won two practice debates, we were mowed down in the first tournament round, 3 to 0. That ended my Osceola debating.

The spring of 1922 brought tryouts for oratorical, dramatic, and humorous speech events. My selection was an adaptation of Robert G. Ingersoll's "Tribute to Thomas Paine," which I had used in Missouri. I had done well with Bob and Tom, except on occasions when a judge had been offended by their ideas; since both Paine and Ingersoll were considered agnostics, and maybe even heretics, judges sometimes ruled they were not fit for high-school students to listen to and, accordingly, downgraded the speech on their score sheets.

I won the local oratorical competition, and, along with the winners in the humorous and dramatic categories, the right to compete with neighboring schools. Our contests drew large audiences. The selections, especially those in the dramatic and humorous categories, were entertaining. At the conclusion was the excitement of the decisions on the winners, especially when Osceola won its share of gold, silver, and bronze medals.

I write, of course, of an era when the only competition was the show at the Lyric. As radio was still in its beginnings, people were not bombarded by voices on the airwaves.

The University of Iowa had, very early, sponsored statewide extemporaneous contests. The ability to speak well, extemporaneously, was valued, particularly in the democracies. Anyone might be interviewed or asked to voice an opinion. Early in the season the University mailed a list of twenty topics, on current issues, that participants should prepare to talk on. At the appointed hour, each of us drew a topic that we could keep, or put back, and draw another, but we were then required to speak on the second topic. We were given two hours to study our notes and prepare a seven-minute speech. At the end of two hours, we were called one by one to the platform to give the speech. Judges would score us on content, use of language, delivery, and general effectiveness.

The month before the contest I spent most of my spare time in the City Library, turning the pages of magazines dealing with current events, and writing notes and outlines on each of the assigned twenty topics. I should clarify: this contest was not *impromptu* speaking, which is spur-of-the-moment talk, but tested background knowledge, organization, and presentation. As against memorized orations and declamations, these speeches were composed by the speaker with little "practice." After I had completed a considerable amount of reading, I prepared an outline on each topic, attempting an interesting introduction and a persuasive conclusion.

With a speech on "Iowa's Resources," I survived the local event and moved to the regional. The same topics were again used, since the odds were only one in twenty that anyone would draw a topic he had used previously. My notes contained a few good speeches, a few middling good, and a few that I hoped not to have to use. Heller was with me when I made my draw, and when I unfolded the slip and showed him "Iowa's Resources," he grinned with delight. After several months' residence in the state I had developed pride in being an Iowan and had absorbed much about its agriculture, industry, and people. Iowa had ten thousand miles of railroads; it led the entire nation in literacy. The convert is a notorious enthusiast and often sees details that a native overlooks. So I was doubly pleased to emerge from the contest as the representative of the whole southwest quarter of Iowa.

The state contest at Iowa City was now only two weeks away. The four contestants were sent a revised list of twelve topics that included some from the original twenty; a survivor was "Iowa's Resources." As the rules still allowed a second draw, I figured that I would need to prepare carefully on only eleven topics. After all, two weeks is a short time and one should spend it as best he could. One who had played right field in front of teams of horses and who had

swum in the forbidden waters of the city reservoir was accustomed
to taking high risks.

In Iowa City, the topic I drew first was "The Naval Disarmament
Treaty," only midway in my list of favorites. I stood a moment
clutching the slip, wondering whether I could improve my odds.
Heller reminded me that somewhere in the hat was the topic on
which I had prepared very little. Still, as he left the decision to me, I
drew again. When I saw that the second slip read "Iowa's Resources," I could feel the gold medal already in my hand.

Finally I stood on the high platform in the Natural Science Building, where I faced judges, coaches, parents, and miscellaneous
well-wishers. With the confidence that comes from having a well-
planned speech on a two-time winner, I got off to a good start.
Halfway through, however, I dropped my little sheaf of notes and
saw them spatter on the floor below. For an agonized fraction of a
second I debated whether to continue without them, but decided
not to; I jumped to the floor, grabbed the cards, leaped back to the
platform, and resumed my train of thought. I was like a figure skater
who had fallen on the ice. Though I resumed the discussion easily,
the damage had been done.

As I listened to the others, I persuaded myself that I still had a
chance to win first. The ballot specified percentage points for Gesture and Bodily Action, and I should have realized that my Great
Leap Off the Platform had wiped out my assets in that category, not
to mention the vital category of General Effectiveness. After the
final speech, the judges took an exceptionally long time to compute
their scores. I could only hope.

Many, many times I had sat in the back of an auditorium awaiting
the verdict of judges. Basketball players can keep a running tally of
their team's points; runners can tell whether they are yards ahead or
yards behind; javelin throwers can eyeball distances on the field. I
could only sit, in my private world of tension and doubt, watching
the contest official collect the ballots, add the scores, and take a slip
of paper to the chairman. Never before had I got as far as the state
finals.

I gripped myself as I watched the chairman unfold and smooth the
slip, as he put it on the lectern and looked down at it and out at the
audience, as he mentally began to frame his opening phrases, as he

spoke the usual ceremonial words of thanking one and all who had participated. A contestant begins to wonder how long he can hold his breath and how fiercely his heart can pound without shattering his rib cage. After an age, the chairman announced the winner, a boy from the Iowa City high school. The judges, all from Iowa City, had had to wrestle with the problem of avoiding favoritism and also of leaning backward. Well, I said to myself, I must be second. That award, however, went elsewhere. My hopes sank. I might not have placed at all! My name came next, however, so at least I was not last. Each of us was presented with a full-tuition scholarship to the state university.

I felt more dejected than I ever had in my whole sixteen years. As I walked out of the auditorium with Heller I asked him, "Is there anything worse than losing a contest?" "Yes," he replied, but without much comfort in his voice, "there really is." I wandered alone over the campus, past the iron fence around the central buildings, my speech spinning through my mind again and again. I strolled to the famous Whetstone's drugstore for a malted milk; I had not eaten since morning.

The ride home was twice as long as the ride there. The Rock Island's coaches seemed sootier, the windows grimier, the drinking water warmer. The clicking of the wheels over the rails made no music. At Des Moines I changed and boarded the branch-line Burlington, even shabbier. I dreaded to go back to school, being only a third-placer.

Father was incensed that the officials had used local judges when one contestant was a local boy. He fired a letter to the lady in charge, who answered blandly: "We wish everybody could win." I should have been delighted to be third in the state and win a scholarship, but contestants in any area are seldom elated with any prize short of first. An Olympic hurdler who comes in second is unlikely to say, "Second is real good for me. Gee, I'm lucky just to be here." We live in a winner-take-all world.

At the annual recognition assembly, Heller awarded letters to students who had surpassed in academic, athletic, and speaking events. Better than most superintendents, he knew the value of a public ceremony, not only to honor the recipients of prizes but also to stimulate other students to develop their own varied talents. One by one boys and girls were called forward and ceremoniously presented the cherished, white "O." I went to the platform for "O's" in debate, oratory, and extemporaneous speaking.

A week later came the senior party, the baccalaureate service, and the commencement. All-night class parties were still a generation ahead. We were proud of our class flower, the sweet pea, one of the most popular flowers of that age; our class colors, salmon pink and purple; our class motto, "Out of school life into life's school." I smile now when I think of this, but at the time the choice of flower, colors, and motto seemed elegant. Surely the world was created for the Class of '22.

For the final ceremony, we were seated on the stage of the auditorium. As for the commencement speech, Father could have reported it without hearing it. What I do remember was that as I had a part on the program, I sat just behind the lectern, so close to the speaker that whenever he stepped back, I had to move my feet out of danger. As he rocked forward and backward continually, I was in perpetual motion. I was the most alert person in the auditorium.

A few days later I learned I had been awarded a scholarship to Grinnell College, wherever that was. Now I had two scholarships, and no intention of going to college. I was determined to be a newspaper publisher. For that profession I thought I already knew as much as I would ever need to know.

10

When Don and I learned that the knights of the Ku Klux Klan had come to Osceola, we could not have been more astonished if we had read that the *Sentinel* had endorsed the Democratic platform. One event seemed as plausible as the other.

Already the Invisible Empire had spread through the South, having been revived after World War I. In the exchanges that came to the *Tribune*'s desk, we had read that it was being organized in several of southern Iowa's larger communities. Now we learned that around our own courthouse square, up and down Main Street, and on nearby farms, Osceola and Clarke County people were signing up, taking the oath, and writing their names in blood, or whatever it was they did.

That night in the lobby of the Lyric, Don and I overheard the younger patrons whispering that a full-fledged meeting was then in session in a pasture along the Jefferson Highway, south of town. We decided to check out this exciting rumor, not as investigative young reporters but out of pure, unabashed curiosity. The knowledge that we would be hung up by our heels or burned at the stake if we were discovered did not deter us. We started down the dark road.

We had walked scarcely a mile when we saw the blazing cross atop a hill. From that moment, Indian scouts could not have been stealthier. We climbed fences and moved cautiously across the meadow, creeping behind what few trees and bushes there were, using the cover of the shadows cast by the moon. We had seen enough movies to be on the lookout for guards and soon spotted one at the gate, inspecting those who sought admittance. Other guards were posted; everybody was wrapped in a sheet and wore a pillow-case as a hood, with slits for eyes. One Klansman had climbed a tree to operate a searchlight; its beams, sweeping the landscape, seemed to say, "I'll find you wherever you are," and kept us crouching and alert.

Vaguely I can see twenty, maybe thirty, figures, standing around the cross, listening to a speaker, probably a kleagle or a grand dragon. His voice was partly muffled by all that bed linen but we picked up sentences here and there that gave us the general drift of his message. The Klan, he explained, believed in "100 percent Americanism," which made it a crusader not only against blacks, foreigners, Jews, and Catholics, but also against wife-beaters, drunks, bootleggers, and young men who took advantage of girls in cars parked on country lanes. He used less vim and vigor than we had used in our high-school debates; we decided he would not get far in a tournament.

Actually we were far more curious about who was wrapped in that sheet than in anything he had to say. We speculated, continually shushing each other, about the identity of other sheeted forms. We sometimes felt certain of those who were tall and thin, or short and fat; we thought we recognized a couple of the parked cars; but in the main we could only guess and wrangle.

The speech came to a sudden halt when an uninvited visitor, armed with a shotgun, fired a shot at the spotlight. Someone, no doubt an immigrant, maybe also a drunken wife-beater, was boldly interrupting the ceremony. We saw a Klansman run toward him, but the intruder stood his ground, gun ready for action; other

Klansmen approached, but respectfully kept their distance. The shadowy figure fired another shot and left. They did not bother to pursue him.

Totally absorbed in this turn of events, we failed to notice the approach of a guard. Suddenly alerted, we both let out yells and fled in opposite directions. By a sort of fielder's choice he chased after Don and grabbed him. When I realized I was not being followed, I doubled back to see what awful fate was in store for my one and only brother, and whether I could do anything to avert it. Anyone who has seen a hundred westerns knows that people in desperate situations can be rescued in a variety of ways—suddenly swooping in on horseback, for example, surprising the villain with a well-placed kick while the hero leaps aboard and the pair dashes away despite a fusillade of shots, each of which misses. I saw Don and this unknown guard in what was obviously earnest conversation. I crept closer, looking for a stick or rock, and at the same time keeping on the lookout for other Klan personnel. Finally, to my relief, I saw Don being escorted to the gate. When I caught up with him, he said he had got a lecture on the advisability of minding his own business, was assured that the Klan would not hurt anybody, least of all young, addle-headed boys, and told to go home and not look back. Both of us thought this was sage advice.

Later Don avowed that nothing in this wide world is like racing for your life through a pasture, at night, with a white-robed figure, its sheet flapping in the wind, getting closer every second. Don, too, had seen a hundred westerns and knew what happened when even honorable and totally well-meaning people got caught.

Next morning we saw the cross itself on display in the courthouse park. It no longer seemed threatening, since it was merely an ordinary six-foot 2 x 4 nailed to a ten-foot upright. Half a dozen Van Camp's pork and bean cans, filled with cotton waste soaked in oil, had provided the awesome flames. "Informed sources" said that most of the crowd consisted of out-of-town visitors. Between ourselves, however, we decided that our hometown had been fully represented.

For days I could think of little else. As I walked in and out of businesses and offices on news-gathering rounds, I could not help wondering who was Klan and who was not. I found it difficult to reconcile the Klan I had read about, the Klan that had operated during Reconstruction days, with the genial citizens of our southern Iowa town. Yet the Klan had come as if to stay. During the next few weeks the fiery cross burned in one Iowa town after another, and a year later the Klan was strong enough to hold a convention at the state fairgrounds. Led by a white-sheeted band, hundreds of robed men and women, afoot and on horseback, marched around the track in phalanx after phalanx, carrying large and small crosses.

Still later, at the Madison Square Garden presidential convention, the Klan issue split the Democratic party right down the middle; a plank that would have denounced it by name lost by a single vote. In the fall election an Osceola preacher ran for Congress, proclaiming his connection with the Klan and getting a substantial vote even though he missed being elected. The Klan even sponsored a propaganda movie in the Osceola high-school auditorium, at which Klan notions were dramatized for all who paid the admission charge.

It seemed a lasting virus. When Al Smith ran for the presidency in 1928, the Klan issued the pronouncement that a vote for him was an invitation to the Pope to live in the White House. I thought again of the white-robed figures I had seen, people who no doubt greeted me heartily in the daylight, but at night gathered around a blazing cross, in a pasture just off the Jefferson Highway.

11

If we had paused to reflect, we would have realized that we were in the middle of an unprecedented technological advance. As I have suggested, the radio story, spectacular though it was, unfolded almost imperceptibly. The more visible story was the disappearance of horses with their wagons and buggies. On the farm the horse still pulled plows, cultivators, and manure spreaders, but spent less and less time on the road.

Here is what happened: The peak of the horse and mule population, more than twenty-six million animals, came at the end of World War I. From that point the total diminished, first by half a million animals a year, and later more rapidly. During my senior year, the horse population went down more than a million, reflecting hard times and the decline of farm income. Old animals died and went to what we called the rendering works, and the new colt crop was sharply reduced. A country singer could have lamented: Where have all the horses gone? The effect was much the same as if a million horses a year had been pushed off a cliff.

Automobile manufacturers, meanwhile, were building four million cars a year. During my senior year, Clarke County registered nineteen hundred cars for its ten thousand people, and our farsighted county clerk ordered two thousand license tags for the coming year. People began to say that everybody in the country could take a ride at the same time, provided you could cram seven people into each car. Iowans, however, had a car for every five.

Each year saw new auto dealerships advertising in Osceola papers. You could buy Fords, Chevrolets, Overlands, Buicks, Dodges, Oaklands, and Nashes right off the floor. The *Tribune* advertised Ford coupes for $348, Overlands for $695, Nashes for $985. This was a time when experienced printers were earning the equivalent of five Fords every year, two Overlands, or a Nash and a half. If you craved an eight-cylinder car like a Hupmobile ($2,350) or a Cadillac ($3,000), you need go no farther than Des Moines.

Dealers claimed constant improvement of their product: the powerful motors of the newer models did not vibrate like the old-timers. Knowing people warned against secondhand cars: never buy one, they warned, without first taking it apart, which anyone could do with a screwdriver, a crescent wrench or two, and a pair of pliers. Trucks were also appearing in salesrooms. A truck, dealers argued, could carry five tons of hay to market or do the work of eight mule teams in road construction. For some time Ford dealers had been advertising a light tractor, called, appropriately enough, the Fordson.

Garage owners began to feature the quality of their service. One offered to overhaul a Ford motor for $12.50, and he was eager that you be pleased with his workmanship. People who regularly winter-stored their cars in their garages, a jack under each wheel to take the weight off the tires, began to change their driving habits. One of our advertisers sensed the trend. "Do not store your car over winter," he urged; "we can keep your motor in first-class condition." As a come-on, he mentioned that you could drive your car into his garage without waiting, with the help of his new, automatic doors. If you had one of the new model cars with four-wheel brakes, you could get them all adjusted for 65 cents. You could get a battery charged for 25 cents, buy a new one for $5, and the best one going for $10.

Garage owners also advertised a new service—they would haul your disabled vehicle in with a special truck they called a "wrecker." They saw a market for salvaged parts from old cars, advertising used parts as being available for those who wanted them. So many things went wrong that cars needed frequent repair, and the lack of parts could keep a car off the road for days. Once when Old Betsy stripped her gears, she was laid up for six weeks awaiting replacements. Eventually dealers advertised, "Buy a second car," the main argument being to have one in reserve when the other was undergoing repair.

Oil was fifteen cents a quart; and don't forget, the Standard filling station declared, "that what castor oil is to a baby, lubricating oil is to a car." Whenever you bought gas you almost always bought a quart of oil, pumped from a barrel. We called it by its full name: "cylinder oil." Since unscrupulous dealers could dilute the good oil in the barrel with worn-out crankcase oil, the oil companies eventually decided to sell oil in cans. High test gas was twelve cents, a figure even then so ridiculously cheap that few knew or cared how many miles he or she got to the gallon. Drivers knew to the last fraction about speeds, or the length of a trip, but simply kept no records on gas consumption. They wouldn't have known what "MPG" meant.

Automobiles became increasingly popular because Americans had grown up with tools and machinery. Our generation, like those before us, built the country with its hands. American boys and girls knew about hammers and saws, nuts and bolts. If a threshing machine or a sulky plow broke down, any of several people around could fix it. The first auto mechanics, in fact, were farmhands and town boys. Everybody rather expected machinery to break down, and generally in busy times. Though these events were vexatious, in retrospect Americans were proud of having solved a problem, bragged lustily about it, and laughed at themselves and at one another for having got upset. A popular song had the refrain, "Get out and get under." Both American know-how and sense of humor were richly demanded by the car. Our finest moments were when we summoned our incredible ingenuity to fix our own cars, and, when we had safely arrived at our destination, to make a rousing story about the experience.

Tire trouble was the most frequent. At first tires were not guaranteed at all; later they were warranted for limited mileage, such as three thousand. They were, of course, made of natural rubber; big firms like Firestone and Goodyear advertised that they each owned several million rubber trees in faraway lands. You could get a fairly good tire for three or four dollars, or you could pay from fifteen to forty. Tread design was capricious, neither scientific nor understood. Firestone incorporated the words NON SKID into its pattern, while Pennsylvania used rows of little suction cups that actually increased friction. Drivers routinely carried extra casings, extra tubes, blowout boots, and full patching equipment, including roadside vulcanizing kits, and a pump. Especially a pump. Front tires of even a small car needed sixty pounds of pressure and rear tires seventy. And squeezing in the last ten or twenty pounds of air was tough going. Low-pressure "balloon tires" were instantly popular when they arrived.

Car radiators needed frequent refilling; a car drank as much water as a horse. Overheated engines brought many trips to a halt. Unexpected chuckholes or unusually rough places could break a spring. Our most alarming accident was when driving in northwest Iowa; the motor suddenly roared, the car lurched violently, and we saw, to our amazement, a wheel roll down the road ahead of us. Even so, we were not permanently disabled; we jacked up the car, retrieved the wheel, bolted it back on, tightened the nuts on the other wheels for good measure, and in half an hour were on our way.

A minor joy was to drive the car on the lawn, crawl under with grease gun, oil can, wrench, and pliers, and leisurely inspect mechanical features while greasing bearings, filling oil cups, and squirting oil into moving parts. One also checked muffler connections, tightened body bolts, and looked for broken spring leaves. Each of these therapeutic activities delighted a driver's soul. Now all has changed. Not long ago a mechanic replaced a muffler on my car. When I got it home, I decided to review what I had got for my $35. I could barely get my chin under the car, much less crawl under it. I envied my neighbor, a real do-it-yourselfer. He had drained the lily pond in his backyard so he could drive his car astraddle it, using the pond as a pit into which to crawl to change oil and to perform other enchanting tasks.

Osceola's two funeral establishments began a Limousine Hearse-Ambulance war. One advertised that its limousine had a handsome streamlined hood with twelve-inch brass headlights, and was powered by a seventy horsepower, Continental Red Seal motor, which any boy would recognize as the finest available. The other took a 4-column ad to describe its new vehicle, which included a casket compartment finished in hand-buffed leather and highly polished American walnut. My recollection is that for a time this type of conveyance was used nationwide both for hearse and for ambulance service; that not until later years were separate vehicles preferred; and that still later funeral directors decided to relinquish the ambulance business to the hospitals. But when my time comes to be hauled away I can think of nothing nicer than to be in a limousine powered by a Continental motor, with big brass head-lights in front, gleaming and sparkling in the sunlight.

Gradually automobiles improved, and since drivers could go faster, they demanded better roads. On the maps published by highway commissions, roads were classified and marked with solid lines, checkered lines, and thin lines. The best were called "improved roads." "Improved" might mean simply a reasonably wide, well-graded road, or, later, a graveled road. A legend that I should hate to see overturned is that in the twenties the Iowa football team played a home game with its sturdy rival, Illinois. Rain fell in torrents during the contest, which Iowa won. The ride home after a game when your team lost is always long and sad, but on this occasion the losers also had to slog through miles of rich, slithery, Iowa mud. Visiting sportswriters filed such scathing descriptions of the Iowa highway system that Iowa citizens, legislators, and highway engineers decided the time had come for hard surfacing. In ten years, the state surfaced 90 percent of its highways.

You could not run a newspaper in the twenties without reporting the constant changes in cars and roads. Don and I, like ten million other American boys, could instantly recognize any make and spot its new features. Inevitably, when cars got trustworthy enough to risk stealing, the improved roads helped the thief's getaway. Cars also got numerous enough to tax, at least through their fuel, starting with a levy of two cents on every gallon.

To attract overnight visitors, Osceola constructed a free tourist camp near the courthouse. Its frame buildings were equipped with bunks, plus a shed for the cars, a separate rest room with a laundry room and shower, and free electricity. Tourists carried their own bedding. I used to check the camp's registry book to note addresses and remarks on the accommodations. One year seven hundred people visited the camp, coming from twenty states and Canada. Nothing revealed more clearly that the car was developing a reputation for long-distance stamina.

Before long, commercial tourist facilities were built on the main highways at the edge of towns. The sign, "Cabins," described exactly that: a cluster of individual units, each with a double bed or two, often with linens, and some kind of kitchenette. All sorts of ingenuity went into the materials used for the cabins and into their design; one we saw was a collection of galvanized iron, six-sided, cone-roofed, corn bins, adapted to overnight occupancy. A central structure housed showers, lavatories, and toilets, as did the Osceola tourist camp. You did not need to register; the owner or his wife counted the number of bodies in your party and collected a dollar or two for each. If the night's business warranted, they would even rent their own bedroom and sleep in the parlor. Nearby residents, seeing this easy money, posted signs, "Rooms," in their front yards and began to entertain overnight guests.

The horse had taken things pretty much as he found them; his alterations to the landscape were slow and gradual. The automobile began changing everything, and in a hurry.

12

One advantage of growing up in a newspaper family is that often you see famous people at close range.

Father first proposed the idea at the supper table: "Colonel Bryan is coming to town next month to give a chautauqua address. Why don't we invite him to breakfast?"

William Jennings Bryan, three times presidential candidate, was, after the ailing Woodrow Wilson, the most famous Democrat in the land. Father's proposal was like inviting, in a later day, a Roosevelt or a Kennedy. His bombshell caught Mother in the act of drinking her customary hot, strong, black coffee. She choked back a sputter. "Invite *Bryan?* To eat with *us? Here?*"

"Why not?" pursued Father. "He'd rather eat in a private home than at the hotel. When he campaigned, he dined with families every chance he got." Father was on solid ground; his newspapers had supported Bryan during each of his campaigns, and they had often exchanged letters. He knew the Colonel well.

Mother, ever hard to faze, regained her composure. As an editor's wife she had fed scores of Democratic bigwigs. "What will we serve him?"

"Pancakes," Father ruled. "The Colonel loves 'em. And you make good ones. Also eggs, sausage, fried potatoes—the usual things."

"And sliced tomatoes."

"And sliced tomatoes."

The breakfast was as good as cooked. "Who'll we invite?" By then Mother had the bit in her teeth, was rounding third base, and was reaching for the bugle so she could blow a clarion call.

"All the Democrats in town," Father grinned and winked at us. "There aren't many." Clell Collier, the auctioneer, for example; Andy Edwards, the county chairman. Shortly they evolved a guest list of five couples. Later they moved the occasion to the Collier home, which had a larger dining room.

At the office, Father dashed a note to Colonel Bryan in Florida. Soon came a reply: he would be delighted to have breakfast with the Reids.

The family's admiration for Bryan was boundless. Mother's sister, my Aunt Grace, born in 1896, had been given the middle name of Bryan. Don, born in 1908, had as his middle name, Jennings. Thus the family had cemented the dates of Bryan's first and last campaigns. Father has described the involvement of even the kids at the 1896 election. On the playground the Republican boys would start a yell, "Hurrah for McKinley!" "And a rope to hang the sonofabitch!" the Democratic boys would retort.

When Father was at Grand River College during the 1900 campaign, writing for the county paper, he bitterly observed that Republican students got free train tickets to go home to vote, whereas Democratic students had to pay their own way. His own explanation of Bryan's losses both in 1896 and 1900 was simple: the Republicans had bought the election. Bryan never had stauncher supporters than Father and Mother and their families.

On the chosen day, Bryan arrived in Osceola to give his chautauqua address. Seated at the head of the breakfast table, he put at ease the group that had gathered, with one political reminiscence after another. Mother and Mrs. Collier busied themselves seeing that plates were heaped and coffee cups refilled. In front of Bryan, Mother placed a stack of pancakes; not the small blobs of a modern franchised establishment, but large ones, each the size of the plate. With his big thumb, the Colonel peeled back the layers of pancakes one at a time, slathering each with a slab of butter. That absorbing task finished, he anointed the stack with half a cupful of syrup, meanwhile keeping up an animated conversation. He then impaled the heap with his fork, carved a triangle four pancakes thick with his knife, and, hoisting the buttered, syruped segment into the air, tucked it into a corner of his capacious mouth and gulped it down, not blurring a syllable.

"My, these are delicious," he exclaimed, interrupting his own line of thought.

Father well knew the details of Bryan's legendary capacity for food. The reason the Colonel bypassed hotels in favor of private homes was simply to get a steady, uninterrupted supply of edibles. At a formal banquet, for example, he was agonized by the delays between courses. During a soup course he would not only wolf his own supply of crackers and rolls but would spear any left unattended on a neighbor's plate. More than once he reached into his pockets for morsels that he had squirreled away to bridge such lapses.

At one breakfast occasion at a private home the host, in anguish, declared: "Colonel, I hate to say this, but I've just looked at my watch and we must be at the station in five minutes. We must quit right now." Bryan's total horror at having to stop in the middle of breakfast was evident. Here was an untouched stack of cakes, fully buttered and syruped. Still, he understood the urgency of the situation. "I'll just take these with me," he decided, "and enjoy them on the train." He thereupon wrapped the cakes in his hostess's linen napkin and stuffed the lot in his coat pocket.

This morning, however, the Colonel's meal was not to be interrupted. Mother liked to recount how, after the pancakes, he waded into the sliced tomatoes. She counted half a dozen and then lost track. You can't beat the routine of training on pancakes and sliced tomatoes if you have to make an important speech. When the time came to leave, Don, age fourteen, had the honor of driving Bryan in our newly acquired Overland to the chautauqua tent, where "The Great Commoner" completely enchanted the crowd, and that afternoon drove him to his next appearance in neighboring Chariton.

Older Democrats knew that Bryan was not only the unquestioned leader of the party but was also king of the chautauqua circuit. His talks, mixing politics and religion, sometimes seriously, sometimes with his bubbling humor, always with charm and grace, stirred audiences wherever he went.

Bryan had an unbelievably melodious and resonant speaking voice. He could have stood at the goal posts of the Superdome and make himself heard in the top rows. No microphones. His big chest, powerful lungs, open throat, and large mouth were part of his natural endowment. Added to these native gifts, he had the charm of simple language, now and then touched with eloquence. When he was thirty-six, he had risen before a tumultuous Democratic convention, at once commanding the attention of the delegates. His absorbing statement of his political philosophy ended with the rousing sentence that immediately became famous: "You shall not press down upon the brow of labor this crown of thorns . . ." It stampeded the convention and led to his first nomination.

A year after the breakfast gathering, Father read that Bryan was to give a Sunday afternoon lay sermon at the Iowa State Fair grounds and proposed to Don and me that we go to Des Moines to hear the speech: "Bryan is getting along in years; we will not have many more chances to hear him." So we went, parking the Overland alongside hundreds of other cars on the grass at the edge of the field. A temporary platform, four feet high, had been built; along one side was a stairway; on top were a few chairs, a small table, and the usual tumbler and pitcher of water. It was a hot, stifling, August afternoon.

Although the Des Moines papers carried only a brief account of the speech, for me it was an unforgettable occasion. Father, Don, and I sat close to the platform, on the ground like everybody else. In his opening remarks, the introducer observed that for once those present could listen to the speaker without paying anything. This remark annoyed Bryan; he countered by mentioning that he had given hundreds of campaign speeches at which admission was free. My reaction was that the tactless introduction had put Bryan on the defensive, and that otherwise he would have opened with some entertaining stories.

Actually, at first I was disappointed; Bryan's speech was not so exciting as I had expected. After a few moments, however, he swung into his normal, inimitable style: partly narrative, partly didactic, packed with imagery, touched with humor. He did not stand or walk around on the platform; he sat on the edge of the small table, swinging his big leg back and forth, fanning himself with a giant palm-leaf fan. Although most of the time he was serious, now and then he would tell a story that made acres of closely packed people roar with laughter. One story was a mid-American version of the prodigal son, who ran away from home, frequented pool halls, saloons, gambling places, and other wicked places, but upon his eventual return the father called in the neighbors to celebrate with fried chicken, mashed potatoes, wilted lettuce, corn on the cob, and similar midwestern delicacies. Bryan's detail was apt, vivid, and plentiful.

After Bryan had spoken a full hour in the blazing sun, his white linen coat soaked with perspiration and his face florid with the afternoon heat, he showed signs of bringing his speech to a halt. By this time he had won me over completely; I hated to think that he would ever stop. At that moment an elderly gentleman seated near us climbed the stairs to the platform and held a parasol so that it shaded Bryan's face. The crowd applauded and Bryan was so touched that he spoke another hour, to the pleasure of everybody.

When he finished, the crowd cheered and cheered. Nobody was in a hurry to leave. We made our way to the edge of the platform. Bryan recognized Father and recalled the breakfast at Osceola. As we left, he shook hands all around and said to Don and me: "I'm glad to meet you again. If ever we happen to be in the same city and you find out about it before I do, be sure to come up and say hello."

Twenty-five years later, as a visiting professor at the University of Southern California, I was invited to talk to the Hollywood Rotary Club. I discussed famous speakers I had heard or read about and told the story of the Bryan breakfast and the Des Moines speech. I did not mention his special greeting to me. After my talk, a gentleman named de Mille stepped up to tell me one of his own Bryan stories. "He had breakfast in our home," de Mille said, "and as he left he took my boyish hand in his own great paw and said, 'Young man, if we ever happen to be in the same city, and you find out about it before I do, be sure to come up and introduce yourself.'" I could not find it in my heart to tell Cecil B. de Mille that Bryan had told that same thing to a lot of other boys.

Father proved to be right in his prediction that Americans would not have many more years to hear the Colonel. Actually he lived only a couple of years after his appearance in Des Moines. He participated in the famous Scopes trial, in Tennessee, in July 1925. Five days after the trial had concluded, he died in his sleep. I remember it was on a Sunday afternoon; and I also remember that some of the papers speculated that he died of a broken heart because of his defeat at the hands of Clarence Darrow.

Father declared this speculation was utter nonsense. Anyone who had survived three campaign defeats, he reasoned, would not be overcome by a courtroom opponent. When Father learned that Bryan had eaten his usual enormous Sunday noon dinner, and then had lain down for the nap from which he never arose, he declared this to be the combination of circumstances that had brought about the Colonel's death. Whenever you eat a giant meal, he quietly advised us, don't go immediately to bed; keep stirring around to help your system cope with all that food. I never saw any reason to disagree with Father's analysis.

II. The Locomotive Set

13

I often wonder why Father and Mother did not send me either to Grinnell or to the University of Iowa immediately after graduation.

Here I had scholarships to both schools, and Father was not one to let a commodity go to waste. When years ago he had been given a bottle of kidney pills, he took one now and then even though he had no immediate need. "It might benefit something I don't know about yet," he explained. One could argue that college also can benefit something one doesn't know about yet. And a scholarship is a valuable item—the Grinnell scholarship, for example, covered full tuition—$200—as much as he could get for eight-page ads in the *Tribune*.

Father skirted the college issue because he was swamped with mortgage payments and needed my help around the office. Moreover, I did not press the point. You would think that during my senior year I would have been swamped with college talk from classmates and former graduates, but actually I heard none at all. Half a dozen good schools were within a two-hour train ride, but each Osceola class had sent only a few students, and most of those quit after a semester or two.

Nationally that year there were only 823,000 college students in a population of 123 million: 1 in 150. At that rate, Osceola should have had fifteen in college, but we were a small-town, farm-oriented community. (Fifty years later the national ratio was 1 in 20.) So, like most of my classmates, I did not think of myself as college timber.

By way of a substitute, I took two courses in the new junior college that opened that fall, one of the first in Iowa, but as they were only slightly rearranged high-school courses, taught by high-school teachers, I quit after a semester. A traveling salesman sold Father a correspondence law course, which promised to qualify me for bar examinations, but after two or three months I bogged down in contracts and couldn't get thrilled by torts.

The following summer, however, even though both scholarships had long since expired, the family began to talk college. The mortgage still hung overhead like a vulture in the sky; I would need to be replaced on the *Tribune*'s work force. Perhaps, however, I could get a linotyping job in a college town. And, fortunately, Don had become not only the principal press feeder, but had taken on other kinds of printing chores as well. My leaving would promote him to the post of number-one boy in the household, the last of the family's "good, cheap help," in the words of our Jewish tailor. And if older brother got a part-time campus job, younger brother could also, some day, look forward to college.

Which college? The standard procedure is to write for catalogues, after consulting with the high-school counselor and older friends. As we had no counselor and knew no alumni, we worked simply from a road map of the sort that was beginning to be distributed free by banks and garages. Somewhere on the map was a town with a college and also a newspaper that needed a part-time student operator. We set out.

Our first highway stop was at the state university, two hundred miles away, all dirt road. Father had suggested that we visit Grinnell, which was on the way, but I was enamored of the university, where I had participated in the extempore contest, and grandly overruled his idea. In Iowa City we located the office of the *Daily Iowan*, the university newspaper, discovered that it had four Linotypes, and, moreover, used student operators. My glowing qualifications as an operator who could set ads as well as straight news copy, and also repair his own machine, lost nothing in Father's sales pitch to the composing-room superintendent. Father covered the ground so well that I hardly had to say anything; in fact, I was not asked any questions or required to demonstrate what I could do. I was signed on, half-time, at 50 cents an hour—$2 a night—$12 a week. With tuition at $35 a semester and a day's meals at $1, the future looked bright.

Now came the problem of getting admitted to the university. The registrar, H. C. Dorcas, who had served in that capacity for many years, filled out the admission forms himself. We didn't bother him with questions about courses and he did not bother us about transcripts. He took Father's word that his son was a bright boy who a year previously had been awarded a scholarship. So many went unclaimed, Mr. Dorcas said, that I might still get one. Don, listening attentively, saw his older brother, in an hour's time, get a job that actually paid money and also a piece of paper that signified admission to the state university. In his mind the mystique of going away to school was speedily dissolved. If his brother could do it, anybody could.

Our mission had been accomplished to our full expectations. We didn't even take time to drive around the campus, but started home. Once again we passed through Grinnell and Father again urged that we look at the college, arguing that we might make a still better arrangement than we had in Iowa City, but I was so charmed with the thought of being a university freshman that I insisted we drive on through.

Two miles west of Grinnell we had a flat tire and as we were still a long way from home, we returned to have the inner tube properly vulcanized. Once more Father wanted to visit the campus, but once more I declined. We hit the road and four miles west of town had a blowout. We came back for further, more complicated repairs. By then it was late afternoon. None of us wanted to face a 110-mile, 4-hour drive, partly in the dark, over hilly roads, so we got a room at the Hotel Monroe and had a big supper.

Next morning at breakfast, Father, owner of the most investigative nose that ever graced a country-weekly newsroom, opened the conversation by observing that "now we had all day to get home" and "it certainly wouldn't hurt" to discover what newspapers Grinnell had "and go visit them." Full of bacon and eggs and basking in the approval of my sire and brother, I graciously assented. Though I always liked to visit newspaper offices to see printing machinery, I had no intention of altering the fantastic arrangements we had made the day before.

At the cashier's post, Father laid down a dollar to cover the tab. "What newspapers does Grinnell have?"

"Two. The *Herald* and the *Register*."

"Where are they?"

"Straight down the street for the *Register*, then around the corner for the *Herald*." When we got where we could see both buildings, Father headed for the *Herald*, which was larger and more imposing.

At the *Herald*, a semiweekly published Tuesdays and Fridays, we met the senior proprietor, W. G. Ray, a man in his sixties—short, stocky, gray-haired; semi-walrus mustache; blunt and spare of talk, but basically friendly. Later, much later, I learned that Ray was a Grinnell alumnus of 1882, the year Mother was born, three-time mayor of Grinnell, and holder of the Iowa "Master Editor" award.

Father could be either succinct or expansive, but since Ray's manner indicated that the conversation would be efficient, he immediately stated our purpose. Not disclosing that I was already indentured to the *Daily Iowan,* he described my talents, adding golden words about my reliable character. I was then eighteen—slight, slender, pale. Ray immediately began to plan possible openings for me at the *Herald.* Inwardly I squirmed, since I did not consider myself a free agent, but as he talked I felt my reluctance vanish. He explained that the shop had a lot of work to do on its two issues a week, and, moreover, printed pamphlets and books, and did a rushing business in journals and ledgers. He topped this handsome, decisive speech by stating the pay—75 cents an hour, a magnificent increase over the *Iowan's* 50 cents. This wage, he added, was based on an output of two hundred lines an hour; I knew I could produce three hundred or more. I somehow got the idea that one who could set three hundred would be paid half again as much as one who set a mere two hundred; maybe even $1.10 an hour. This fanciful notion heightened my excitement.

After this explanation he paused for my reply, displaying the air of a patient man who would give the listener thirty seconds to make up his mind. I needed even less time than that. I was eager to begin quarrying this gold mine. We agreed that I should start the next Monday at 5:00 P.M.—the job would be a night job—ten days before college opened.

Ray's associate, A. L. Frisbie, joined us for the tail end of this negotiation. He was taller and stouter than Ray, ten years younger, and readily made friends. At Grinnell he had been a varsity football player and a Phi Beta Kappa. Where Ray was blunt, often substituting a "har-rumph" for other language, Frisbie was cordial. Ray chopped off the interview with a grunt and walked away. Frisbie filled in with something like, "We will be delighted to have your son work for us. Would you like to see the plant?" He showed us the two Linotypes and the usual equipment of a composing room. We met Frank Clayberg, the operator-machinist, and the apprentice, Louis Wisecarver. In the basement we saw newspaper and book presses and the machine that ruled the horizontal blue and vertical red lines of the bookkeeping journals that were the predecessors of computer printouts.

Don was fascinated. Here was an office that employed many people, even young people. He could see that big money could be earned running a machine, and, more to the point, his brother was going to latch on to some of it. Not only was it big money, but it was outside money; like most kids, Don and I thought money earned working for someone else was more spendable than money earned by working for your own father and mother.

All these facts he filed for future reference. Obviously an operator could go to college anywhere. In less than twenty-four hours his brother had been offered two elegant jobs.

Now that the matter of financing a college education had been settled, the lesser question arose: Would Grinnell accept me? Other than it had once offered me a scholarship, we knew little about Grinnell. We did not know, for example, that it considered itself "the Harvard of the West" and had formidable academic standards. It looked both at high-school grades and at something called character. The registrar, Bethana McCandless, did not seem upset by the fact that we wanted to enroll then and there, without ever having given her previous warning. She told us that a year's bill—tuition, fees, room, board—was a flat $625. This sum was awesome compared to state university charges, but then the wages offered by the *Herald* were also awesome. She not only enrolled me but also consulted a chart and assigned me to a room with two others in Smith Hall. As the buildings were never locked, she explained, I could move in at anytime. The admission process had taken all of ten minutes.

Father asked about scholarships, indicating that a year ago I had been awarded one.

She did not dispute that audacious claim, but confided that the college happened to have one scholarship left. Father seized this opening as promptly as if he had learned someone was in the market for a set of sale bills. "How do we apply for it?" I recognized the line of questioning. ("Old man Purcell is going to sell off his stuff? How much has he got? When is the sale? Where does he live? How do you get there?")

"The committee meets day after tomorrow to make its decision."

"Who's on the committee?" Father had his notebook out. Eventually he learned that only one member was in town—John W. Gannaway, professor of political science. In moments we were at his home. He himself, a short, stocky, smooth-shaven, partly bald man in his late forties, greeted us and invited us into the parlor. Father made his pitch and received the expected answer that my application would be given every consideration.

We returned to the Overland, drove around the campus, looked at its cluster of nineteenth- and early-twentieth-century buildings, though we had no idea which was used for what, and, for the final time, started home. We had asked no questions about the college itself—only how to enter it. No one in living memory had gone to Grinnell from Osceola. But Father must have thought that Grinnell looked pretty fancy compared with the single building of Gallatin's Grand River College, which he had briefly attended the previous century.

I wrote Ray, confirming our agreement, and asked him to clarify the hourly rate. In a full explanation of perhaps three lines he reassured me that I could work half-time or more at 75 cents an hour, whether I set two hundred lines an hour or three hundred. That statement removed part of the glamor, but not all of it. A few days later I learned I had been awarded the remaining scholarship.

In anybody's book, Grinnell College is a highly regarded institution. It is famous for distinguished teaching. Its students have done well in graduate and professional universities. I am proud to be an alumnus. I entered Grinnell, however, not for any of the foregoing reasons, but because Somebody Up There caused the Overland to have two blowouts, until we finally got the message and crossed the threshold of the *Herald*.

Early in September we returned to Grinnell. The curving dirt road went through three small towns, then in and out of the heart of Des Moines, then through five more towns to Grinnell, past acres of cornfield stubble and groves of bronzed oaks and red and purple maples. We parked outside Smith Hall, to be my college home for four years, and took my bundle of clothes, my Royal typewriter, and a tennis racket to the designated room. The building was deserted; the sounds we made echoed along the empty corridors; the room had the smell of freshly used cleaning solution. In minutes I had distributed my belongings in dresser and closet and was entirely settled.

Suddenly there was nothing more to do and little more to say.

After an awkward pause, Father said he and Don had better start back so they could get home before dark. Rather than being left alone, I decided I would ride as far as downtown. At a promising corner Don stopped so I could get out, but I hesitated to make the break and said I would ride to the city limits. That point quickly arrived. We said a third, final round of good-byes. Father said, "Now be sure to write." Don said, "Remember Mother's advice, don't carry all your money in one pocket." I thought of my single, ten-dollar bill. As they drove away, I stood at the roadside and watched. A few rods down the road, Father waved and Don honked a farewell honk. The Overland got smaller in the distance, kicking up vast clouds of dust as it rolled along. No other cars were on the road. Finally the Overland disappeared over a hill; soon the dust settled; I trudged back to town.

In every child's life comes a time to leave home. Ties are not instantly snapped, but visits to the parental nest get shorter and further apart. Little by little, more of the child's personal possessions are moved to another home base; the bedroom or part of a bedroom left behind, the dresser drawers, the space in a closet, are gradually taken over by other children and other purposes. Or the parents move, and in the new home no territory whatever seems to belong to that specific child.

That autumn day was the beginning of my home-leaving. School was to keep me away nine months of the year; vacation jobs out of town filled the summers. Even so, I thought of these breaks as provisional, flitting, temporary. For the time being we can let them stand that way.

14

For an hour I wandered idly, then at 4:30 entered the Poweshiek Cafe for supper. The odds are it was roast beef and mashed potatoes that had long abided on the steam table, served with two slices of white bread and a slab of butter, followed by pie, the universal dessert. At that hour I was the only customer in the long, dark, cheerless room. Restaurants like the Poweshiek kept students happy with dormitory food.

I was not worrying about finances, as I had the ten-dollar bill and knew I could earn more before school actually opened.

Well before 5:00 I was at the *Herald*. Its front office had partitioned spaces for the students who edited the college publications,

for Frisbie, for Ray, and the rest of the staff. One of these was Pearl
Haag, who was not only bookkeeper and payroll clerk but also general overseer who knew the status of jobs in progress and which
printer was working on what. These days she would have the title of
administrative vice-president and an office of her own.

I began the ritual that I was to follow hundreds of times, opening
with "Hello, Mr. Ray," a greeting acknowledged by a glance and a
grunt. His instructions were almost as brief; either he handed me a
stack of news copy or told me where to get it. On Fridays, he added,
"Don't forget your pay," and Pearl, on hand to see that I did not
forget it, gave me a small envelope filled with the week's earnings in
bills and coins. Often Ray's instructions were, "See Frisbie." Then
the pattern was, "Hello, Mr. Frisbie," followed by a lengthier response: how are you, how's school, what do you hear from home,
and finally by ample instructions to guide my evening. In the back
shop, Frank and Louis, tidying their final galleys of type, were
ending their long day. On this first visit, Frank gave me all sorts of
heady advice: this will be your machine, here is the style sheet, here
are the tools, there is where you go for extra metal, don't forget to
turn the motor off when you leave.

Others in the shop were also getting ready to quit: Isobel, a
red-haired, ball-of-fire woman, who, like Mother, was a competent
printer; Bill, printer and pressman; and half a dozen others whose
names have slipped away past all recovery. In minutes the building
would be emptied and the doors locked. Lights would have been
turned off, except for the small, shaded bulb that illuminated my
keyboard. So my memories are of working alone in a dark building,
night after night until 10:00, midnight, or later.

My first assignment was to set a genealogy of Amos Judd, a Vermont settler of the seventeenth century, his fifteen children by two
wives, and their descendants. The book described the births, marriages, achievements, and deaths of several generations. Even in
1923, people were interested in their roots.

The Judd book, my first introduction to family history, was
America's story in miniature. The Judds fought in every skirmish,
rebellion, and war, surviving cholera and other classic fevers,
gradually moving west and south into nearly every state in the
Union. Sometimes a Judd went west and simply disappeared.
Sometimes the author could discover much about one Judd but little

about another. When a household destroys its letters, clippings, and other records, it slams the door on its branch of the family. I spent many evenings working on this long book, moving through the Revolution, the Civil War, the Spanish-American War, World War I, and the greater and lesser events in between.

Publishers, printers, and operators live in a world of deadlines: long-term, such as having the ballots printed a month before the election; midterm, such as setting an ad on Monday so the advertiser can see the proof Tuesday so he can return it Wednesday; and *right now*, such as: "Can you stop what you're doing and set me this line in 14-point Century Bold caps, 30 picas, so I can make this correction and get this form to the press?" There are also regular deadlines, such as those demanded by press day, so the new issue will be in the post office in time for the 7:45 mail. Every piece of job work had a deadline written on its ticket: "Promised Wed. A.M.," "Promised 3:00 P.M. Fri.," and so on. I never, never saw a job ticket reading, "Customer in no rush. Job can be delayed. Any time will do."

One Wednesday when I arrived at my usual 5:00 hour I found everybody feverish, even Pearl, who routinely could handle three requests simultaneously, and Frisbie, whose calm was normally unshakable. A power failure had brought to a halt Linotypes, presses, paper cutters—everything that had a motor. Electric service had just been restored, but half a dozen critical deadlines had already passed, and the lost time had to be made up right now. Typesetting had fallen far behind. Could I work extra hours—all night if necessary? Ray showed me a pile of copy several inches high, his abbreviated mumblings intoned in a worried key. Isobel stood by, waving special copy she needed for jobs now past due. Frisbie explained they disliked imposing on me, but the situation was critical.

For me it was a supreme moment, to be printed on parchment, bound in full calf, and lettered in gold. I looked at the group, thumbed the heap of copy, made calculations, and assured them that I could and would set it. "All of it?" queried Ray. "All of it," I replied, in my best Horatio-at-the-bridge, thumb-in-the-dike, Leonidas-at-the-pass, eighteen-year-old voice. A linotype operator is seldom offered the main role in a drama.

My huddle of spectators dispersed, some for the day, as if they had been set free; a few for supper break before coming back to work overtime. Obviously they could not proceed with either ads or jobs until the type was set. I tackled the urgent materials first that required assorted sizes of type and lengths of line. Then I settled down for the long bout with news copy. Actually I was not eager to be up all night as I still had lessons of my own to prepare. Even college students are known to have internal power failures that cause them to fall behind.

I worked with intense concentration, feeding lines through the machine faster than it could accept them—a feat known as "hanging the machine," the result of the keyboard mechanism being inherently faster than the casting mechanism. Many operators can do this for a while; I hung the machine for ten- and fifteen-minute stretches. Midnight came, with my leaving my chair only at the intervals necessary to dump the accumulation of lines into galleys and to hang fresh pigs of lead above the melting pot. The printers had long since gone home.

When I finished the last sheet, it was 2:00 A.M. I had set nineteen galleys (columns), heaping the available table space with galleys two and three deep. I entered "9 hours" on my time sheet and walked the dimly lit blocks to Smith Hall.

As heroics go it was not like scoring two touchdowns in the last minutes of play, but in its own area it was a classic performance.

Next morning the office force, viewing my immense output, could hardly believe the nine-hour figure that I had turned in, except for the sensible reason that workers do not cheat themselves on their time sheets. When I appeared that afternoon, Ray expressed doubt that I had done the job as quickly as I had indicated, arguing that I had misfigured. But when Friday came, he flashed a rare grin when he greeted me with his customary, "Don't forget your pay."

Occasionally he asked me to take the train to Montezuma, fifteen miles away, to run the machine for his son-in-law, Dave Sutherland, editor of the *Montezuma Republican*. Working on the *Republican* was much like working on the *Gilman City Guide*, as the *Republican* had only a single dilapidated typesetting machine. When it broke down, putting Dave behind, he flashed an S.O.S. to Grinnell and I hopped the Minneapolis & St. Louis to his rescue. The track from Grinnell to Montezuma was a short, stubby spur, on which a single mixed train of a coach and two freight cars shuttled back and forth, an authentic relic of overexuberant railroad planning. I enjoyed these expeditions, since I would be paid for travel time, given supper money, and lodged in the Webber Hotel, which featured both electric lights and steam heat. No one can forget his first experience with an expense account.

On one trip I finished at 11:00 and walked to the Webber to get a room for the night. The clerk, talking to a friend in the quiet, deserted lobby, interrupted his conversation long enough to advise me that he had no rooms left whatever.

I stood there, puzzled, hardly knowing where to turn. I had flipped the *Republican*'s night latch and could not get back in. I saw a sofa in the lobby and asked if I could sleep on it.

The clerk, who recognized me from previous visits, had a better idea and asked his friend, "Do you suppose Old Jake would mind having this kid sleep with him?" I got the impression right away that the practice of sharing a room with a stranger was not entirely new.

"No, Jake won't mind. Take him on up."

We climbed the single flight of stairs and stood outside Old Jake's room. The clerk opened it—it was not locked, of course—and called: "Jake! Jake!" Jake mumbled sleepily.

"Jake, we've got a kid here who has no place to sleep. The hotel is full. Can he climb in with you?"

"Sure, sure." Jake was still not entirely aroused, but he rolled to the far side of the bed, hardly giving me a glance. The clerk turned on the light just a moment so I could get my bearings, then turned it off, and departed. I stripped down to my underwear and in minutes was sound asleep.

In the morning I quietly put on my clothes. A china pitcher and bowl were on a stand but I did not bother with these niceties. Across the bed I could see the massive, blanketed form of my benefactor. I crept down the stairs and entered the lobby, now deserted.

Here in the center of a small Iowa town I had stumbled onto a survival of frontier days. People share beds and rooms today with strangers, but only in the presence of blizzards, earthquakes, or tornadoes that make travelers and residents homeless—events that remind us again that we are, at best, members of the human family and, at most, can survive only with the help of others. In minutes I was on the train back to Grinnell.

As it happened, this was my last trip to Montezuma.

15

My college career was shaped mainly by the demands of the *Herald* but partly by those of the community.

Grinnell, a town of 5,000, was on the double-track Chicago-to-Denver route of the Rock Island, later famed as the Route of the Rocket, and still later, for its losing struggle to survive. Crossing the double tracks, after running through the campus, was the less-distinguished Minneapolis-to-St.-Louis branch of the M. & St. L., locally known as the Maimed and Still Limping. Though its passenger service was deplorable, there was nothing maimed about its 2:00 A.M. fast freight, the roar of which regularly hurtled new freshman women from their beds, panicked by terror, sure that Doomsday was upon them. After the first week, though, even they did not hear it.

A well-graded dirt road, the White Pole Trail, connected Grinnell with Davenport on Iowa's eastern border. Westerly this road went to Des Moines and on to Council Bluffs–Omaha. Bus service was still to come. As late as 1928 I bought a $11.20 round-trip ticket from Des Moines to Chicago on a newly established line, but the bus left Des Moines seven hours late. Nobody seemed to know where it was or when it would arrive, so I spent most of those hours anchored to the depot. The bus took all night and the next day to complete the trip. Not until the mid-1930s was long-distance service at all dependable.

When the road was dry, the sixty-five-mile drive from Grinnell to Des Moines took two hours. When the road was wet, the wise driver stayed home. A factor that increased travel time was that the road went through the main street of every town on the way. In just a few years, however, drivers would make sixty miles an hour on good dirt or gravel roads—a mile a minute.

Although the airplane had been around for two decades, it was still, in the minds of level-headed people, a single-engined biplane creature, used for stunt flying. No discerning person would be seen in one. The men who paid $5 at state fairs for a short ride fully realized that they were flirting with danger and were immensely relieved to get their feet back on the ground. Every now and then a news item reported a fatal crash. Only the largest cities boasted "aeroports." Towns were beginning to identify themselves, however, by painting their names in large letters on the roofs of buildings, to help pilots check their positions. The reliable, all-weather way to travel was by train.

Radio, used feebly in the 1920 campaign, continued to grow. As early as 1922, Iowa had twenty broadcasting stations. I recall seeing a set in Ray's home and a few scattered through the men's halls. The physics department owned a radio with two sets of headphones and a loud speaker. Before I was graduated, I heard a broadcast of a football game.

I make these statements to locate Grinnell and the college in time as well as in space. Sixty years later, neither task is easy. Students had to adjust themselves to a stern code. Because of the newly ratified Eighteenth Amendment, the sale of liquor was banned. To this federal law, the college added its own inflexible rule: a student caught "possessing or consuming" liquor was expelled. Although bootlegging abounded, Grinnell students simply did not have the drinking habit. I pass over the colorful exceptions, but on the whole drinking was more prevalent at large universities than at small, religious-oriented colleges. A quip was circulated about Iowa playing Indiana—Hawkeyes in the stands on one side, Hoosiers on the other. After the game, empty bottles of a nondescript sort were found under the stands and tallied. On the field Indiana defeated Iowa 27 to 14, but in the stands Iowa outdrank Indiana 87 bottles to 42. As Will Rogers said, Prohibition was better than no liquor at all.

The town of Grinnell had passed an ordinance forbidding the sale of cigarettes; pipe tobacco and cigars were allowed, but not cigarettes. To counter this restriction, one student who had a railroad pass regularly made out-of-town trips and returned with a suitcase full of cartons. All smokers knew that they could pick up a supply of Chesterfields, Lucky Strikes, or Camels from his dresser drawer at anytime, leaving fifteen cents per pack. In that way he financed his education, so the end was glorious though the means were shady. Men were allowed to smoke in the dorms but not elsewhere on the campus. The rule did save a lot of litter.

Few women smoked; those who did, did so privately. One afternoon I was startled to see two women, not students, smoking in Candyland, and stared at them in a mixture of awe and fascination. Smoking became so popular with women, however, that a year or so after I was graduated the college provided a special smoking room for them. Though to most people it seemed a sensible way of handling the situation, this flagrant recognition of women smoking needed to be explained carefully to parents and alumni. Ray was one of those who thought the city's anti-cigarette ordinance was ridiculous.

Against this background of public morals, the college imposed its own rules, explained year after year by upperclass students to freshmen. After the first day or two, no automobiles were allowed on campus until the spring break. This spartan regulation was accepted without complaint, since most families had only one car anyway and needed it at home. No one felt deprived; classrooms and entertainment spots were in easy walking distance. What astonishes me at this point is that Sunday dates were forbidden until after the spring holiday—the idea being that Sundays were designed for men to enjoy the companionship of men, women the companionship of women. Upperclass men and women successfully sold this notion each year to new students.

The marriage of students automatically canceled their registration. Don and his steady date, Dorothy Graves, also a graduate of Osceola High School, were secretly married the summer before his senior year. But the marriage was discovered at midyear, so both were required to leave the college. Students already married were not admitted, even though they could have lived off campus. It took World War II, with hordes of mature students financed by the GI bill of rights, to put a sudden end to the no-marriage ban. Without their tuition, colleges would have perished. My speech professor, Ryan, commented years later on the irony of this situation: "The tuition of married students saved Grinnell."

No musical instruments could be played after 8:00 P.M., Sunday through Thursday; no card playing in club rooms on Sunday; no smoking in the men's dining room when ladies were present; lady friends could be entertained in the men's halls only between 7:00 and 10:00 P.M. with proper chaperonage and due notice to house chairmen; coats must be worn to dinner Sunday noon.

Women were locked in their cottages by 10:00 P.M.; on party nights the hour was extended to 11:00. This rule, solidly approved by society, was enforced on large and small campuses alike. If a woman checked in fifteen minutes late, she was assessed a "minor"; if more than fifteen, a "major." Three minors equaled a major. After three majors or nine minors, she was "campused," which meant that for a week she must be in her room by 7:30, could not go to any campus function without being accompanied by a member of the Women's League Board, and could not talk to any men, least of all the one she was going steady with, for more than three to five minutes. Her escort, realizing that he deserved punishment as well as she, often atoned by sending her candy or flowers.

In the light of modern freedom such rules seem quaintly Victorian, if not horrendously medieval, but, other than an occasional protest in the *Scarlet and Black*, we accepted these regulations as we accepted the coming and going of the Rock Island. As this decade was known as the Roaring Twenties, characterized by scandalously short skirts, red hot mammas, John Held's cigarette-smoking flappers and coon-skinned draped cake-eaters, along with speakeasies and bootleggers, I can only conclude that because of our sheltered existence our roaring was muted and muffled. But not too sheltered; booze could still invade the men's halls, and one student financed his education by selling contraceptives.

Grinnell's academic reputation attracted outstanding students. In any group you could hardly swing a cat without hitting three or four high-school valedictorians or salutatorians—archaic words once used to label first- and second-place students in a graduating class.

Perhaps we felt our lives were overly governed, or, in language that is more contemporary, that we were missing grand opportunities for self-actualization. However, we were too busy studying to worry about such possibilities. We deftly evaded the rules when we could but we did not mobilize against them.

The faculty also moved in a system with rigid boundaries. Like us, they had to meet standards set by their superiors. The president governed mainly because of his abilities, but he governed partly because, as I heard one of them put it, upon his installation he had been invested with an aura of magnificence that added to his influence. He could expect to survive fifteen or twenty years with little criticism from anyone. Presidents did not resign, they retired. Not until the campus rebellions of the sixties did we see many of these ancient practices crumble.

. . . Well, one can reflect, rules are different today . . .

And, Mother might have said, rules were different when she went to college.

I find it hard to think of Mother as a one-time college student; she had had only a bit of grade-school education. Yet she attended Stephens College in 1903, when she was twenty-one; she was a piano teacher and came to Stephens for more music. After only part of a term, she caught the measles and had to go home.

"I'm glad you asked about Stephens [she could have told me]. I was terribly homesick. I missed the farm. But, I kept telling myself, as long as I could walk down Broadway and see a horse, I would stick it out.

"Our teachers were so much stricter than yours . . . we were actually afraid of them. They gave such long assignments . . . and were so critical.

"You say you had so much to eat you didn't always go to breakfast . . . well, we never got enough to eat. On days when they served spareribs, I could get only two or three and had to fill up on bread. We looked forward to food boxes from home.

"You say you could keep your girl friends out until 10:00 or 11:00. And you could go anywhere with them. We couldn't go out *at all*, unless with a chaperone. Of course the school couldn't keep track of so many of us, so we *managed*. But we had to be in at 9:00, and what's worse, we had to blow our lamps out by then.

"Well, since you ask, we went to bed as we were supposed to, but we didn't sleep. We made a tent out of the covers, put the lamp under the tent, and wrote letters to our fellows. Oh, we were *very careful* about the lamp and kept the blaze low.

"No, we didn't have a clinic—that's why I had to go home. They didn't want a girl with measles around the dormitory. I guess I might as well tell you another reason—I heard the fellow I was interested in was beginning to look at another girl. . . . You're asking too many questions . . ."

. . . Mother, you or some other girl might have burned down the whole dormitory. The Great Stephens College Fire of 1903, they would have called it, and you would have gone down in history along with Mrs. O'Leary and the cow. And they called *us* the Roaring Twenties!

16

For the first ten days I had Smith Hall to myself. Then, overnight, the building filled with forty boys, two of whom moved in with me. I left for my evening's work and when I returned at 10:00 they were just getting ready to go to bed. I saw each remove his clothes and don a cotton jacket and a matching pair of pants. Later I learned they were pajamas. It had never occurred to me that people had special clothes to sleep in. In fact, it seemed stupid to go to the trouble of removing one set of clothing only to put on another set. I went to bed in my BVD's—that famous make of sleeveless, one-piece, drop-seat, light-weight underwear ("Next to myself, I like BVD's best" was one of the first of the famous catchy ad slogans, like Bon Ami's "Hasn't scratched yet" and Ivory Soap's "99 and 44/100 percent pure"). I was outwardly calm but inwardly shaken. Next day I wrote Mother about my predicament. She scoured Osceola and finally located a pair; when they arrived, I felt respectable. My roommates probably thought I had simply left them at home, and I did not care to reveal the full depth of my ignorance.

On registration day I was counseled by a marvelously knowing senior, Margaret Henley. To this completely charming young lady I readily confided my interest in becoming a newspaper publisher, along with my liking for debating and speaking. She enrolled me in English, French, mathematics, and public speaking, plus a two-hour elective with the modest title, History of the World and Man. She discussed the advisability of taking required courses first and had an eye for good teachers. "Your English professor," she confided, "is chairman of the department and a Harvard Ph.D., so he should be especially good." He was Paul Spencer Wood; eventually I took more courses with him than with anybody.

After leaving Margaret, I passed tables where sat the representatives of student activities. I now think of them as vultures preying on tender freshman bodies. I was easily conned into ordering a *Cyclone,* the yearbook, which took a precious $5 bill. I must have thought a yearbook would give as much space to freshmen as to anybody. I could not have been more wrong. When I arrived at the office of Louis V. Phelps, the treasurer, I had only $10 left.

I quickly saw that the students ahead of me in line were better fortified to confront the treasurer than I was. From their conversation I could overhear that they were armed with checks from home that covered their semester bills of between $250 and $340. I suddenly realized I had overlooked a major detail of college life. When I reached the head of the line and revealed my name, Phelps reached for my statement. As I had a $100 credit from my scholarship, he said easily that all I would need was $219.50.

I tendered my $10 bill. "I'd like to pay this on account."

"Well," he said grimly, "that leaves you a balance, payable now, of $209.50."

"I don't have it."

"You what?"

"I don't have it. I have to work for it first."

He looked like a man who had opened the safe and found the cash box missing. "How do you propose to earn it?"

"I'm a linotype operator at the *Herald*. I work nights."

He wanted to know how much I could earn by this unusual process, and how much I could pay each week. I told him I did not know, as some weeks I worked more hours than others. I also had other expenses, such as books.

He processed this iconoclastic information reluctantly, something short of computer speed. Behind me the line grew restless, but curious. Obviously one of their own was about to be impaled. This could be fun to watch. Phelps knew that what he said would be overheard. College authorities do not relish bending a rule in public.

"You bring a written statement from the *Herald* that you are an employee. Then each Monday you come to this office and pay something on account. You will need to have the total bill paid by the end of the semester.

"Now," he went on, and here the script became taut, "if you don't make your payments, we have ways of seeing that you are not allowed to go to class." This statement was calculated to make me shudder, along with any others in the line who might be financially overoptimistic.

Undoubtedly he had worked out similar arrangements with other students, but surely well in advance, and with a better ante than ten dollars. Next day I furnished him with a letter from Ray, who, I learned later, had also made a supporting phone call. In the semesters that followed the treasurer's staff became accustomed to my Monday afternoon visits.

So many bonds interconnect the students of a small college, so many classes and friends in common, that little distinction was made between those who needed to work and those who didn't. One group was as respected as the other. This attachment later made our class reunions memorable. Since eventually we would all be graduated and become internationally famous, present inequalities were transient. On graduation, well-paying jobs for all would be abundant. It was the American dream.

17

That freshman year I had classes with the heads of two departments: English and speech.

Being chairman was in itself a respected credential. Chairmen did not rotate in and out of office, as they did in many college and university departments decades later, but were put there to stay. The chairmanship represented seniority, outstanding academic achievement, and the ability to command. When one man wore out on the job, the administration turned to another. Only infrequently did a woman attain a professorship, let alone a headship. I can recall only three female full professors: Eleanor Lowden in English, Caroline Sheldon in French, and Luella J. Read in art.

Our freshman English class of twenty gradually assembled, knowing that the head of a department was on the way. If a senior, bent on mischief, had stood outside the door saying, "Remember, your professor is head of the department; when a department head enters the classroom, students are supposed to stand," we would have stood.

We knew that everybody called him "Mr.," even though he was both "Professor" and "Doctor"; but then, every male teacher was called Mr. Even President John Hanson Main, Johns Hopkins Ph.D. and later LL.D. from four institutions, was called Mr. Main (or, behind his back, "Prexy").

As we suspected the head of a department would be especially tough in freshman English, we awaited his arrival with trepidation. He entered with quick step—a slender, slightly stooped man, with thinning hair, and a high forehead. He carried a green-felt drawstring bag half-full of books, which he fanned out on the desk. Later we learned that the green bag indicated that he had studied at Oxford. He seated himself, picked up his class roll, looked at it, looked at us. I remember his ingratiating, thin-lipped smile, and his twinkling eyes peering through rimless glasses, as if he were already beginning to chuckle inwardly over the good things he had in store for us.

He took his watch from his pocket and laid it on the table, in itself a comforting gesture.

I recall that all at once I needed to start writing things down, and that I, like other students, had no supplies. The young man next to me opened his leather-covered, loose-leaf notebook, the Grinnell seal embossed on the front. Even before Wood entered the room, he had methodically written the date and the name of the course with what was obviously a new fountain pen. So at the outset I learned that some students plan ahead better than others. I am a quick study and saw that I would need a fountain pen and a leather-bound, loose-leaf notebook, bearing the college seal, as soon as I could replace the ten dollars that the college treasurer had lifted from me.

Wood had an extraordinarily wide range of interests. Why was I amazed that he could refer to current songs, movies, athletic events, with apt, often humorous connection to whatever we were reading? Perhaps because my other teachers, no doubt equally well informed, had never quite related to the student's pool of experiences with his informality. Moreover, he seemed as much at home with the literature of the still-young twentieth century as he was with the eighteenth, as familiar with Sinclair Lewis, H. L. Mencken, Carl Sandburg, and T. S. Eliot as with Dryden, Pope, and Johnson.

Freshman English consisted partly of grammar, rhetoric, and the study of short selections, ending with the Old Testament in a translation that emphasized the book as history and literature. Mainly, however, the course consisted of frequently writing three- or four-page themes, plus long papers that successively illustrated expository, argumentative, and narrative prose. Despite my inner conviction that I could write as well as anybody, Wood kept me on a diet of B−'s and B's. Even with regular conferences, at which he returned my accumulated themes bearing these lowly grades, with lengthy suggestions, I persisted on my B plateau. Gradually I began to realize that a writer has to do his own thing, not somebody else's thing; that the "style" for theme writing was not elevated and bookish; that the proper topic for a theme was one that was rooted in the writer's own beliefs and experiences and that could be set down in language that was specific and personal. Once I had grasped this timeless wisdom, I wrote a theme about what it was like to run a typesetting machine in the dead of night at a newspaper office.

Wood coughed up an A, and from then on it seemed I could do no wrong.

18

Mark Twain once wrote that if he were a pagan, he would erect a statue to Energy and fall down and worship it. I offer no observation about my own religious leaning, but I would like to erect a statue to Luck right alongside his.

In my first public-speaking class, I had an indication of her favor.

I had looked forward to the course, even though I did not know the name of the teacher. With thirty others I met one morning in an auditorium that would seat two hundred. We disposed ourselves haphazardly on either side of the center aisle. Moments after the bell rang, a stately figure with iron-gray hair and full but carefully trimmed moustache, walked jauntily through the door at our right, banged a few keys on the piano as he passed it, and stopped in front of the small stage, where he stood, cheerfully, looking us over. He carried a textbook and a packet of course cards.

In later years we used the word *courtly* as one that well described him.

"Good morning," he saluted us, in a rich, full voice. "This bit of protoplasm standing in front of you is named Ryan." I was pleased that I was familiar with the word *protoplasm* and, like any good printer, could spell it.

"First, I am going to divide this class into two groups." He shuffled the packet to reassure us that what followed would be a completely random operation. "The names of those I read will join the other class at the end of the hall." He nodded in that direction. He then intoned fifteen names. Their owners slowly, even glumly, walked past the piano, out of the auditorium. For some reason I felt pleased that I was among those that Luck had picked to stay.

Ryan then regrouped us on either side of the aisle, two by two, explaining that when he asked one of us to speak, he wanted that person to have a quick route to the platform without needing to squeeze past several bodies.

"Your text is *Fundamentals of Speech* by Charles H. Woolbert," he continued. Speech teachers will recognize that title as one of the two or three books widely studied in the twenties and thirties and becoming established as a classic, to be reviewed with respect in graduate seminars. Like any discipline, the field later had a hundred texts, most of which never saw a second edition. "Woolbert is the only author whose psychology is right." Reading a sample, Ryan commented that the book was "outstandingly behavioristic." Those were the days of John B. Watson and behaviorism; since then ten schools of psychological thought have come and gone.

Woolbert, a professor at the University of Illinois, with a Ph.D. from Harvard, was one of the nation's most distinguished professors of speech. His Ph.D. was in psychology; in all the world there was only a single Ph.D. in speech. Ryan's own degrees were a B.A. from Cornell and an M.S. from Chicago, in English. The few speech courses he had taken were taught in the Department of English at Cornell. These esoteric details, however, I did not know until long afterwards. Right now I was getting acquainted with the bit of protoplasm.

Ryan was a dedicated believer in the necessity of public speaking in business, professional, and public life. "Public speaking is the most important study in the curriculum," he assured and reassured us. The way to learn to speak well is to make numerous short speeches. "Newton, Iowa, is the home of the One-Minute washing machine. Grinnell is the home of the one-minute speech." Even a brief speech, however, should have a useful purpose. A speaker should not merely scatter "beautiful sunshine," which we quickly saw was his term for B.S. To be able to present a message in a short time called for organization. "Every speech should have an introduction, a central idea, a body, and a conclusion," he insisted. "Approach the idea, state the idea, develop the idea, leave the idea."

We chose our own topics; the day of teacher-assigned subjects or memorized selections from revered orators had long vanished. In fact, Ryan and his Cornell teacher, James A. Winans, were primarily responsible for burying this classical practice. Before we spoke, we handed in a one-page outline of what we proposed to say. An outline that failed to show an introduction, central idea, body, and conclusion was bounced back to its creator.

Ryan would not tolerate notes; we must become able to look at our listeners. We could avoid the no-notes rule by memorizing our talks, but he quickly detected the flat cadences of memorized deliv-

ery. To steer us further toward a natural fluency he would sometimes say, "Although I asked you to prepare a one-minute talk,
today I actually want you to talk two minutes." This shift required us
to scratch together and sort out instantaneously any germane information. Though he kept to the assigned time limits, calling "Thank
you" when the deadline arrived, we quickly saw that if we had a
genuine idea, he would yield us additional time. Another device
was, after collecting our outlines, to hand each of us another student's outline, let us study it and then give that student's talk.

Ryan himself used the short speech to explain principles. "I am
going to step over here and make a little speech about 'The Four
Ways to Begin a Speech.'" A minute later we knew the four ways:
Anecdote, Personal Experience, Illustration, General Statement.
The initial letters spell A P-I-G. Another speech was on the four
ways of concluding: Summary, Hortatory Appeal, Illustration, Personal Reference; in a word, S-H-I-P. Years afterwards you could
rouse any of his students from deep slumber and he or she could
summon from memory those mnemonic devices and the idea each
letter stood for.

At times we had a written examination. On those days Ryan wandered around the classroom, reading over our shoulders what we
had written. If a student opened with a scrawl, he gently tore the
sheet from the blue book and talked firmly about legibility and
margins. "Start over," he advised, "make it neat; make it *look* like a
good paper." He might correct a sentence, or say, in a hoarse
whisper, "You didn't answer the question. *Answer the question that
is asked.* Now the first part can start like this . . . ," still in a stage
whisper. What kind of an examination was this, in which the teacher
helped the student *during* the class hour? Was this exercise really to
teach us to order our thoughts in writing as well as in speaking, and
not merely to give us a grade?

Some students, especially those who went on to graduate and
professional schools, said later that Ryan had taught them the basic
principles of examination writing. Others went so far as to allege
that Ryan had taught them to think.

One day he demanded: "What is the most important thing in
life?" We were taken by surprise, for we were sitting there stuffed
with one-minute speeches, eager to purge them from our systems,
and not delay the ordeal by answering a stupid question. Still, doing

what we were asked, we offered guesses: love, religion, home, and family, even the one-minute speech itself. Each was rejected. Finally he revealed the answer: *health*. To teach the importance of health was a major part of his pedagogy. He had known students, teachers, business and professional men, whose careers had been shattered by nervous breakdowns or other debilitating ailments; hence, good health was a prized jewel.

This point being made, he asked us to name the second most important thing in life: again, the answer was not home or mother, but *economic independence*. Every young person should strive not for riches but for the ability to stand on his or her own feet. Next he demanded, "What do you know today?" We were proud to be able to answer promptly, and we did: "Nothing!" I suspect that third question was included mainly to keep the discussion from getting too solemn. Still, he observed, considering that so much needed to be learned, we should adopt the humility of the scholar.

Shortly afterwards he opened the class with review questions. "What is the greatest thing in life?" "Health!" we roared. Years before, went a rumor, Ryan had been desperately ill; that experience made him resolve to teach students to appreciate this one great gift. If on a rainy day anybody came to class improperly attired, Ryan sent her or him home through the rain to get rubbers and raincoat. "No need to try to teach you to speak," he declared, "until you learn to take care of your health." We were also able to recall the correct answers to the other two questions. After our responses came a pause, and then: "I may never be able to teach you anything more meaningful. Class dismissed." We were amazed by this turn of events but we remembered the point.

Years later Ryan was guest of honor at a public banquet at which many Grinnellians were present. One speaker, a former student, remarked: "When Professor Ryan kept telling us, 'Boys, wear your rubbers,' I never knew he meant those dang things you put on your feet." The crowd roared. Nothing is funnier than an in-joke, understood and relished by those present. Ryan could not have been more delighted.

Ryan's ideas were printed on individual leaflets and were later incorporated in his one book, *Successful Speaking*, published by the *Des Moines Register*. My copy is the fifth printing. For twenty years he drove to Des Moines, teaching public speaking in an evening

class to business and professional people. Everybody who was anybody in central Iowa took his course; in all, more than eight
thousand. Through these contacts he frequently addressed state and
national conventions of business organizations: banking, lumbering,
retailing, and others. Before addressing any group he read widely in
its professional journals—to learn the current issues in the grocery
or undertaking business, for instance—and counseled his listeners
about the art of communication in their own fields, citing their
problems and circumstances with infinite understanding.

Once I asked him about his speechmaking to business and professional people. "You must saturate yourself with their concerns," he
said. "You must pore over their house organs and trade journals
until you have absorbed their language. How can you help them
with their problems of communication until you learn what they
need to communicate about?"

"And I'll tell you another thing," he went on. "You must get them
to see that their calling is important. For example, say to the lumber
dealers, 'Your job is not selling boards, nails, cement, doorknobs.
You are helping people construct homes, businesses, churches,
schools. Your job is really building a community, a nation.'"

Speech was not a required subject, but 90 percent of the students
took it.

Ryan had the gift of phrasemaking. "Do not make the gods weep"
was his reminder to avoid dullness and make ideas compelling. "A
fool convinces me with his reasons—a wise man with my reasons.
Seventy-five percent of your speech is made by the audience."
"Abraham Lincoln made the greatest three-minute speech ever delivered, the Gettysburg Address; the greatest twenty-minute speech
ever delivered, the Second Inaugural; the greatest one-hour address
ever delivered, the Cooper Union Address." One can offer compet-
ing candidates, but he would not be able to escape the contagion of
Ryan's admiration for Lincoln as a speaker and years later would
recall the vivid way in which he had stated these judgments.

In 1947, Ryan retired and moved to San Diego. Two years later,
as head of the department at the University of Missouri, I invited
him to join our faculty. His former students at Des Moines learned
that their professor was returning to the classroom. When Ryan first
visited the office I had assigned him, he found it filled with pots,
vases, and boxes of flowers that they had sent.

I wondered if Ryan were as good as I remembered. Perhaps my adult judgment would not support my youthful enthusiasm. I asked him to give a lecture to the five hundred students enrolled in our beginning public-speaking course. I introduced him without fanfare. At once his magnetic personality filled the lecture hall and his magic combination of ideas, imaginatively stated, gripped his listeners—mostly mature GIs, back on campus after World War II. They were as moved as I had been, a quarter of a century previously.

I am proud to have been one of his students and still wonder whether my career would have been different if I had been sent to the class at the end of the hall. Who was it said life is half virtue, half Luck?

19

Fortunately, students do not have to face individually, head-on, the formidable structure known as college. Inner groups help give them identity, share their burdens, and confound the authorities. These groups make college life possible, even enjoyable.

In my instance, the largest of these groups was what became the Class of '27. At the outset we were labeled as raw material that could amount to something only under wary supervision. Our women followed rules governing number of dates and hours to be spent in study halls. Our men escaped these indignities but suffered others. Each had to wear a beanie, a scarlet and black skullcap surmounted by a button. If he failed to wear it, he could be paddled by an upperclassman. Moreover, on meeting any upperclassman, he was required to salute by touching the button. Failure to button resulted in being swatted. The command "hands to ankles" frequently rang across the campus.

In small, helpless bands we were herded together and confronted with these regulations, being assured that they were designed for our ultimate welfare. We also learned that, early in the semester, we would one night be routed from our beds, and, clad in pajamas, would be marched to the golf course and compelled to run a gauntlet of our superiors, each armed with a paddle. This ordeal was known as the "pajama parade." We readily saw that the clash of a couple of hundred paddles on our thinly clad bottoms would produce bruises that would linger for days.

Each in his own way braced for the ordeal. Many suffered practice swings from their fellows in order to toughen the hide. Others went to bed clad not only in sleepwear but in underwear as well. Some contemplated inserting, between hide and BVD's, the cardboard rectangles that came with laundry-finished shirts. Should these precautions be discovered, the penalty could be frightful. Still, human beings take desperate risks when survival is at stake. Not knowing which night would be the night added to the agony.

Finally the bleak midnight moment came when we heard shouts, heavy footsteps, and the slapping of paddles. We were marched to the golf course, cordoned off, and one by one forced to run past the long line of eager, expectant, yelling men. We could see the victims ahead of us, each running for his life, and could hear shouts and the cracks of paddles on taut flesh. Days before we had calculated that if one ran close enough to the man in front, the paddlers might not be able to give him full attention. If, on the other hand, one dawdled and allowed a breathing space between him and his precursor, he would get everybody's artistic, follow-through blast. Each had to fight his own battle; later, back at the dorms, we could attend to one another's wounds.

The art of hazing, which we called *prepping*, was practiced in other ways. In one hall, preps were required to enter and exit through the fire escape. In another, they were compelled to try out for the glee club, whether or not they had ever screeched a note. I have to think with compassion of David Peck, the famous Men's Glee Club conductor, as he suffered through that long list of assorted loons and crows. In still another instance they had to shine every pair of every upperclassman's shoes. Of course, at any time they could be dispatched on menial errands such as fetching a hamburger from Ken Miller's basement snack bar or a book from the library. In later years each freshman had to saw out, sand, varnish, and decorate a paddle to be used exclusively to swat him with.

Another event, the torchlight parade, staged before the first football game, gave us a different sense of group membership. I swelled with chauvinistic pride as I fell in line with seven hundred others, marched to the gym, selected a torch, and continued downtown,

Two segments from the annual All-College photo, taken in front of the library and chapel. We knew it was picture-taking day, but that made little difference in our attire. White shirts and ties were standard for the men; skirts, not slacks or jeans, and heavy, loud-striped stockings (in season) for the women. In two years the skirts would be shorter. (Grinnell Collection, 2 December 1925.)

stopping here and there for yells, later returning to the football field, the scene of the morrow's battle, for hot dogs and mustarded buns. I did not report at the *Herald* until it was over, and although my late start kept me at the keyboard until after midnight, the glow of the evening was worth it.

I got in on the last gasp of a centuries-old college and university tradition known as the literary or debating society. On some campuses it bore a Greek or Latin name: Demosthenean, Ciceronian, Athenian; on others it bore the name of an institution: Oxford Union or Etonian Literary Society. In groups like these, Burke, Fox, Gladstone, Webster, Clay, and countless others polished their skills in composition and delivery. Woodrow Wilson, who studied or taught at half-a-dozen institutions, was the most ardent advocate of the tradition. If the campus had no society, he organized one. At Princeton he persuaded the baseball team to disband and form the Liberal Debate Club instead.

Often these clubs were started on campuses that had little formal provision for teaching writing and speaking. These young men and women, generally those interested in public service, teaching, the ministry, or law, saw that their future success hinged upon the ability to write and speak. Accordingly they organized a club, selected officers, drew up a constitution, and scheduled programs at which they debated or read papers.

Amazingly enough, this custom was still surviving at Grinnell my freshman year. Grinnell had eight societies, with names like Forum and Ionian, for men; Philadelphica and Aegis for women. Most of them had nineteenth-century origins. Each had about forty members.

Every fall the societies held open houses to which those who wished to join were invited. The ritual was as close as we ever got to fraternity or sorority rushing. Old members looked over the new crop and we in turn inspected them. They presented us a sample program, told us about past achievements, and served us tea and cookies. Eventually invitations were matched with acceptances and I became an initiate of Forum.

We knew that initiation ceremonies would give our upperclass friends still another chance to bring out their paddles, and that we would be subjected to other indignities. I speak only for the men's clubs; the women were possibly more genteel. A favorite routine of

Forum actives was to tie one end of a string around a raw oyster; the active held the free end while the pledge, blindfolded, swallowed the creature. Once the oyster had been put down, the active pulled it back out. Afterwards we took a pledge of loyalty that we were told went back to 1906, the founding year. We were then given a hearty welcome and were served refreshments that we were allowed to keep down.

The second meeting was duller; only a dozen attended. The reason I am so ready with this figure is that at the last minute I was asked to be the speaker, and the best topic I could think of was to tell the brothers how to operate a linotype. Though I brought pictures, spare parts, and sample slugs, I cannot believe that what I said was exciting. Even so, attendance at subsequent meetings was no higher, and other clubs fared little better. When midyear came I found myself on a committee that decided to abandon the men's societies and organize Grinnell Forensic for the relatively small number, about twenty, who were genuinely interested. So, unfortunately, I never got to be on the tendering end of a strung oyster. Eventually we became a chapter of Delta Sigma Rho, a national honorary forensic society. The women dissolved their societies completely.

The smallest of a college's inner groups is one's roommates. My first two were congenial, but when they transferred to other schools, I joined four others in a group known as The Syndicate. The word itself recalls the gangsters and mobs that constantly made the front pages. Our territory consisted of four rooms; we bunked in two, used one as a club room that featured a nonstop game of bridge or cribbage, and crammed five desks into the fourth, which became our official study hall. For a year we had a senior, Eugene Woodruff, a chemistry major, from Iowa; two of my own class, Alden Greene, also a chemistry major, from Illinois; and Wendell Metcalf, a mathematics major, from Iowa; and successively two underclassmen, Keiffer Wenger of Illinois and Gaylord Knudson of Iowa.

To our credit, we took our study room seriously, agreeing at the outset that no conversation was permitted at anytime. I must confess that someone, hitting a tough spot in his reading, at times muttered a quiet, perplexed "Dammit!" This observation was not considered talk, which would be an infraction of the rule, but more of a prayer, permissible at all times.

We shared a variety of interests. We attended athletic contests, lectures, and concerts; we were active in track and band. We helped each other in wondrous ways. When I realized I simply must learn to dance, it was The Syndicate that encouraged the venture, helped teach me basic steps, and advised about dating girls who would not be too critical.

College authorities, reflecting the school's parent clientele, had been reluctant to believe that the new style of dancing, in which the gentleman held his lady close and snug, was respectable. They were, of course, certain that dances should not be held on Sunday, and that they should be chaperoned. To disarm both parents and alumni, the college called the weekly gatherings not dances, but a more innocent term, *recreation hours,* which we promptly shortened to "rec hours." A girl could write her mother that she had a date for a recreation hour, which would seem like a wholesome kind of fun. From our point of view the weekly rec hours, augmented by the house parties put on by each men's hall and women's cottage, and the all-school events such as the formal dances, were the absolute hub of the campus's social life. To miss them was to miss everything. We knew the situation was artificial but we lived with it.

A rec hour consisted of twelve dances, each numbered, and included nine or ten fox-trots plus two or three waltzes. The reason for numbering the dances was to allow the boy to trade specific dances in advance. At the formal dances, the exalted music for the grand march also gave couples a chance to form a stately promenade around the floor. Evenings were thus well structured; except for last-minute dislocations, everybody knew who his or her partners would be. The music was excellent. A favorite campus band called itself "The Mississippi Six." Its personnel changed from year to year, but was lively and good fun. Typical fox-trot numbers were "Oh Joseph," "Tiger Rag," "I'll See You in My Dreams," "Shanghai Shuffle," and "Copenhagen." Typical waltzes were "All Alone," "Let Me Call You Sweetheart," "Seventeen." Many of these were new; today it is difficult to believe that once there was a time when nobody had ever heard "Alabamy Bound" or "Dinah."

As I have never been able to stand on the sidelines and watch other people have fun, I plunged in, short on grace but long on determination. My first date was with a hometown girl. She was startled to hear from an Osceola boy who had never dated anybody

Couples posing in front of the fireplace in the lounge in Central (later Main) Hall on the occasion of a formal dance. The Roaring Twenties had moments of elegance and refinement; the "red hot mammas" were really ladies, at heart, and their escorts, gentlemen. Given a change of costume, the play of light and shadow would convince anyone that this picture came straight out of Rembrandt. (Grinnell Collection.)

and doubly startled to be invited to a rec hour. Still, as she loved dancing and felt that being left without a date on a dance night was the greatest of human sufferings, she accepted. Starting, of course, with my willing roommates, I traded the full number of dances, so she would not have to struggle with me all evening. Moreover, I kept up a lively conversation with her and each of my other partners, a way of distracting them from my erratic meanderings. In short, I did what every beginner does. On balance, I suspect she had a good time. The appeal of melody and rhythm, the chance to meet new people, the occasional moments when steps flowed smoothly so that two bodies could move as one, the colored flood-lights that were turned on during the waltzes, the general fun of being at a party, the refreshments afterwards, the noisy groups of students arriving at the girls' cottages only moments before the doors clanged shut, the last-minute compliments and good-nights—all of these made up what we called a rec hour.

A dance date was the only real date; a movie date by comparison was insignificant. A girl could bestow only a certain number of dance dates, and an even smaller number of engagements for formal dances, such as the Christmas formal or the dance sponsored by her own cottage. At these points competition became keen. Preferences had to be brought into the open, which led to discouragement.

In retrospect I am not surprised that the guys and girls of the campus were so devoted to dancing. Of course the alternatives were both limited and lonely. During a rec hour the men's halls were almost entirely deserted; practically every fellow, some after considerable phoning, had secured a date. The big parties were not dinner-dances, or dances preceded by singing or stunts, they were dances, pure and simple. Couples assembled even before the orchestra began playing. Few would be late; they wanted to enjoy at least part of Dance 1 together since Dance 2 would be traded. They seldom sat out dances; and they clapped heartily after every selection. Not until after the "Good Night, Ladies" did they think about the somewhat hurried downtown refreshments. A few years later, the universal tune to close the evening was "Good Night, Sweetheart."

The twenties produced the most sentimental, melodic, appealing music ever written. I have mentioned a few titles: others that were introduced or reintroduced were "Always," "Cecilia," "Collegiate," "Five Foot Two—Eyes of Blue," "I Love My Baby," "Sleepy Time Gal," "Who," "Yes Sir That's My Baby," "Red Hot Mamma," "Bye Bye Blackbird," "Baby Face," "Half a Moon," "Mary Lou," "Smoke Gets in Your Eyes," "I'd Climb the Highest Mountain," "Blue Skies," "Girl of My Dreams," "Three o'Clock in the Morning," "I'm Looking Over a Four-Leaf Clover," "Me and My Shadow," "My Blue Heaven," "I Wonder What's Become of Sally." And anyone who lived through the Roaring Twenties can double the list, from memory. Musical novelties also swept the campuses overnight: "Barney Google," "Horses," "Where do You Worka John," "I'm Just Wild About Animal Crackers," "Crazy Words—Crazy Tune."

We danced to composers, singers, and bands, of gigantic reputation: Irving Berlin, Eddie Cantor, Billy Rose, Ira and George Gershwin, Oscar Hammerstein II, Jessica Dragonette, Duncan Sisters,

Gene Austin, Kate Smith, Sophie Tucker, "Fats" Waller, Rudy Vallee, Paul Whiteman, Fred Waring, Duke Ellington, Ben Bernie, Wayne King, Benny Goodman.

This was the era when the American musical came of age; when the king of instruments was the saxophone; when electrical rather than acoustic recording was developed; when radio went coast-to-coast; when player pianos were popular; when jazz and the blues again fired the imagination; when silent movies were displaced by the talkie. Considering this vast exposure, coupled with the fact that both tunes and words readily gripped the mind—oft-repeated phrases and predictable rhymes like June-moon, Dinah-finah, true-you, Mary Lou-I love you—little wonder that we learned melodies and choruses wholesale. Every generation cherishes the music of its youth but I hardly see how the tunes that grew out of the twenties and the Great Depression can be surpassed. We did not realize it, but American music, like American movies, became loved by young people around the world. Americans who traveled overseas after the war heard their songs everywhere: restaurants, hotel lobbies, nightclubs, resorts, railway stations.

Once I made a list of things learned during my freshman year. In no particular order, here they are: An astonishing amount of information. A better grasp of the arts of writing and speaking. A rudimentary knowledge of auction bridge. An immense fascination with dancing. I have since compared my list with those of others who have tried to compact the freshman experience into few words. One thought he most prized the ability to use a library. Another that she acquired a deep appreciation of music. Another the lessons to be learned from competitive athletics. Still another the insight that led to the choice of a career. Even at Grinnell we discovered in retrospect that each of us had attended a different college.

On the whole I felt I got a fair return on my weekly ten-dollar payment tendered every Monday afternoon at the office of Treasurer Louis V. Phelps.

20

College is like a clock store. At the outset all timepieces are set at the same hour, but some run faster than others. At intervals the master of the store resets them so that again, for a time, they tick in unison.

At the beginning of a semester, all clocks read the same. Another occasion is the day before a holiday, when students and teachers have to meet identical deadlines. Most classes face tests, so that students who have procrastinated needed to reset their individual clocks to match those used by the teachers. Term papers and laboratory notebooks, assigned long in advance, suddenly fall due. On both sides of the M. & St. L. tracks lights burn late as everybody tries to catch up on homework.

We barely had the energy to meet classes that final day. Our minds were bulging with odds and ends of information that might have to be disclosed in examinations. After our last class, we hustled to our rooms to pack for the journey home.

Most colleges had a rule designed to prevent students from starting the vacation early or returning late. Everybody must follow the school clock. At Grinnell we were fined a dollar for each class missed the two days just before or the two days just after a holiday. Hence, classes were well filled before and after vacations. With few exceptions we departed and arrived exactly as the school calendar specified.

Two of my sharpest memories are of the exhausting days that preceded each vacation, and of the mob of two hundred students that collected at the Rock Island station to catch the 5:18 westbound train. We were the locomotive set. The long, narrow cindered platform was jammed with excited, laughing students, eager to go home—yelling back and forth, making last-minute dates, shepherding personal belongings, glancing toward the horizon for the first sign of the approaching train. Finally someone would see a puff of smoke or hear a whistle; the mass would compact itself as each individual inched toward the place where he thought the passenger cars would stop.

Then the locomotive swung around a distant curve so that all could see it; there was a warning whistle; seconds later the train roared past us, steam hissing, bell ringing, brakes squealing; and finally stopped two full car lengths ahead of the main part of the mass. The train was as long as it would ever be: baggage cars, a mail car, numerous coaches, a parlor car, a few Pullmans. Well-dressed passengers already aboard looked at us amusedly, indulgently. The Chicago-to-Denver Limited did not exist exclusively for us, though we acted as if it did.

We rushed aboard, flashing our tickets. Although the Rock Island had put on extra coaches, even then most of us had to stand, or sit on our luggage. We and our suitcases, laundry bags, portable typewriters, and an occasional ukulele flowed in and around the adult passengers, mainly from Chicago and Davenport, plus University of Iowa students, who already occupied the choice seats. Conductor and brakeman inched through the coaches, collecting tickets for Newton, Colfax, Des Moines, Omaha, Denver. Well before each stop the conductor bellowed the city name as he went through car after car. When, in an hour and a half, he reached the outskirts of Iowa's capital city, he called out "Dee Moines-s-s," using the official Rock Island pronunciation; each car came to life as forty or fifty men and women students collected luggage from floor and racks and prepared to dismount. A horde of students lived in Des Moines; still others went beyond; a few, like me, changed to another train for the rest of the journey. The master winder had adjusted our clocks to the same hour.

These splendid movements of people by rail have long since been abandoned; most students now ride home in their own cars, or hitch a ride, making dates from notes thumb-tacked to a central bulletin board: "Ride wanted, Erie, Pa., or nearby, will share gas," "Driving to Minneapolis, Tues., can take three riders." Often the revealing phrase appears: "Leave anytime." Nobody worries about dollar days. Other students flood bus depots, and, in the larger cities, airports; neither was available in the twenties. Yet I remember how shocked we were in 1977 to find that there were no buses from Bruges to Paris. They didn't exist; in Europe there are still plenty of trains.

Not all students left in the first exodus. On the evening before each major holiday, the college sponsored a formal, $4 dance, which was, for most students, the wages of a day and a half. Men wore black tuxes with stiff white shirts, and studs; women wore long, sleeveless gowns. The dance was not held in the dilapidated gym but in the women's dining room with its vaulted cathedral arch, copied from an Oxford dining hall. Your partner would be an extra special person, either your Number One or the best available date from your preferred short list. Sometime during the evening, each couple took time out to pay its respect to the faculty chaperones. Like the programs for the house parties, formal-dance programs were also printed—a little like bridge tallies—and the girls hung these trophies around their mirrors, dangling from the frames like so many scalps. By intermission the marble floor, inflexible and unyielding, would have added to the aches and pains of bodies already exhausted by sleepless nights spent in last-minute study. But no one noticed. Not until they got home and had slept around the clock would they realize how weary they had been.

No one could have been welcomed home with greater affection than I was. Though our apartment was only a two-block walk away, I was met at the depot by the whole family, all insisting on taking my laundry bag. I was given the honor of driving the car, a real treat, since I would not have been in a car for weeks. If I arrived on a press day, as, for example, the Wednesday before Thanksgiving, we went straight to the back shop to finish printing, addressing, and bundling. On other days we moved directly to supper, which had been held up until I arrived.

Father's opening remark always was, "Son, you look peaked," Mother following with "Your eyes look tired." The lines became part of a ritual. If someone had skipped them, Don, whose sense of humor brightened every meal, would have supplied them: "Don't you think Loren looks peaked?" They inquired about school-work—which courses I liked and which ones I didn't, and what grades I would probably get; who were the boys in The Syndicate I was always writing about; and had any new girls appeared on the horizon? They talked about advertisers, which new ones had come over from the *Sentinel*, and which old ones we had lost to it; how much more was still owing on the mortgage; what was new with uncles, aunts, and cousins. I was waited on, catered to. But next morning—and this was also part of the ritual—I was no longer a guest but a member of the family. For the rest of the holiday I was tendered only the regular, standard affection.

In three days, or in the instance of a Christmas holiday, three weeks, I was fully ready to return to school. I feel awkward writing this statement, but there comes a point when college seems like the real world, and home merely a place to pass through. Surely countless other young people have had the same feeling. At any rate when

I and other early arrivals returned to Grinnell, we found many who had returned even earlier, on the station platform to meet us.

Back at school a typical midweek day went like this: Both the men's dining hall, a long, narrow basement area with plastered-over beams, and the women's handsome, high-ceilinged dining room, opened at 7:00. One student, Ted Peterson, was in charge of the men's dining quarters, and another, Mary G. Jones, was in charge of the women's. Only a few tables would be set, as hardly a fourth of the students appeared for breakfast. Waitresses in the women's dining room and waiters in the men's, all students, appeared with trays of scrambled eggs, or bacon, or both. Pitchers of milk and coffee had already been set out, along with boxes of cereal. Ted or Mary G. supervised the serving, directed latecomers to seats, locked the doors at 7:15, and kept an eye on students as they left to make sure no comestibles such as sugar or toast or butter were smuggled to individual rooms. Even then, the amount of candy made from such contraband was considerable. I showed up for breakfast two days a week, apparently happy to do without food until noon.

Classes started at 8:00; no classroom was more than a five-minute walk. Four hours later, students headed for the noon meal, first hurriedly checking the mailboxes.

Luncheons at the men's hall fell into two eras: one uncivilized, one civilized. The routine was to rush to the dining room so tumultuously that save for the efforts of the headwaiter, we would have broken down the doors; most of us had had nothing to eat since the previous evening. We swarmed to our customary seats; whoever found himself nearest the bread platter tossed a slice to everybody else. We did not speak of passing the bread; we "dealt" it. As soon as a waiter appeared, carrying a serving dish of vegetables and a platter of meat, half-a-dozen hands reached for the meat, another half-dozen for the vegetable; the winner served himself a hearty portion and passed the shabby remains to a neighbor, who took a full third or fourth. In seconds both dishes were empty and the table only partly served. Not until the waiter had returned with fresh supplies did the others get food; sometimes a third trip was necessary. By then the bread would be gone, and a new stack would appear, greeted by the cry: "Deal the bread!" We kept the waiter on a trot refilling dishes. In fifteen minutes we were out of there, having

Rock Island Lines

Table No. 1—CHICAGO, ROCK ISLAND, OMAHA AND COLORADO.—Westbound.

June 14, 1920.	Mls.	9	7	13	5	29	209	17	17	207	121	125	321	21	19	19	11	129	133	143
Central time. [LEAVE		AM	AM	PM	PM	PM	PM	AM	AM		AM	AM	AM	PM	PM	PM	PM	PM	PM	PM
Chicago + ... ô	0	*1 00	*10 05	*6 25	*10 00	*11 30	*1 10	*7 00		*9 00	8 45	*10 45		*1 00	*5 30	†6 06	*6 00	k12 50	*2 32	†4 07
Englewood + ... ô	6.6	1 15	10 20	6 38	10 15	11 45	1 25	7 15		9 15	9 00	10 59		1 16	5 43	5 17	6 13	12 45	2 47	4 28
Auburn Park .... ô	8.6	—	—	—	—	—	—	7 22		—	9 08	—		†121	—	—	—	12 56	2 55	—
Washington Heights + ô	11.9	—	—	—	—	11 58	—	7 30		—	—	11 13		1 28	—	—	—	—	—	4 35
Blue Island .... ô	15.7	—	—	—	—	12 05	—	7 40		—	9 35	11 20		1 36	—	—	—	1 26	3 27	4 43
Tinley Park .... ô	23.5	—	—	—	—	12 20	—	8 00		—	9 50	11 36		b —	—	—	—	1 37	3 45	4 55
Mokena .... ô	29.7	—	—	—	—	12 30	—	8 10		—	10 02	11 46		b —	—	—	—	1 45	3 56	5 05
New Lenox .... ô	33.9	—	—	—	—	—	—	8 16		—	10 08	11 53		—	—	—	—	1 52	4 11	5 09
Joliet + ... ô	40.4	2 01	—	6 35	11 05	12 50	2 13	8 30		10 05	10 20	12 06		2 16	4 35	6 06	7 02	2 05	4 22	5 20
Minooka + ... ô	51.4	—	—	—	—	1 08	—	8 53		—	AM	PM		2 35	—	6 26	—	PM	PM	PM
Morris + ... ô	51.8	—	—	7 05	11 40	1 25	2 45	9 10		10 40	—	—		2 52	5 08	6 42	—			
Seneca + ... ô	72.0	—	—	—	—	1 42	—	9 28		—	—	—		3 11	—	6 56	—			
Marseilles + ... ô	77.3	—	—	y —	—	1 52	—	9 38	bβ	—	—	—		3 22	—	7 06	—			
Ottawa + ... ô	84.5	—	—	7 35	12 12	2 10	3 18	9 52	11 10	—	—	—		3 37	5 57	7 18	—			
Utica .... ô	94.1	—	—	—	—	2 25	—	10 06	b —	—	—	—		3 50	—	7 31	—			
La Salle + ... ô	99.1	—	—	7 53	12 34	2 40	3 40	10 20	11 31	—	—	—		4 05	6 00	7 41	—			
Peru + ... ô	100.1	—	—	—	b —	2 45	—	10 25	—	—	—	—		4 10	6 03	7 45	—			
Spring Valley + ... ô	104.4	—	—	—	—	2 52	—	10 35	—	—	—	—		4 20	—	7 53	—			
Marquette + ... ô	107.8	—	—	—	—	—	—	10 40	—	—	—	—		4 25	—	—	—			
De Pue + ... ô	110.0	—	—	—	—	3 05	—	10 45	—	—	—	—		4 30	—	8 02	—			
Bureau + ... ô arr.	114.2	4 00	12 42	8 22	1 07	3 20	4 15	10 55		11 52	—	—		4 50	6 28	8 18	8 43			
Peoria + ... ô arr.	161.4	—	10 05	—	—	6 20	6 20	1 30		1 30	—	—		6 55	—	10 05	—			
Tiskilwa + ... ô	122.4	—	—	—	—	—	3 32	AM 11 08		PM	—	—		5 05	c —	PM	—			
Wyanet + ... ô	128.7	—	—	—	—	—	3 40	11 18		—	—	—		5 14	—	—	—			
Sheffield + ... ô	136.6	—	—	—	—	—	3 55	11 35		—	—	—		5 28	7 01	—	—			
Mineral .... ô	142.0	—	—	—	—	—	4 03	11 45		—	—	—		5 36	—	—	—			
Annawan + ... ô	145.7	—	—	—	—	—	4 30	11 52		—	—	—		5 42	—	—	—			
Atkinson .... ô	151.0	—	—	—	—	—	4 30	12 02		—	—	—		5 50	c —	—	—			
Geneseo + ... ô	159.1	—	—	d 5	h —	4 35	12 16		—	—	—		6 03	7 35	—	—				
Green River .... ô	167.9	—	—	—	—	—	4 45	12 30		—	—	—		6 15	—	—	—			
Colona .... ô	169.7	—	—	—	—	—	4 48	12 35		—	—	—		6 18	—	—	—			
Carbon Cliff .. ✕ .... ô	171.8	—	—	—	—	—	4 55	12 40		—	—	—		6 22	—	—	—			
East Moline .... ô	175.3	—	—	—	—	—	5 05	12 51		—	—	—		6 32	8 00	—	—			
Moline + ... ô	179.3	5 31	2 04	9 54	a 32	5 22	1 05		—	—	—		6 50	8 10	—	10 07				
Rock Island + ... ô arr.	181.2	5 38	2 10	10 02	2 40	5 30	1 10	PM		—	—	PM		7 00	8 20	—	10 20			
Rock Island ...... lve.	181.2	5 55	2 15	10 12	2 50	6 20	1 15	11 40		—	*5 45	7 10	8 30	—	10 30					
Davenport + ... ô	182.8	6 07	2 26	10 25	3 05	6 33	1 25	1 50		—	6 55	7 20	8 40	—	10 40					
Walcott .... ô	195.0	6 28	—	—	h —	AM	2 12		PM	—	7 18	PM			PM					
Stockton .... ô	199.3	6 36	—	—	h —	5 22	2 19		—	—	7 27	—								
Durant .... ô	202.0	6 40	—	—	h —	5 25	2 25		—	—	7 33	—								
Wilton + ... ô	207.7	6 51	—	—	h —	2 36		—	—	7 45	—									
Moscow .... ô	211.2	6 57	—	—	h —	2 43		—	—	7 52	—									
Atalissa .... ô	216.0	7 05	—	—	h —	2 53		—	—	8 05	—									
West Liberty + ... ô	221.4	7 15	3 18	11 25	4 08	3 26		—	—	8 15	—	9 40								
Downey .... ô	226.8	7 25	—	—	h —	3 31		—	—	8 22	PM	PM								
Iowa City + ... ô	236.0	7 45	3 41	11 50	4 35	3 52		—		8 38										
Tiffin .... ô	244.8	8 00	—	—	h —	4 09		—												
Oxford .... ô	251.6	8 11	—	—	h —	4 24		—												
Homestead .... ô	256.6	8 20	—	—	h —	4 35		—												
Marengo + ... ô	267.3	8 32	—	—	5 25	4 57		—												
Ladora .... ô	273.8	8 49	—	—	h —	5 11		—												
Victor .... ô	278.8	9 01	—	—	h —	5 23		—												
Brooklyn + ... ô	287.6	9 18	—	—	6 00	5 40		—												
Malcom .... ô	293.6	9 32	—	—	h —	5 54		—												
Grinnell + ... ô	302.6	9 55	5 18	1 43	6 27	6 30		—												
Kellogg + ... ô	313.7	10 18	—	—	h —	6 55		—												
Newton + ... ô	322.7	10 37	5 47	2 17	7 05	7 15														
Metz .... ô	328.5	10 47	—	—	h —	7 27														
Colfax + ... ô	334.6	11 03	6 05	—	7 30	7 40														
Mitchellville + ... ô	342.5	11 12	—	—	h —	7 52														
Altoona .... ô	348.8	11 25	—	—	h —	8 05														
East Des Moines .... ô	357.1	—	—	—	h —	8 23														
Des Moines + ... ô arr.	357.7	11 50	6 50	3 25	8 20	8 30														
(Camp Dodge.)						3 01														
(Fort Des Moines.)						PM														
Des Moines ...... lve.	357.7	11 50	7 05	3 40	8 35	8 50														
Valley Junction + ... ô	362.5	12 20	7 28	4 00	8 57	9 15														
Commerce .... ô	366.2	12 27	—	—	9 05	9 22														

In the twenties, the Rock Island operated four trains a day each way between Des Moines and Chicago. Westbound Train 7, and its counterpart, eastbound Train 8, later known as the Rocky Mountain Rocket, was the favorite home-going train at holidays for students at Grinnell, the State University of Iowa, and other colleges and universities along the route. We avoided trains like No. 9, a local that stopped everywhere and lingered lovingly at each stop.

salvaged half an hour for precious personal matters before afternoon classes began.

We liked only a few things; exotic food, like pickled beets or stewed rhubarb, was left untouched. Once, during exam week, when the chef (slyly?) served eggs and brains, we fled en masse.

In a letter home, Don appraised the situation: "It takes a wide-awake fellow to eat in the dorms. I do not get to read the paper at the table here. Once I tried to read your letter during lunch and was hungry all afternoon."

These paragraphs describe what I have called our uncivilized era. I like to think that we inherited this behavior from juniors and seniors, and not from our dear fathers and mothers. Then a new supervisor appeared and was horrified by what she saw. We did not fit her image of students attending the Harvard of the West. With uncommon tact she met with house chairmen and appealed for at least a shadow of decorum. Surely we acted decently at home; and even if not, surely we did not want to go out into the world bearing the table manners of Iowa hogs. She was amazingly successful; in a few days we were dining like the cultured human beings our mothers hoped we would be. We were courteous, thoughtful, even genteel.

My college day ended at 5:00. By 10:00, when I had finished at the *Herald*, the campus was deserted. The period for dating was over and the girls were safely barricaded behind Quadrangle doors. A bridge game might be going on in the club room. By midnight most lights were out.

People who have attended college forget how hard they had to work; the highly competitive atmosphere is charged with tests, problems, reports, experiments, translations, hundreds of pages of reading, and occasional term papers. But finally it's Friday, inevitably the busiest day of the week but carrying its own promise. A larger number of students than usual greeted Friday by showing up for breakfast. Nearly everybody had three or four classes to tick off, and a fair share of quizzes or other special worries; Friday was no day to trifle with. Whatever my last Friday class, whether it was 11:20 botany or 1:20 English, I finished it with the special anticipation that one bestows upon the week's final hurdle.

Then came a great letdown. We could spend the rest of the afternoon and the next two days as well, as we pleased: games, sports, loafing around. We had assignments, but these could be spaced—even momentarily disregarded.

After World War II, huge segments of the professional world went on a five-day schedule. Millions of people still had to work on Saturday and Sunday to supply food, goods, transportation, and other necessary services, but other millions could look to Friday as the final, ultimate day of the workweek. But we of the campuses invented the notion (I overlook bankers and other special types). I have studied or taught on a dozen campuses; in all the world there must be no feeling quite like Friday—surviving it, not with flying colors, not brilliantly, but surviving it; just being on your feet when the last bell rings, your white plume bedraggled and your standard drooping, but both intact. And Friday leads to Saturday, the morning when you awake to realize that for a while you are no one's slave. Heaven must be something like that.

21

Sometimes when I awaken in the misty dark of night and stir the mix of words and pictures that are loafing around in my mind, I speculate upon what a young man would think if his Guardian Angel appeared and announced, "I'm going to give you a glimpse of the girl you are going to marry. You will be able to see but not touch. And when you actually meet her in real life, you must not let on that you've seen her before."

Surely one could not refuse such an invitation.

My Guardian Angel would have taken me to North High, famous old Des Moines school, that served thousands of boys and girls, mostly out of middle-income families, before it was finally moved and rebuilt. I can imagine floating through brick walls and entering a classroom where twenty seniors have collected: laughing, chatting, some standing, some already seated, waiting for the teacher. Guardian Angel, saying nothing, would have let me look for a while, and in this moment of moments, I would certainly have stared intently at every girl in the room. Finally, a specific girl would have been indicated with a gesture—"That's the one"—and every other young person would have faded away as I stared at one sharply edged image: a girl of appealing height and build, blue eyes, blonde hair, a concentration of animation, energy, vitality. My single, teasing glimpse promised more than it revealed, since personality is not conveyed in a glance.

How does one converse with his or her Guardian Angel, anyway? Should I ask questions, starting with simple ones: "Can I be told her name?" "What's her family like?" "What's she interested in?" "When and where will I meet her?" "How can you be positive she's the one . . . and that she will like me?" Surely the best approach is to say, "Tell me about her."

Well, Guardian Angel might respond, you are one of a thousand eighteen-year-old men in this part of the world, and she is one of a thousand sixteen-year-old women, so to start with you are a million light-years apart. She will thread a complicated maze and make a thousand correct turnings before she arrives at the center, where she will meet you, if you, starting at your entrance to the maze, also make a thousand correct choices. Nothing else I can tell you at this time has useful value. Besides, are you sure you really want to know? And would anyone really want to know, years ahead, who the Other Person is to be? At this point, the mix of words and pictures fades away.

A thin layer of facts will be enough for now. Her family name is Towner. Her father is an electrical contractor; her mother is the daughter of a Fort Dodge lawyer and sister of a Hearst newspaper manager. Her given name, inherited from two grandmothers, is Mary Augusta. Her peers, unable to manage Augusta, call her Gussie. Later groups of friends will shorten it to Gus. So, I think wryly, one of these friends will be me, and I will become very fond of a girl named Gus. Other names are, possibly, more romantic. I can hum enchanting melodies about Sue, Sally, Rosie, Irene, Margie, and Mary Lou, but, come to think of it, my sparkling, dancing, imaginative age failed to create a tune about Gus, even though its ingenious composers could sing that they were crazy over horses, or wild about animal crackers. I'm saving my unrestrained applause for the musician who will compose a delicate, haunting, evocative melody to a girl named Gus. And now when you meet her again a few pages further on, you must not let on that I've already told you about her.

She took a first small step in the maze when, early in her senior year, she applied for admission to Grinnell, not knowing that I was already there, waiting. On the form she could write down that she was on the tennis team, the school paper, the YWCA board, the judicial board, the French and dramatics clubs, the student council. In due course she was accepted; moreover, she was awarded a tuition scholarship plus a table-waiting job that would pay for her board.

Further ahead she did not need to look. Right now those May and June days rushed past like a comet in the sky. With the 580 seniors of Des Moines's four high schools, including the 177 from North, she was full of preparation for the single, citywide commencement. Des Moines's daily newspapers proudly boasted that its school system was graduating the largest class in its history. The *Register*, the *Tribune*, the *News*, the *Capital*, printed pictures of every graduate and also surveyed their expectations: 350 would enter a profession, 40 a business; the rest, undecided. Twelve, all boys, would become physicians or surgeons; 23, all girls, would become nurses. Law would claim 22 boys, but only 2 girls. Girls who entered business indicated that they would become stenographers or office managers, not corporation executives. Who was the liberated woman? (Their daughters and granddaughters, that's who.)

The seniors of these four, big-city high schools shared the same kind of events as the graduates at Osceola, 65 miles south, at Gilman City, 150 miles south, and at nearly every other high school in the land. There were senior banquets, with class wills, class poems, class prophets. There were high-school assemblies, with awards for service, character, dependability. The American rites of graduation vary little from school to school.

The 580 seniors joined forces for the final ceremonies. The baccalaureate speaker told them that qualities of character formed in their younger days would play as large a part in their eventual success as any combination of specialized skills acquired later on. What could be more perceptive? The commencement speaker, a survey of North High graduates at hand, could praise this large, cosmopolitan class for reflecting most of the national origins that had made the land great, for flowing into a wide variety of vocations that would serve humanity, and, best part of all, for planning (most of them) to make Des Moines their future home.

Of course it mattered little whether any of them heard him. Their task was to sit quietly, and before long each would receive a diploma. Perhaps the most astonishing fact is that well before midnight the new crop of alumni were home in bed. The twenties, roaring though they might be, did not feature all-night parties for the celebration of high-school commencements.

Next day Des Moines shook itself and went about its business. Its newest skyscraper, the Equitable, was to be dedicated. Its newspapers turned their attention to the renomination of Calvin Coolidge and his decision to select Charles G. Dawes as his running mate. Two rich men's sons, Richard Loeb and Nathan Leopold, were accused of murdering young Bobby Franks; a prominent lawyer bearing the name of Clarence Darrow undertook to defend them. In short there was good news, indifferent news, and bad news; on balance, however, the nation not only seemed stable and prosperous, but would continue in that delightful state forever.

22

Eventually I became a sophomore, which is something like being a corporal—not quite so exalted as a real officer, not quite so lowly as a private. If the months continued to speed by, I would become a junior. Courses piled up in neat stacks labeled English, history, French.

A student is fortunate if he has a single outstanding teacher; I had several. One was a professor of history—Cecil F. Lavell, a product of the Canadian undergraduate system. His teachers, he once said, did not make him work but did make him want to work; they "opened doors that could never be closed again." Who can write a more eloquent statement of the purpose of education? He left King's College "with a belief in fairies and a belief in law—much the same thing of course—and very little faith in machinery." He became an assistant professor of education at Teachers College, getting to know such disparate people as John B. Watson in psychology, who believed in fairies not at all, and Edward Lee Thorndike, who believed greatly in such machinery as mental measurement, word lists, dictionaries, and other methodical efforts.

In 1913, four years before he came to Grinnell as a member of the history department, and a dozen years before I walked into his classroom, Lavell, then forty-one, was on a train, fitfully attempting to sleep. Suddenly he awoke to the realization that he did not know where he was going, why he was there, or even who he was. In search of answers to these unsettling questions he fished into his pockets and found letters that told him his name and his occupation. He also learned that he was bound for Detroit, but he could not discover why he was going there or what he had planned to do once he arrived.

In this situation many would have returned home to locate family and medical help. Lavell found enough money in his pocket to do these things, but, as he described his mental state, "I began to feel a sort of shrinking horror of the unknown world from which I seemed separated by an impenetrable wall." Deep down, he felt he could not go back to the life he had left until he had wrestled further with the strange malady that had assailed him.

The alternative was to get a job—not teaching, as he would need to produce identifying credentials, but at unskilled labor. For the next two years he worked at strenuous jobs: on a railroad, repairing tracks, and unloading cars; in an ice plant, moving blocks of ice; at a lumber mill, handling heavy timbers. I find myself trying to imagine the frail, slender man I knew spending twelve hours a day pulling, pushing, lifting, shoveling, as he struggled with the elusive problem of linking his present with his past. At times he visited a library and so picked up a few threads of his former intellectual career. Librarians and fellow workers were astonished to see the books this ill-clad laborer devoured: history, philosophy, literature. Once he peered into *Who's Who in America* and, to his amazement, found his own name.

Still, he could not yet go home; his past was too hazy, too unreal. One day he showed a friend to whom he had revealed his secret, the title page of Thorndike's *Educational Psychology*. This man, a perceptive Russian Jewish tailor, remarked: "Well, you must have been a friend of Thorndike." The comment passed unnoticed, but later, when both were cleaning the kitchen, Lavell on his knees scrubbing, the tailor halted his mopping and reflected: "It would certainly be funny if Thorndike could see you now." Instantly the image and personality of Thorndike flashed across Lavell's mind, and at that moment the present linked hands with the past. Later an acquaintance on the police force discovered a photo that had been distributed at the time of Lavell's disappearance and showed it to him; this further confrontation with his real identity, reassuring him that family and friends missed him and were seeking him, confirmed his decision to return to New York.

Lavell's strange adventure is now only a dim memory in the minds of a few alumni. At the time my generation was in Grinnell, however, it was a familiar story; we heard the details from schoolmates and from Lavell himself, who occasionally narrated this experience in chapel talks. From those talks I recall two vivid comments: one was that although his fellow laborers often used rough language among themselves and continually played practical jokes on one another, their innate sensitivity tempered their language and their behavior to him. Another was the genuine kindness and the helpfulness they reflected: showing him how to use their simple tools efficiently, forgiving his clumsiness and ineptness, understanding his bone-weary exhaustion in his early days as a physical laborer, and in general maintaining a "We've all had to go through this" attitude or "Everybody sometimes accidentally hits another fellow with a pick." They felt no superiority or inferiority in his presence but simply a profound sense of the necessity of working together to get the job done. Their attitude also speaks eloquently of Lavell's own innate graciousness and humility.

With little effort I can see his class. Fifteen people are sitting in the back rows of a room on the top floor of Alumni Recitation Hall; in front is a scattering of empty chairs. Twenty other students, mostly male, are absent. The bell rings and the teacher appears, now a professor of the history of thought, whatever that is; the course has an equally comfortable title, Philosophy of Education. Standing in the corner nearest the door, he pulls a small black book from his coat pocket and calls the roll, without so much as giving us a glance; twenty-five responses, such as "present" or "here," come from the fifteen attenders. On one occasion George Gains, the college cheerleader, and possessor of a deep, bass voice, three times successively intoned "here" when the names of three different absentees were called. Lavell smiled, hardly looking up; neither he nor Gains were fooling each other, both knowing that attendance and grades were baubles and that even hardened nonattenders would end up with at least a C.

The letter, if not the spirit, of roll calling being complied with, Lavell began his lecture. Still standing with his back to the door, he paced three steps toward the opposite corner; then backed three steps toward the originating corner; and thus throughout the hour. I find it impossible to sort out what he taught in any single course I had with him; how can one distinguish among Beginning Lavell, Intermediate Lavell, and Advanced Lavell? Names like Rousseau, Michelangelo, da Vinci, Cavour, Mazzini, Garibaldi, Bismarck, Disraeli, floated over our heads, along with whimsical observations bolstered with allusions to literature, the Bible, and, especially, the Greeks. He added a new dimension to my education, sending me to the library, on my own, to learn more about one of his Italians, Frenchmen, Germans, or Greeks. He opened doors that could not again be closed.

We were never required to write term papers. Nor was there any heavy laying-on of quizzes, or even of invitations to ask questions. Occasionally one was asked, punctuating the hour like a thunderbolt; Lavell, as astonished as the rest of us, nevertheless dealt with it in a way that made the questioner feel that he had opened up a brand-new line of inquiry. After the answer, or maybe during it, the questioner subsided, and the lecturer resumed his monologue. On the day of the final, the entire class for the first time being present, Lavell dispatched scouts to locate six or eight extra chairs.

Lavell was a superior chapel speaker. His favorite themes were from *Alice in Wonderland*. Lewis Carroll's fantasies almost met their equal in Lavell; sometimes it was hard to tell when he was reading from the book and when he was inserting a bit of his own whimsy. If a student organization asked him to appear on a program, it might request particularly that he bring along *Alice*. If, sixty years later, you asked Grinnell alumni and alumnae a question such as, "Who used to read about the Cheshire cat?" Cheshire-catlike grins would break out all over the place: "Lavell!" And a few would begin (more or less) to quote fragments from the book:

> "Cheshire Puss, . . . would you tell me, please, which way I ought to walk from here?"
> "That depends a good deal on where you want to get to," said the Cat.
> "I don't much care where—" said Alice.
> "Then it doesn't matter which way you walk," said the Cat.
> "—so long as I get *somewhere*," Alice added as an explanation.
> "Oh, you're sure to do that," said the Cat, "if you only walk long enough." . . . (And vanished.)

But, of course, the Cat reappeared; and when Alice asked it not to vanish so suddenly, this time it vanished quite slowly, beginning with the tail and ending with the grin. Upon which Alice made her famous remark that she'd often seen a cat without a grin, but never a grin without a cat.

Each year the seniors conducted a ballot to select their six favorite speakers for the senior chapels; Lavell was invariably one of those chosen. He described our complacencies in an understated manner, touched with gentle irony, that won our attention and delight. "The most diabolical thing in the world," he once said, "is intense conviction concerning matters that are not important." "Luckily," he would observe, "life is not either real or earnest." He described intelligence and foolishness in a way that made it difficult to see where one began and the other left off. Many truly intelligent discoveries seemed foolish to sensible people. Even Columbus and Galileo were viewed as fools.

Once he told us:

> This is something like what a college really says to its graduates.
>
> You do hereby receive your degree, not because you know much, for you do not, but because you have dared to open doors, . . . because you have dared to look at your own ignorance and not draw back. . . .
>
> If it is a paradox, it is a true one, that a liberal education is of value largely insofar as it liberates us from the burden of our wisdom.

Lavell's chapel talks found their way into print in college and community publications. At times he had those he liked best printed in small booklets. They bore titles such as *The Inadvisability of Arriving at Conclusions,* or *What Is Intelligence?* the latter a Socratic dialogue inquiry. Late at night, at the *Herald,* I occasionally found copy for one on my tray, to be printed in a special typeface he liked, one that required emptying the machine of ordinary newspaper type mats and running in the other set, an operation that took half an hour then, a couple of seconds half a century later. As the college still has a few of these booklets in its collection, I contributed in my own way to the preservation of his chapel eloquence.

If he made it to the Happy Isles, his oft-quoted phrase, he well knows that one of his students put some of his best stuff in type.

I wrote part of this narrative one summer in London while reading at the British Library and awaiting materials for my own re-

Cecil F. Lavell (History), John P. Ryan (Speech), two of Grinnell's well-liked professors. Others remembered are Norris (Biology), Conard (Botany), Sherman (Chemistry), Stoops (Philosophy), Payne (History), Spencer (Greek), Rusk (Mathematics), McClenon (Mathematics), Strong (Economics), Steiner (Applied Christianity), Peck (Music). And still others, depending on who's making the list. Our professors had studied not only at Harvard, Yale, Johns Hopkins, Chicago, and Cornell but also at Leipzig, Freiburg, Oxford, Toronto, Munich, Heidelberg, Berlin, Geneva, and the Sorbonne. A fourth of them were in *Who's Who in America*. (Grinnell Collection, 1927 *Cyclone*.)

search field. I found three of his books in this distinguished collection, a small circumstance but one that would have pleased him. One title, *Imperial England*, written with his colleague, another Canadian, Charles E. ("Peggy") Payne, appeared the year it was published on the *New York Times*'s list of the one hundred outstanding books of the year. Another, *A Biography of the Greek People*, was even closer to the topics he talked about, to that select class of fifteen ardent believers occasionally augmented by a group of floaters who at least wanted to be aware of the meeting place so they would know where to go on examination days. The third was a slender edition of a chapel talk that I had set up at the *Herald*.

I scanned this small heap of books at my desk in the British Library's tall, domed, circular reading room, then put them gently to one side, and reflected upon this historian, philosopher, writer, speaker, and also, for a time, section hand and mill worker, who drew from these varied adventures in his classroom lectures and chapel talks. He taught fifteen years after we were graduated, dying in Toronto in 1948 at the age of seventy-six.

23

We were citizens of our own cosmos, with its classes, roommates, rec hours. And we were citizens of a real cosmos, with its business and politics. The real world kept going through a boom-and-bust economy that at times supported our education, at times handicapped it, and at still other times halted it. Never believe the Great Depression hit unexpectedly, like a hurricane, that week in October 1929; all sorts of little storms, starting in the early twenties, preceded it. Our generation of students lived with a host of economic uncertainties, one of them being the likelihood that at anytime one or more hometown banks would suddenly close their doors. Bank failures were then a natural, to-be-expected catastrophe, like floods, droughts, and tornadoes.

How can I describe a bank *failure?*

One day you enter your favorite bank, a picture of eternal solidity with tellers behind ceiling-high grating, operating through small pass-through slots in barred windows, and with officers well concealed in private cubicles. These outward signs proclaim that here your cash is tenderly cared for. The place is hushed, the loudest sound being the click of the lever-operated adding machines. You tender your money and bankbook (we did not use the term *passbook*); you see your currency fingered, your coins stacked in piles. "Fifteen eighty-five," announces the teller, and then, deferentially, "is that what you made it?" You nod; he enters the sum in your book, rubber-stamps the date, smiles, returns the book, and scoops your offering into his drawer. Other patrons cash checks, make deposits in 4 percent savings accounts, get change, pick up pads of checks.

Here is a system that will endure forever, like the Packard Motor Co. Yet next morning you see a typewritten note on the door: "The bank is closed," together with sentences about receivership.

One day you could withdraw your money without a ripple; the next day you cannot even get back your fifteen eighty-five. If only you had known, you keep saying to yourself.

On occasion the word circulated in advance that a certain bank was no longer sound. Americans tend to exploit impending shortages: we hear that toilet paper or Mason jars are in lean supply, or that saccharin is to be banned, or that Cadillac is making no more convertibles, or that diesel automobiles are the kind to buy, and immediately the lines begin to form. When rumors assail a bank, the result is a run; lines form, depositors withdraw their money, and even if the bank was not in danger of closing, now it is forced to.

During the twenties and early thirties, a hundred million Americans learned the banking business the hard way. In Iowa, people got uneasy about all banks. As Father exchanged with thirty or forty Iowa newspapers, now and then he could read that a bank had suddenly locked its doors. Each closing meant that marginal businesses, operating on a shoestring, went bankrupt; and that scores of retired people lost their lifetime savings. As Osceola's three banks were advertisers, Father kept a checking account in each one but was careful to keep his balances low by paying his bills promptly, so that in case a bank let go he would not lose a large sum.

I really believe he thought all three banks were sound. Their officers were solid citizens; they lived in the big houses, drove the Buicks and Chryslers, and in general showed other signs of prosperity. A drive for funds to support community projects could count on them for generous contributions. They were eager to make loans to farmers to buy land and plant crops, and to livestock breeders to buy feed or build herds. Nobody could see risk in this type of business. "You can't go wrong buying land," I heard a banker say; "they're not making any more land."

Nevertheless, Father operated with built-in prudence. He trusted no savings accounts. As fast as he got a few hundred dollars ahead he called Gates, the mortgage holder, and made a payment. One morning I was in the *Tribune* office when he handed Gates a check. "Now you'll cash this right away," Father said. "Of course," Gates agreed. Father and everybody else knew that in the wake of a bank closure, people who had been slow about cashing checks rushed back to the makers and demanded reimbursement; so the makers, who thought they had paid the debt once, out of funds now swallowed up by the bank's receivers, now had to go through the agony of paying again, out of fresh cash in their tills.

I got my first lesson on a spring day during my sophomore year when I read that the cashier of one of our banks had gone to the courthouse park early one Saturday morning and had shot himself in the head. People hurrying to work early found his body lying across a bench. The national examiners had closed his bank the evening before. His lovely daughters were schoolmates of Don's and mine. He had been one of the town's esteemed citizens: president of the Chautauqua, member of the Country Club, active in the Business Men's Association.

He was fifty-one. I have often thought that if he had stayed alive even a few months longer he would have seen that what happened to his bank also happened to scores of others in southern Iowa. He might not have made that early morning walk to the courthouse park. He might have realized that he was a victim of circumstances. Before long another Osceola bank failed and a third kept open only after drastic reorganization that cost officers and directors their personal wealth.

Banks were caught up in the economic forces that bankrupted other firms, and individuals as well. A thin line separated bad judgments from illegal actions. It turned out that bankers were no more infallible than, well, newspaper editors. To the depositor, the bottom line was that the reorganization of a closed bank was a slow, costly process, as those who had borrowed money from the bank could not immediately repay, and, worse, many could never repay. Hence in a year's time a depositor might get back only 10 percent of his money, or less, with further payments widely distributed. Receivership was a costly process.

I had opened a small account in the Citizens National Bank at Grinnell, though my balance was modest because of my weekly payments to the college. As banks furnished free checks, made no service charges, and were nice to know, I felt like a substantial citizen whenever I poked my currency through the barred windows, saw the sum entered in my bankbook, and received the thanks of the institution.

The Citizens National Bank was housed in modest quarters, especially when contrasted with the nearby Merchants National Bank building, which to the untrained eye seemed to be trimmed with slabs of marble and decorated with gold leaf. At school one morning when I heard that there was a run on the Citizens and I went down to withdraw my $18.50 investment in its entirety, I found myself at the end of a line half a block long. I have seldom seen people so worried, and the sight of fortunate depositors emerging from the front door, some of them carrying cigar boxes obviously crammed with currency, was encouraging in one way and discouraging in another: the bank had not closed yet but might any minute. None of the forced joking and joshing that went on was funny to those far back in the line: "Did you take it all?" "Need any help carrying that heavy sack?"

A bank official walked up and down the line telling people that the bank would stay open even past its regular 3:00 closing hour and inviting patrons to stay for hot coffee and doughnuts after they had transacted their business. He said "transact your business" with a twinkle, since everyone knew that only one kind of business was being transacted. And as the line grew shorter and I could see that the tellers' windows were still open, I could also see piles of currency, in neat bundles, on display in the front window; police officers and sheriff's deputies, armed with shotguns, stood on guard. Here was a bank that had a million dollars in deposits and had most of it on display. Officials of the Citizens had telephoned banks in Des Moines to arrange for a few bales of currency to come in on the morning train. In other words, the Citizens Bank was in sound financial condition.

I picked up my $18.50 and just for fun asked the teller if I could have a calendar and an extra checkbook; he smiled and gave me both. On the way out I also snitched a doughnut. A couple of days later, however, I returned and redeposited the money, since the bank had weathered the storm and was still in business. The man ahead of me had brought back a shoe box full of currency and handed it to the teller. "I want to put this back in the bank," he said. "I've been worried sick all week, hiding it first one place and then another."

In the months that followed, the Citizens Bank doubled its capital and acquired the building of the Merchants. For a long time it was the only bank in town. But depositors of other banks were not so fortunate. One year a thousand banks were wiped out, and half of the nation's banks closed or merged before the Great Depression ran its course. I regret to say I did not absorb as much from my experience with the Citizens as I should have and later had an encounter with another bank that did not turn out so well.

24

That summer I decided to go to Chicago and get a job in a newspaper composing room. I did not need to leave; I could have worked in Osceola and, by living at home, would have netted as much; but I was determined to go to Chicago.

Why Chicago? Des Moines was Small City, and too close; Chicago was Big City, and just the right distance away. Osceola offered nothing new; Chicago promised adventure. Besides, deep in me is the urge not to do any one thing for too long a time; in later years, even in the settled boundaries of my professional career, I found ways of achieving variety.

This trait is buried in my genes. My Grandfather Reid, age sixteen when gold was discovered in California, was one of the thousands who came off the farms to go West to seek their fortunes. As he died before I was born I never heard him describe his exploits, but I know that he had exciting years in the West before he returned to Missouri, married, and settled down on a small farm. A dim memory persists of seeing pieces of quartz in an upstairs trunk at the family home, and of being told that they were souvenirs of the gold rush.

At seventeen my Grandfather Tarwater went West to work for the Department of the Interior as a surveyor for the general land office.

As surveying became too tame, he hired out as a guide for one of Custer's generals in the campaign against Sitting Bull and the Sioux. Later he helped bury the dead after Custer's disastrous battle and still later pursued the victorious Indians through the Dakotas, Wyoming, and Montana. He also served as scout in other campaigns. How well he must have known those plains and mountains, designated on the old maps as Nebraska Territory, penetrated only by the western trails and a single railroad. When once I asked Aunt Grace why he had not related these thrilling adventures to his oldest grandson, her reply was direct: "You didn't ask him. If you had, he would have told you quite a story." I now wonder if there are others around to whom I should be directing questions. Often the best tales (make that *history*, if you like) slip away unrecorded.

My father had published the *Guide* only a few years when he, too, feeling restless, went to Texas to look at a newspaper property, went to Oklahoma on a similar search, went to Montana to file a claim in the great land lottery—but finally returned to Missouri. In his lifetime he edited and published six different newspapers. My Aunt Frances homesteaded in Montana, and two sets of uncles and aunts went to California long before the migrations of the twenties. So I inherited honestly the urge to move around.

At spring vacation I knew better than to ask Father's permission, directly, to spend the summer in Chicago. I blandly asked him about going to New York to run a machine. That, he observed, was the stupidest idea he had ever heard of. Next day I inquired if he thought any better of the idea of my going to Cleveland. He answered promptly, "No!" but added that if I came around with an idea that had any sense to it, he would consider it. We compromised on Chicago.

Father did more than agree; he mulled over his vast store of newspaper connections and dashed a letter to a Grand River classmate, Pope Yeaman White, who was with the W. D. Boyce Publishing Company as editor of the *Saturday Blade*. Certainly hundreds of other former paper carriers are still around who were agents for the *Blade* and for its companion periodical, the *Chicago Ledger*. And there are thousands who belonged to the Lone Scouts of America and devoured its official magazine, *Lone Scout*. Boyce also published it. Lone Scouts were found in small towns and rural districts not large enough to have a Boy Scout troop; the idea of the organization was to give these isolated boys a chance to work for merit badges and to earn degrees just like their fellows in the Boy Scouts. Back in Missouri, I had read *Lone Scout,* and, more than that, several of the little hand-drawn, mimeographed, or even printed "tribal magazines" that individual Lone Scouts published, and for that matter, still publish. In fact Don and I edited and published our own tribal magazine, *The Wigwam,* but as our subscription list seemed limited to our uncles and aunts, we abandoned the venture after a few issues.

The *Saturday Blade*'s editor cordially replied that I was welcome to stay with him while I looked for work.

In early June I arrived at the Boyce plant, a Loop building of six stories, met White, and explained my hopes. He introduced me to the plant foreman, who advised about getting a job. The first step was to report to the International Typographical Union. Although ITU had a four-year apprenticeship requirement for full membership, I felt my newspaper experience was an equivalent and did not anticipate any difficulty. White also helped me locate a room on Springfield Street, just off Chicago Avenue, far west of the Loop, for thirty dollars a month, including breakfast, laundry, and mending.

Early Monday morning I talked to the Union secretary, Carl Berreiter. Summer employment opportunities were sparse, he said. As newspapers were unionized, I was ineligible until I was officially taken into the ITU, but I could make the round of nonunion shops and see what was available. I was not to reveal my interest in joining the Union; he explained that since he had men working everywhere, he could keep me under surveillance until he decided what to do about my application.

Not until 11:00 did I get started calling on nonunion firms—so-called composition shops that specialized in setting type for printing establishments. Firms subcontracted for linotype composition because they needed special typefaces, or because the material to be set was complicated, or because their own staffs were swamped. Composition shops represented a specialty that performed an invaluable service to the printing trades.

My procedure was to walk into the back office of the firm, locate the shop foreman, and interview him. I was then twenty, but like any of Horatio Alger's young heroes I knew I should walk briskly toward the foreman, avoid shuffling my feet, and look at him intently with clear, blue, honest eyes. Invariably he began by asking how old I was, and I told him. He inquired how fast I could set type, and, being modest, I said 5,000, which was far below my true speed. I will not bother to explain this system of reckoning, except to say that 5,000 was like a stenographer typing forty words a minute, which is standard, when sixty is good and eighty is blazing. His next question was "What kinds of setting can you do," and I replied, truthfully enough, "Anything." Country newspapers do not breed specialists. He asked me, with a thin smile, if I were a boozer. Drinking was almost an occupational ailment among printers. I could say I wasn't.

The first shop foreman had nothing available. Neither did the second, third, or fourth. The fifth advised me to be sure to give my age as twenty-one, otherwise nobody would be able to hire me. I interviewed steadily through the luncheon hour and deep into the afternoon. The magic number of twenty-one did not seem to help. I was getting further and further down my list of shops. Four o'clock and four-thirty came and went and I still had not had a single glimmer of hope. Hard times had hit the big-city printing industry as well as the small towns and countryside. I was as bone-weary and discouraged as a mortal can be.

Shortly after 5:00 I found myself climbing the stairs to the second floor of the Smith-McCarthy Typesetting Company, located on South Dearborn Street, near the station. Operators on the day shift were leaving and a few on the night shift were straggling in. I was told to talk to the day superintendent, a man named Horace. I asked him if he had a machine job.

He looked at me sharply. "How good are you?"

I was exhausted, depressed. I had been beaten down all day. I had wandered from the land of "Nothing right now" through "Leave your name and we'll call you if anything turns up" to "We're not hiring anybody at all." I had nothing to lose. "I can do 7,000."

Immediately he gave me gimlet-eyed attention. "Can you do anything besides straight matter?"

"Of course. Display, tabular, whatever you've got. And I can look after my own machine."

He was incredulous but had to ask one more question. "How old are you?"

This was it. "Twenty-one." If the roof fell in, so be it.

After an agonizing pause, during which he was sorting my state-ments into two piles, "Probably true" and "Probably not," Horace said: "One of my men quit just a few minutes ago. Right now we do have a little rush of work. When can you start?"

I knew the answer to that—learned it years before from Horatio. Luck and pluck, he had written; pluck and luck. Even though I was more dead than alive, a skinny horse that had plowed corn all day, I answered: "Right now."

"Okay. Take the head machine over there." He pointed to a row of eight. "Begin with what the operator there has been working on."

I found a stack of copy marked for size and style and saw the point at which the previous operator had marked where he had stopped. His machine was still running; I looked at the slug he had last set, still warm, and checked its wording against his notation. Weary as I was, I knew I had made some interesting claims about speed that I now had to live up to. The job on the copy tray was simple enough. In thirty seconds I could tell the machine was a good one. I needed all the help I could get.

After an hour, the night superintendent came over, introduced himself as Buck, and indicated that he was going to start me on a new job that required different kinds of type and varying line lengths, involving mold changes and magazine shifts. Only a fully experienced operator could handle this new assignment, but it called for nothing I had not previously done a thousand times. I scanned the pages and asked technical questions mainly to verify the instructions. Buck watched me a moment, then went back to his own work; but as soon as I finished this job he had others of a similar sort.

At 10:00 everybody went out for luncheon; a night worker's life is turned upside down. Most businesses were closed; the streets were dark. Chicago did not waste much electricity on South Dearborn Street. The half dozen of us were the only ones in the small, dismal restaurant. Though the food had spent long hours on the steam table I gulped it like a farmhand. We were back at work in half an hour.

By 1:00 I was exhausted; muscles aching, eyes burning, bones grating against one another. At the water cooler I bathed my eyes and splashed my face. To shift the agony to other muscles, I fre-quently left my chair to walk around and check an imaginary mal-function. The operator next to me, a red-haired woman named Helen, was struggling with every page—she was new to the craft. When she saw that I was machinist as well as operator, she asked for advice with her mechanical problems. I was grateful for any bit of talk or change of activity that would help keep my eyes propped open.

I had no idea how long we were supposed to work. Two o'clock came with no sign of anybody quitting; so did 2:30. A few minutes before 3:00, however, I could see signs that our shift was coming to an end; operators tidying their machines, floor men heading for the washroom, lights being turned off. The foreman, whose name was Rosie, stopped by to see if I had a final question. Finally, finally, the night was over.

We rushed down the stairs in a cluster and fanned out in different directions. I walked north up Dearborn, across to State, up State to Chicago Avenue, where I knew I could catch the owl car to my new Springfield Avenue address, many blocks away—a long ride for a body that by now was totally consumed.

I paid little attention to the other passengers in the crowded streetcar. I found myself dozing, though I knew I must stay awake; even so, I rode three blocks past my stop. Somehow I dredged up the energy to walk back and locate the house in which, somewhere, I had a room. The landlady, Mrs. Curran, had left a light burning. Never was a human being more deserving of sleep.

At work the next evening, Horace greeted me with: "You didn't do anything like 7,000 last night." His tone, however, indicated that he hadn't expected me to. "That's right," I replied, "but I wasn't on straight copy." He knew that, too. Those were the last words spoken on either side about 7,000.

I know now that in interviewing and in other life situations as well a person must have a realistic appreciation of his assets and his shortcomings. He should not understate the one nor puff up the other. The world is not likely to put a higher value on you than you put on yourself. The question is, "Can you do the job?" and if you can, the answer is not "Maybe," or "I think so," but "Of course." Dizzy Dean, the flashy Cardinal pitcher, stated the idea in his own colorful language: "If you really done it, it ain't bragging."

The equipment at Smith-McCarthy's included seventy-five magazines and twenty-five extra sets of mats—a way of saying that, excluding duplicates, it could offer printers a choice of 150 or more different sizes and styles of type. At the beginning of the summer, the firm had had seven operators on the night shift. I heard a lot of talk about pay scales; the day foreman received $65 per week, the night foreman $48, other operators $46 or $48. At that time union operators were getting $63, and the rumor was that *Chicago Tribune* operators got $80 or $90. The enviable place to work, however, seemed to be the R. R. Donnelley Company, nonunion printers of telephone directories and other large-order publications: $5 or more per week over the scale, plus fringe benefits, if you could master the art of setting telephone directory entries, which called for appalling accuracy and concentration. To set scores of entries like "Stoppenbeck Ruey 1803 So Narragansett FI 8-2239" calls for a careful eyeballing of each consonant and vowel, the kind of care that one does not need with "The farmers had to sell their livestock and agricultural implements." Getting into Donnelley's, however, was tough; it hired only after detailed investigation and would have nothing to do with anyone who was tainted with any kind of union connection. After I had worked a few nights I asked how much I was to be paid and was surprised to learn that I was down for $55 a week, payday every other Friday.

One afternoon I walked to the Boyce plant and visited with Editor White. He was so intrigued by the wages I was making that he thought I should chuck Grinnell and stay with linotyping. He himself had become discouraged about editing as a profession; he had to work six days a week, plus home assignments for evenings and Sundays, continually struggling to get enough decent copy to fill a weekly. Somehow I had thought that big-city editors wallowed in privileges and other riches. He assured me that, contrary to popular belief, many city editors and reporters dreamed of the day when they could save enough money to make a down payment on a country weekly. I told him that the ideal person to run a country weekly was a man with a strong wife and three kids. From my own experience I was positive that two were not enough. Between us we gave the newspaper profession a hard time.

After a night or two I adjusted to my new life. I had breakfast every morning at 10:00, Mrs. Curran often having coffee with me. She was a good-sized Irish woman, blonde and blue-eyed. She fussed at me for eating so little, like, for instance, cornflakes, and urged me to have eggs and toast as well, though after a few mornings she gave up on me. But as her own family had left for the day, she enjoyed our visits and I did also.

After breakfast, I had a seven-hour stretch of free time in which to enjoy Chicago's art galleries, museums, cinema palaces, and other entertainments. An afternoon movie at that splendid temple of Balaban and Katz's, the Chicago Theatre, was far more stirring than one at the Lyric in Osceola. The Chicago had an enormous screen and an organ with several keyboards and banks of stops. The organist played a short concert at each performance, with colored lights swirling over organ and organist. He could imitate various kinds of instruments; his shrill notes were exciting and his deep notes rumbled back and forth across the theater's arching dome.

A highlight was the afternoon I went to the Roosevelt Theatre to see Rudolph Valentino in his famous comeback movie, *Monsieur Beaucaire*. Valentino had had a disagreement with Famous Players-Lasky for casting him in inferior scripts and, for a time, had stopped making pictures. I stood half an hour in a long line that started at the Roosevelt and wrapped around the block. Once inside, the audience sat expectantly as the movie got under way. When finally, in a dramatic setting, Valentino himself appeared, extravagantly dressed, the hundreds of *oh*'s and *ah*'s revealed an adulation never duplicated until Elvis Presley's era. Silent films would be tame fare today, but we found them entirely satisfying. our imagination supplied anything that was lacking in talk, sound, or color.

Though sound movies had not yet been perfected, I did have an opportunity on another afternoon to hear the DeForrest talking machine. We were told that the voice was recorded on the film at the same time the picture was taken, so that the synchronization was particularly good. We saw and heard a man talking, a woman singing, a banjo quartet, and a saxophone solo. You could tell that words matched lip movements and that the banjo tones marched along with the plucking motions.

One Sunday afternoon I took an excursion on Lake Michigan to Milwaukee and back. The ship, *Christopher Columbus*, seemed like an ocean liner; I had never been on so huge a boat. We spent five hours on the way, a couple of hours in Milwaukee, and five hours back. Another Sunday I visited Riverview Park, mainly to check out its eight roller coasters, bearing such names as "Cannonball," "Jackrabbit," "Greyhound," and, most spectacular of all, "The Bobs." Anyone with a teaspoonful of sense would start with an easy ride and work up, but I began with the giant "Bobs." Our train of cars was pulled up a track several stories high before starting down its steep, wild twisting course. Gravity and centrifugal force were extended to their outer limits. The second ride found me better prepared; but at the end of the third I felt my body had endured all that could be expected of a body.

My favorite eating place was the Automat. As you entered, you passed a cashier and bought twenty-five or fifty cents worth of nickels, enough for an enormous meal. You then picked up a tray and walked past rows and banks of glass-windowed pigeonholes, each with a slot in which to insert nickels, and a crank to open the window so you could reach into the pigeonhole and retrieve the item of food on view. Behind a window, for example, might repose a piece of delicious raisin pie, the sign indicating that its price was two nickels; you fed your money into the slot, turned the crank, opened the window, and the raisin pie was yours. When the pigeonhole was empty, it was refilled from the back by an attendant. Tempting salads, hot plates, drinks, chocolate layer cake with thick filling and icing were made accessible by inserting nickels into slots. The world lost something special when the Automat vanished from the big cities.

Mrs. Curran often urged me to see Garfield Park. "It's only a few blocks away," she said. "The flowers, shrubs, and trees are fabulous." One morning she confessed that she herself had never seen it, though she had lived a lifetime in that vicinity, a statement that startled me at the time; but as the years went on I discovered that the world had thousands of people who lived close to a Garfield Park, a Washington Monument, or a Gateway Arch, and had never visited it.

As I had just missed a payday and had to exist on my rapidly diminishing capital, I was relieved when the ghost finally walked, as printers put it, and I received a check, with a serial number, printed on safety paper, the $110 spelled out in check-protector figures, and signed by two officers of the firm. I had never seen anything so magnificent; Ray had always paid me off in tired old currency. Saturday morning, down to my last twenty-five cents, I took the Chicago Avenue car downtown and located the bank on which the check was drawn, but it was closed and would not be open until Monday. "Bankers' hours," as the world called them, were unlike those of decent people's.

Unruffled, I walked around the block, found a large bank that was open, and presented my check to the teller. He glanced at it, front and back. "We can't cash this check," he said, coolly. "We don't know this account. We have no information about—who is it? — the Smith-McCarthy Typesetting Company."

I was dumbfounded. I had had no such difficulty with Grinnell banks, though actually I had not had much experience with checks. But since this teller acted like a bank president, I saw no reason to argue. I sought out a still larger bank; a modest sum like $110 shouldn't embarrass a thoroughbred institution. I got the same answer. We don't know this account. We don't know you. Take this check to the bank it's drawn on. My explanation that it was closed aroused no compassion.

As my check looked as genuine as a hundred-dollar bill, what with its engraved lettering and bold signatures, the numbers representing its value carefully shredded into its forgery-proof paper, I simply couldn't give up. I decided to go to still another banking mausoleum and hunt up a lady teller. She would take a single look at my honest face, note the residue of cup grease and graphite under my fingernails, perceive that I was a genuine workingman, say "How would you like this, sir?" and fork over the money. Already I began to feel better.

The lady teller was understanding when I explained my predicament. "All right," she said as she looked at me and at my check, "I'll just need some identification."

I had no driver's license, social-security card, credit card, Red Cross blood-type card, or other ID such as every workingman carries today. I had to admit I had no way whatever of identifying myself. "Maybe you have a letter from home," she observed, helpfully, reaching toward a stack of bills as if eager to pay me off, "or a membership card, or something with your initials on it." She paused, still ready to count the currency, if I could give her any encouragement at all.

I went through my pockets again but I knew in advance that they were empty. I did not even have a lead slug or the micrometer I often carried, which might at least have shown her that I was a printer. Suddenly I had an inspiration. "Would you accept a laundry mark?"

"I might. What laundry mark?"

I loosened my collar and pulled the inside of the neckband into view, so she could see the identifying name put there by the laundry. I craned my neck and leaned forward so she could read the label. "What do you see?" I offered, confidentially.

"I see 'Alden Greene,'" she replied.

"Oh, goodness, he's my roommate at school." In a day when dress shirts were white, it was never hard to get the wrong shirt.

She smiled, returned the bills to their slot, and handed me my check. Now she not only had no reason for cashing it, but had a good reason for not cashing it. "I'm sorry," she said.

I had enough loose change to take the streetcar back to my room. Somehow I had to survive until Monday. I had nothing to eat Sunday except the free breakfast that came with my lodging. Mrs. Curran, a lady of true motherly instincts, with boys of her own, was delighted when on this particular Sunday I asked not only for cornflakes but also for bacon, eggs, and toast. That gorgeous meal lasted me until Monday morning. I walked the miles to the Loop, cashed my check, had a mammoth luncheon, and went to an afternoon movie.

Nowadays when I visit Chicago I mingle with the crowds along State Street near the corner of Madison Avenue, touted to be the world's busiest intersection. As I watch people come and go I reflect that sixty years ago I walked along State and Dearborn, after 3:00 in the morning, when those same crowded streets were deserted except for an occasional drifter or late worker. Now and then a partly filled owl car came along. I strolled the long blocks to Chicago Avenue never molested, unafraid, enjoying the sleeping city. At Chicago Avenue, however, on the streetcar, I invariably caught up with a score or more Polish women who had finished cleaning offices in the nearby skyscrapers. Now that their work was over, these women seemed happy and excited, chatting in their native tongue as they boarded the streetcar to rejoin their families asleep at home.

On the car also was a group of Yellow Cab drivers who had finished their night's work. I had never before seen a cabdriver close-up. In my conversations with them, I learned that Chicago had three thousand Yellow Cabs, driven by all kinds of people, old and young, most of them only until they could find something they liked better. They talked about the places they had been and the customers they had served. They grumbled about the meager 20 percent of the take that they were allowed to keep but looked forward to the time when they would qualify for 30 percent. Their average share of six or seven dollars a night left them hard pressed, they explained, to make expenses. They knew that finding really good jobs was next to impossible; if they complained, their places could easily be filled. Lots of people could drive taxis.

As our car swayed and rattled along Chicago Avenue it began to pass block after block of small establishments labeled with Polish signs. You would have to go to Warsaw to find a greater concentration of Poles. At every stop we lost a few cleaning women and a taxi driver or two, each, upon leaving, saying good-bye to friends before disappearing into the nighttime shadows. Next morning I shared the talk with Mrs. Curran.

One morning I read an ad in the *Chicago Tribune* that one could take dancing lessons from professionals, and for only $15 become graceful and irresistible. I visited the studio, dreaming about becoming graceful and irresistible at a Grinnell dance. The fortyish, slenderish lady in charge assured me that such good things could be in store for me. Moreover, she would personally instruct me. I handed over the $15.

Although the studio, on the second floor of an ancient brick building, was dark and sparsely furnished, it had an area that would pass for a dance floor. On a table at the side were a Victrola and a stack of records.

She escorted me to the floor and demonstrated a few steps, holds, and clutches, which I awkwardly duplicated. She kept repeating that the ability to dance well depended largely on mental attitude; I must manage my partner with a strong, positive air. We had a few dry runs so I could get limbered up. She finally settled on one or two maneuvers that seemed within my capabilities.

She gave the crank of the Victrola a few turns and put on "Cecilia." I cannot recall how many time she played and replayed "Cecilia." Sometimes she promoted me to "Sleepy Time Gal" but sooner or later I was back to "Cecilia." I not only saw her in my dreams, but during the day as well.

In my own persistent way I stuck it out for the full series of lessons. The last afternoon she confided: "You're doing fine—you're on the edge of greater things—you owe it to yourself to sign for the intermediate course." I decided to quit while I was still ahead.

Midway through summer I noted that fewer operators were showing for work. One evening I appeared but Buck sent me home, saying there was nothing to do. As I started down the stairs, however, I heard Rosie yelling; I turned, and he beckoned me back. "It's all a mistake," he said; "Buck just now found a big job that had fallen into the wastebasket." So I was spared that particular evening, but from then on was given only two or three nights of work a week. A downturn of the business cycle had hit linotyping. Eventually I was the only operator on night duty. One Friday I looked at my diminished paycheck and as there was little work in sight, I suddenly decided I had had enough of the big city, and said good-bye to Buck and Rosie. Next day I boarded the Burlington's Denver Limited and in a few hours I was home. On the way it dawned upon me with a start that I had forgotten to visit Garfield Park. Sorry, Mrs. C.

All in all I had saved $110, more money than I had ever had in my life. I had become a member of the International Typographical Union and had a membership card to prove it. I had learned about the printing trade in a giant city, including helpful facts about the mystique of interviewing for a position. I had observed furthermore that thousands of Americans do not speak English, and that the streets of Chicago at 3:00 in the morning were as safe as the streets of downtown Osceola. I had heard a theater organ and a talking film, and I had ridden a lake steamer. I had mastered the city's most dynamic roller coaster. I had visited the headquarters of the famous Lone Scout organization. I knew about city banks and banking. I was a full-fledged member of the twentieth century.

August was drawing to a close. In a few weeks I would be back at Grinnell.

25

I first saw her on the platform of the Rock Island station, on a cool, misty morning, with a group of girls, there to meet the Des Moines train. I was with The Syndicate and other dorm mates. Each autumn the first campus arrivals met the later trains to greet their friends.

When I was growing up in my small Missouri town, meeting the trains every day as a paperboy or reporter, I never dreamed that I would first glimpse my love on a depot platform.

She was now a sophomore and I a junior. Already she had spent a year at Grinnell; I had heard her name in conversations with students from Des Moines, of whom our hall had several: Frank Dewey, Sam Elbert, Ted Lovejoy, and others. She was a good student, I had heard, fond of tennis, basketball, and swimming, and invariably to be seen at chapel, concerts, lectures, dances.

For some reason we had never met.

That first view was from twenty feet away: a mop of blonde hair, a heavy coat to fight the morning chill, Argyle stockings. She was a little shorter than I; in other words, a perfect height. So this, I thought, is Gus Towner. She and the other girls were lively, animated, eager to greet the friends who were expected. In moments the train whistled its advance notice and soon came into view; growing larger and larger, it threatened to run us down; the first cars whizzed by as if they were not going to stop at all, but the squeaking of brakes told another story. The long chain of coaches and Pullmans stretched the length of the platform. As conductor and brakeman emerged, putting their step boxes down, students swarmed both out of those authorized exits and of others they opened for themselves; most of them were met by friends on the platform. The welcomers seized hand luggage and waited while the newcomers made arrangements with the half dozen draymen available to have trunks delivered. Nobody had had breakfast, but that could wait.

She left with her group, I with mine. Weeks passed without our meeting. The *Herald* filled my evenings, and though we were both English majors, she, as a sophomore, was taking courses I had already completed.

One December day three of my Des Moines friends planned a bridge party and invited me to join them. Their dates were Des Moines girls and they suggested that I escort Gus Towner. We reserved the lounge of the YM-YW building. Three of the girls, including my partner, had never played bridge. That was no problem, however, since they had a week to learn.

We did not bother to invite a chaperone. We had learned early in college that, particularly when rules are vague, we should never inquire officially about them or the powers will protect themselves by saying no. If something is not expressly forbidden, or only vague-

ly forbidden, go ahead and do it. You will not have put people in a
position where they have to make a decision. It's a policy I have
followed religiously.

The evening of bridge was short of tournament caliber. The boys
were good players, but the girls—well, they learned the night before in a cram session. My partner had astonishing luck. Once when
I was dummy she played a fabulous hand. Three times she successively led clubs from dummy and trumped in her own hand, glowing
with pleasure at her newfound skill. I looked questioningly at my
opponent, but since he smiled indulgently and said nothing, I saw
no reason for asking her to replay the tricks.

She had the high score and won the prize, a set of three brass
ashtrays. None of the girls smoked—but then, we had not anticipated that any of them would carry away the prize.

Minutes before 10:00 we adjourned and walked the girls to the
Quadrangle. It had hardly been a date at all, but more of a party.
She was comfortable to be with and easy to talk to. In the weeks that
followed we sometimes met on the campus or in the halls between
classes, smiled, and said hello. We were both fully wrapped up in
activities to which we were already committed. Neither of us really
expected anything from the other.

26

Meanwhile Don, a senior, had developed into a fine debater. He
and his teammates successively won the state quarterfinals, semifi-
nals, and finals, each by a unanimous decision. Imagine half a dozen
consecutive 3-0 verdicts—half a dozen shutouts—eighteen judges
listening, agreeing, approving. Don and his two colleagues swept
through opposing high schools like grasshoppers through a
cornfield, winning tuition scholarships to the University of Iowa.
Without difficulty, Don got a linotyping job at the *Daily Iowan*, so
when the fall term opened we left for different campuses.

After a couple of weeks, the promised job was suddenly swept out
from under him. Another student, a former employee, had unexpectedly decided to return to school, so the foreman explained that
he needed to give the job back to its original holder. From this
shaky reasoning there was no appeal. Not enough work was available for both.

All of this Don phoned me the next day. What to do? We decided not to trouble Father and Mother with this puzzler until we had chewed on it awhile. I offered to explore the possibilities at the Grinnell newspapers. Ray said he could start Don at only fifty cents an hour but could give him as many hours a week as he wanted. The registrar said Don could be admitted, and the treasurer offered to let him pay his bill on the installment plan.

That evening I phoned Don. As he had not located anything of interest, the Grinnell opportunity suddenly became attractive. He thought he could get his fees and room rental refunded. Actually he retrieved every penny, despite ambiguous regulations; he had not been a star debater for nothing. So the state university lost in this casual way a student who became one of Iowa's best-known news-papermen. Don was not disappointed about leaving; he said the upperclassmen didn't even take enough interest in him to paddle him.

Twenty-four hours later he was a full-time student at Grinnell. Like me, he had come there in a roundabout way. We called Father and Mother, who were secretly delighted to have their sons to-gether and proud that we had worked out the transfer between ourselves.

In retrospect I realize that nobody had asked to see Don's tran-script or had needed a letter from the high-school principal attesting to his character. No one said, "We'll review the situation; come back Monday." No one demurred, "Well, possibly, but we'll have to see him first." No one carefully explained, "We've just completed regis-tration and since we have not yet made an exact count of this year's enrollment we'll have to ask you to return later when we know where we stand." No one bemoaned, "Trouble is, he's missed freshman orientation," for the simple reason that, in those days, there wasn't any orientation. You came first and sent home for your pajamas later.

The people I talked to made decisions on the spot. One does not find this situation in modern times, on the campus or anywhere else. Both of us were able to get into college at a time when a lot of regulations governing admission were still to be invented. Several rules we did have had to be outgrown, but, even so, at some point between the founding of William and Mary and the multiversity of two centuries and a half later, higher education made an unfortunate turn. Now there are forms to fill out, procedures to follow, chains of command to be pursued, signs that say "Wait Here," "Sign Below for an Appointment," "P through T Go to Room 124." Computer printouts become longer, with more columns, yet meaningful information is difficult to get. Even this system can work, and when it does, it is because of intrinsic reasons: diligent students who know the score and can ask the right questions, administrators who know not only the rules but also the exceptions, and good teachers who can cut the red tape, supply the missing links, identify the centers of authority, and make decisions without summoning a committee.

27

During my junior year I decided there must be a better way of getting an education than by spending five hours out of each day pounding a keyboard. Cramming study into parts of afternoons and weekends was demoralizing. I decided I should work full time for a year and then finish college without the burden of a part-time job. Two months at Chicago had convinced me I could do it.

Others were unhappy with Grinnell for a different reason: word had spread that the trustees were planning to dismiss members of the faculty and staff because the state of the economy compelled a $20,000 reduction in the budget. The trustees proposed to put the professor of Latin on leave without pay, assigning his courses to the professor of Greek; to make cuts in music and economics; and to abolish most of the public-relations staff. Those concerned faced personal disaster. A professor of English confided to a small group of us, with respect to the full professor about to be given a leave that he did not want, that "chairs in Latin are extremely difficult to find."

As I reflect upon this crisis—the year was 1925—I am astonished at the amount of talent that $20,000 would buy. I am even more astonished that a college president would recommend this summary dismissal of teachers and others of long service, even in the days when a president was almost a law unto himself, governing as he wished, with little fear of being reversed. Little mechanism existed for hearings, reviews, or appeals.

Even in this seemingly hopeless situation, professors and students did what they could. The faculty worded a strong request to the trustees to reconsider the proposed changes in the instructional staff (though it was not so interested in rescuing the publicity people). But the long discussions among students were especially convincing. It did not matter that the persons involved were not the most popular or even the best teachers; nor did they have any special reputation as scholars. It was enough that they were men who commanded respect. It did matter that a principle was being assaulted without consulting those most concerned. Many students who had never had and would never take a class in music or economics, much less Latin, declared that the quality of instruction would suffer irretrievably and vowed that they would transfer to another college. Others circulated petitions in the dormitories, with 90 percent of the students signing. Word got around that they would rather have the budget balanced by a tuition increase than by the drastic method proposed by the trustees. It was a remarkable demonstration of student support of their professors.

The campus mood deepened my own, already depressed, spirits. And then unexpectedly I saw a way out. On my way to work one afternoon, I stopped at the post office to buy stamps, and, as always, I paused in front of the bulletin board to read the accumulation of posters. Ever since my Gilman City days, where Father and Mother ran the post office, I had been fascinated by the flow of "To Be Posted" bulletins that came from the Third Assistant Postmaster General in Washington. Here would be front and side views of a man wanted for robbing a mail train at Topeka. *May be armed.* Here is a photo of a man sought for breaking into and entering the post office in Springfield. Name is given and also aliases. *Beard may be false.* Money orders imprinted 876100–876199, Galveston, Texas, are stolen; *if seen, notify Postmaster General.* Buy Postal Savings Certificates: *2 percent interest.* Counterfeit money is abroad in the land. Enlist in the U.S. Coast Guard. Also on mimeographed sheets were lists of openings in government departments.

On this visit to the post office, making my usual faithful stop at its bulletin board, I noted that the Government Printing Office in Washington had vacancies for printers, linotype operators, and proofreaders,$1 an hour and up. In years of bulletin-board watching I had never before seen a request for operators. Late that night I wrote a letter describing my qualifications.

When weeks passed with no reply, I decided the government had located scores of operators and would continue to function without my talents. The college trustees, meanwhile, impressed by student unrest in their concern for their professors, and by the possibility of a few students leaving, reviewed its decision and planned to keep the entire staff, solving the crisis by increasing tuition $50. Though this was a jump of 25 percent, most students reasoned that a diploma from a college that maintained its quality was worth the extra amount. So I was feeling better about remaining at Grinnell. Then, two weeks before the end of the semester, came a telegram that I could have a job—$100.80 for every two weeks, plus vacation time, and other delicacies. Here was a chance to live and work in the nation's capital.

I showed the telegram to Ray, who this time gave me his absorbed attention. He was not worried about replacing me and had no objection to my leaving, but he talked earnestly about the importance of getting a college degree. He argued that once a student left the campus he often did not return. He mentioned employees of the *Herald*, who, having taken positions before completing their studies, had never been graduated.

I assured him I would return to Grinnell, under circumstances where I could be a full-time student.

Days later I was at the *Herald* for the last time. Frisbie told me how pleased he had been with my work and hoped I would enjoy being in Washington. I then saw Ray, whose face wore the frustrated look of a publisher whose pressman has printed a big job in black ink instead of blue. He was so aggravated that he needed a moment to realize that I had come not to set type but to say goodbye.

"Don't forget your pay," he growled. In the lines of that troubled face, however, I saw the edge of a smile. Pearl gave me the money and a hug, sort of. Next morning I boarded the Rock Island, this time going east, not west, and not with two hundred others but by myself. In no time at all I had left Grinnell behind and was staring at the passing miles of snow-covered Iowa prairie.

At Chicago I transferred to that sumptuous railroad, the Baltimore & Ohio. During the few remaining daylight hours my nose was pressed against a window, as I had not been east of Chicago since I was seven. When night came I curled up on my coach seat and got what sleep I could, aroused frequently by the blast of a whistle, the stop at a station, or the roar of a passing train. At daybreak I made my way to the diner, determined to get a hearty meal regardless of cost. Before long I would be receiving the fabulous wages paid by the Government Printing Office.

The hour was so early the diner was empty. The black waiter waved me grandly to a seat at a table covered with a crisp, white cloth, with gleaming china, and sparkling silver. Here was an ambience I had never experienced.

"Good morning, sir," he said, in as resonant a voice as Billy Bryan's, chock full of hospitality. "Could I bring you a cup of hot coffee to help you start the day?"

This young sir of twenty-one, whose still-twisted body and rumpled clothes clearly indicated a night spent on a coach seat, had never received such attention. Not at the Grinnell dining hall, not at home in Osceola, not back in Gilman City.

Never in my life had I drunk coffee. Here, however, was an offer not to be refused. "Yes, please," I nodded, in the friendliest voice I could summon at that bleak hour. In seconds the coffee was before me, black and steaming—not a cup but a full pot. He filled a cup and set it before me.

Now that I had it, I debated what to do with it. Should I pour it in a saucer and let it cool, like my grandfather? Well, no, not in a Pullman diner. Should I adjust and modify it? Sugar and thick cream, in silver-plated vessels, were at my fingertips. Ryan used to quote Talleyrand as declaring that coffee should be black as night, hot as hell, and sweet as a woman's love. I decided to go Ryan and Talleyrand one better, omitting the sugar as well as the cream. The coffee was strong, full of character. I grimaced.

The time had come to proceed to the breakfast itself.

I picked up the heavy, starched linen napkin, a full two feet square, and spread it over my lean shanks, trying to act as if I had done this every morning of my life. I turned my attention to the menu, a four-page folder, each page as big as a letterhead, and read the entries, set in 14-point type, the few lines richly spaced—the use of wide margins in a display being in itself a form of opulence. I passed up the oatmeal and let my eyes drop down to the bottom line where the heavy stuff was featured: hot cakes, ham and eggs, and such luxuries, accompanied by a lavish assortment of fruits and juices. I wrote my decisions in a firm hand on the order pad. The waiter picked it up, expressed his approval of such a handsome selection and his intention to serve it forthwith, and disappeared into the kitchen at the end of the car.

In moments came my dish of stewed prunes—seven or eight beauties, gently spiced, each as big as a golf ball. I took a good fifteen minutes to consume them all, reflectively munching as I watched twenty miles of scenery slip past. The waiter, attentive without really seeming to be, removed the bowl, which was on a saucer, which was on a small plate, and soon reappeared with my main dish, under a radiant silver dome. This he deftly removed and there, on a large hot plate, was a generous slice of ham and my three lightly browned, over-easy eggs. He set the toast, wrapped in a napkin, alongside, readjusted salt and pepper shakers and butter dish, so all would be in readiness. He added more iced water to the water glass and topped off the cup of coffee. How different all this was from a college dining room! Out of hundreds of breakfasts eaten away from home, this was one I was to remember forever. I suspect the cost was as much as eighty-five cents. It was my first experience on a diner, and I remember it as fondly as I do the service, much later, on the Twentieth Century Limited, the Panama Limited, the Super Chief, and other splendid American trains. As the years rolled on it became increasingly difficult to get a superb meal, with elegant service, on anything that moved. Anything.

At Washington's Union Station, I alighted with my possessions in a laundry bag, the sure sign of a student. Actually a case, thinner than the average suitcase, it was a heavy cardboard box, inside a canvas covering, fastened with web straps. For a few pennies one mailed the bag home, filled with dirty shirts, underwear, socks, handkerchiefs. One's mother washed and ironed the contents, added cookies or other edibles, reversed the address card so it now displayed the name and address of her beloved college boy or girl, and mailed it back. Only affluent students patronized town laundries.

I threaded my way through the giant waiting room where hundreds were collecting at assembly points waiting to depart, standing around private heaps of luggage, waiting for trains to be called, or, like me, headed for the exits. All the great lines of the East served the nation's capital—the Baltimore & Ohio, the Chesapeake & Ohio, the Pennsylvania, and others—and I had arrived in as grand a train as any. Outside the station I saw the Capitol, a sure sign that I was in the right city. And across North Capitol Street was the Government Printing Office, a plain-looking, boxy, seven-story building.

Suddenly I realized I had made no plans beyond this moment. I had nowhere to go. With my Chicago experience in mind, I bought a copy of a newspaper, hunted up a bench, and looked through the "Rooms for Rent" ads. In minutes I had located a couple of prospects. The room I rented was small and dark, but it was close to the city's axis.

As I had an afternoon to sightsee, I strolled along Washington's famous avenues, each named after a state. If I had had a long loaf of bread to carry under my arm, I would have been a dead ringer for another young printer, Benjamin Franklin, who, two centuries previously, had gone to Philadelphia, also to make his way in a big city.

III. The Linotype Connection

28

Bright and early Monday morning I faced my new employer, The United States Government.

To a small-town boy, that first encounter went off without show of emotion. On either side. I exhibited my telegram and was directed to the medical office for a physical examination. In minutes The Government had stripped me to my delicate underthings and in that helpless condition started asking me questions of a personal nature. I was then allowed to reassemble myself and was sent to the composing room where I located the superintendent, Bill Skeen.

Over a twenty-year period I worked under as many gruff, laconic, demanding, and stern-tempered foremen and plant superintendents—and later department chairmen and deans—as anyone living. Not until the forties did I even occasionally meet a friendly, relaxed type of executive. During the period of my earlier years some phenomenon, not yet fully charted, had eased the half-sourpuss, overbearing sort of man into what might be called middle-management positions. In a dozen growly phrases Skeen assigned me to Linotype No. 49, indicating its general location, and also the spot where I could pick up a batch of copy.

I stopped at the desk of a stout, wheezy, red-faced copy dispenser, a Dutchman named Van Hook, and told him I was newly assigned to No. 49. He handed me a take consisting of two typewritten sheets that were part of a Supreme Court decision. "Now 49," he said, "go over there, show it to your machinist, and he will adjust your machine for you."

I was learning fast: my new name was 49, and I was to have the services of a professional machinist, a luxury I had always done without. With my curiosity full-blown, I asked him the questions that were stirring inside me. How many Linotypes are there?—144. Are they all on this floor?—No; 72 on this floor and 72 on the next. What is on the other floors?—Presses, Monotypes, editing and proofreading rooms. Do we go outside for lunch?—No, there's a cafeteria on the top floor. Is it true the Government Printing Office is the world's largest printing establishment?—You're damn right. Four thousand people work here, and if you don't hurry along there will be only 3,999.

By this time others behind me were awaiting their takes, so I left to find Machine 49. I was surprised that Van Hook had given me such a small amount of copy but later realized the system was designed for speed and flexibility. Divide a long Supreme Court decision in twenty parts, so that twenty men can work on it at the same time, and in half an hour it is completely set up in type. For a single operator, a morning's work might consist of a piece of a court decision, a couple of pages from a *Farmers' Bulletin*, two sheets of description of a newly awarded patent, another segment of a court decision, a bit of a Department of State document, part of a House or Senate bill. Late in the day operators would get takes for the next morning's *Congressional Record*, though most of this periodical was handled by the night shift.

The productivity of the Government Printing Office was incredible. Guides who took visitors through the plant liked to say that we could set the whole Bible in six hours, and print and bind it in another eighteen. In such an enterprise, my share would be merely to set the equivalent of half of Genesis. The typesetting for the book you are now looking at could be completed in less than an hour.

Arriving at 49, in a section of eight Linotypes, two rows of four with the keyboards facing the aisle, I located the machinist, whose name was Wick. He showed me a thick, red book lying on my copy tray. "This is the *Government Printing Office Style Manual*," he explained. "GPO style is different from anything else in the world. For example, GPO capitalizes a lot of words that other stylebooks don't."

"Right now," he went on, "your take is rubber-stamped 'Fol. Lit.' That means you are to follow copy literally, with no changes of punctuation, capitalization, or anything else. You're working on a Supreme Court decision, which cannot be altered by operators, proofreaders, or editors. That's also true of treaties and statutes. Your next take, however, may be a *Farmers' Bulletin*, marked simply 'Fol.' That means the editor expects you to do the routine editing necessary to make the copy conform to GPO style. Sometimes it's a congressman's speech and isn't stamped at all, which leaves a lot to the operator; he can correct the grammar, if he feels like it."

I learned to capitalize Army, Navy, Government, President, Treasury, Bureau of Engraving and Printing. I learned to stick in a comma on "Fol." copy wherever it was humanly possible to insert a comma; but even then the proofreader would find places to write in

comma that I had never dreamed of. I learned to hyphenate
to-morrow, to-day, to-night, which everybody else in the nation had
stopped doing years before. I learned these and other matters the
hard way, by failing to make the necessary changes and having my
errors show up on the proof.

Just as Wick had finished his explanation, the bell rang. I did not
need to be told that lunchtime had arrived; I was swept up into the
mass of a hundred hungry men headed for the elevator. Skeen was
there to see that we did not overcrowd it.

The cafeteria offered variety, and for thirty-five cents you could
have all you could possibly eat. I saw that several of the men were
hurrying their meals in order to have time for a frame of duck pins.
This game was played on alleys smaller than standard bowling alleys, and with smaller pins; each player was given three rolls instead
of two. Scoring, however, was much as in bowling. I learned to
divide my thirty-minute lunch into ten minutes for eating and
twenty for duck pins.

One noon I saw a printer reading a book in Greek. I had had a
course in Greek literature in translation, but here was a man who
could read the original. I noted that his selection was Hesiod's
Works and Days, which I had studied a few weeks previously. I was
curious to know if he had gone to college, and he shook his head.
"But Greek is meat and drink to me," he insisted. I pondered: Here
I am, a college junior, spending my lunch hour bowling. And here
he is, a man of slight formal education, reading Hesiod in the original. At home that evening he must have said, "I met a printer today
who said he had read *Works and Days*," and his wife must have
replied, "Oh come, now."

Our lino section had its own talent, though: several lawyers, a
chiropractor, a dentist, and a physician. We also had among us a
musician who had written a 250-page opera, but was still setting bits
and pieces of Supreme Court decisions and patent specifications.
Everyone mentioned our dentist with sympathy, because after
spending years of spare time studying and getting his diploma, he
was afraid to quit his job. But I also learned of another dentist who
did not leave his job even after he got his license, but then one
spring was discharged; he had to start practicing and thus was forced
into making scads of money. In life we never know whether something that happens to us is going to be good or bad.

As I had been told, I was started at the basic wage of $1 an hour. I learned that if after serving a three-hundred-hour tryout period I maintained a higher average, I would be paid $1.05, and that still higher speeds qualified an operator for $1.10 or $1.15.

Weeks later, in an idle moment, I told Wick that if he would speed my machine to seven lines or more a minute, and if I could persuade Van Hook to give me decent copy, I would try for the world record. These conditions were met and I spent an exciting two hours on the project, though nobody quite knew what the world record was, nor what kind of copy or type size was standard in this sort of competition. So although we attracted attention on the floor with our show, we never knew whether any records fell. Moreover, the International Typographical Union did not encourage this sort of activity. Although technically Uncle Sam ran an open shop, most of us held union cards, and unions are not fond of wage differentials based on output.

With seventy-two operators on our floor chewing away at copy, no one person got more than two or three takes from the same public document. An astonishing variety of information passed across my copy tray. I learned about the diseases of sheep and how to keep bees from swarming. I knew the condition of the loose-leaf book market in Guatemala, and could tell you how many upright pianos were manufactured in Finland. I read how to appear as a witness in a congressional committee hearing and not reveal any information, and how to make logical arguments before the Supreme Court without troubling too much with facts. Would you like to know how to tell good grapefruit from poor ones? Or good cabbages from soft ones? Or choice rutabagas from inferior ones? I learned, since I set parts of bulletins on each of these subjects. Would you be at all interested in the balloon-tire market in Belgium? Did you ever feel the need of practical information on the cost of keeping a yacht? From the lino section of this mighty plant, I saw all and knew all, like Pathé News.

One day Van Hook gave me a job to correct that consisted of page proofs of an old bulletin. I studied it and returned it to his desk and said, "Van, this book isn't machine set, it's handset."

I do not know how I could tell the page was handset; people develop an expertise they cannot always explain. How does a Treasury man spot the subtle differences between a superb counterfeit and a genuine bank note? My botany professor, Henry Conard, could identify trees two or three hundred yards away. On field trips when I would ask him, for instance, "How do you know that's a white oak?" he would start feeling for words that might carry meaning, concluding candidly, "It just looks like a white oak." To this printer who had begun his trade fifteen years previously in a country office, the pages *looked* as if they had been printed from individual type characters, not from machine slugs.

Van Hook scanned the page, insisted that it was machine composition. I shook my head. "Show it to Skeen," he said, finally.

The foreman glanced at it and ruled that it had been set on one of our machines. "Well," I countered, "unless you're positive, you'd better look at the pages themselves and make sure." We would be the laughing stock of the whole GPO if we couldn't identify our own product. He stuck to his guns, so I started back to my machine.

Before I had gone far, however, he called me back and said, "Here, Reid, let that job go, it isn't important; here's a hot one." So I took it.

Later Van Hook, grinning, asked me: "Did you say you learned the trade in a country shop?" "I sure did," I replied. "Well, Skeen just asked where in hell you learned anything about hand type and I told him."

That was the day I became something more than just 49. But I have to reflect that our generation was filled with men and women who acquired all kinds of useful skills in home, field, or shop, that were to become completely outmoded. Few will turn aside to glimpse a person who could distinguish between hand and machine composition or for that matter who could listen to the sounds of an ailing machine—linotype or locomotive—and spot what was wrong with it.

29

Those years and the twenty that followed represented the absolute peak of typesetting-machine glory. Human beings never mass-produced a more ingenious combination of wheels, belts, gears, and levers. The Linotype had no electrical or electronic devices (though later these appeared briefly) but depended on gravity, springs, the drive of gears, and the thrust of odd-shaped wheels called cams. Its beauty was functional; to the casual eye it was graceless, top-heavy angular. Nearly all its insides were exposed, easy to get at for repair no one thought to design a cover to hide its graceless edges. Nor was much effort given to silencing its clatter. It was created by a German machinist named Ottmar Mergenthaler, not by a designer or stylist It came in only one color, gray. You could make 90 percent of its adjustments with a micrometer, a screwdriver, and a small wrench.

Already the Linotype had been on the scene a quarter of a century in printing's five-century history and would be on its way out in another quarter century, but while it was around it was the monarch of the composing room. I do need to mention that it had a strong competitor, the Intertype, so similar in design that if you could operate and adjust one, you could operate and adjust the other.

What I did every day would have taken five or six compositors setting type by hand. Moreover, the solid lines of type that I produced were infinitely more manageable than lines of separate and individual type characters. Yet in the 1980s an operator of computer equipment, often a young person who had learned the typewriter keyboard in high school, can produce more than one of us who had served a four-year apprenticeship or the equivalent—and what he or she turns out is simpler still to handle than the lines of type that seemed so revolutionary to us.

As the years stack up behind us, fewer and fewer people remain who recall the sounds of the machines that made the industrial revolution: the threshing machine and the steam engine that powered it, the noises of the locomotive and the click of wheels moving along unwelded tracks, the engines and grinders of a grain mill, the clatter of a telegraph in a railroad station, the whirring of the insides of a telephone as one cranked it to summon the operator.

The Linotype with its several thousand parts played its own tunes not so brisk as "Tea for Two" or as sustained as "It's Three O'Clock in the Morning," but combinations of both. The operator presided over a keyboard with ninety keys—more than a piano—a key for each small letter, capital letter, figure, and punctuation mark. First came the clatter of individual matrices in response to the keyboard, each matrix a little larger than a postage stamp, with the mold of one letter carved out of one edge, and as thick as the letter for which it served as a mold. As the keys were struck, these matrices dropped out of their magazine, or container, onto a moving belt that speeded

A corner of the Government Printing Office's ninety-machine linotype section in the 1980s. I recall no women operators on the day shift in 1926, although scores were employed in the proofreading and bindery sections.

The photo gives a good view of the ninety-key keyboard. If Mergenthaler had arranged his keyboard like a typewriter's, the changeover from hot-metal linecasting to photo-computer systems would not have been so revolutionary. (Photograph courtesy of Government Printing Office.)

each matrix into an assembling frame, which held the line of type. When the line is assembled, bearing the words, for example, *Now is the time for all good men to come,* this assembling frame is lifted to exactly the right height, when a metallic click indicates that the line of matrices has been snatched from the frame and is being slid along to the left, thus leaving the assembling area and entering the casting area. Meanwhile the assembling frame is lowered to its starting position so the operator can finish the phrase, *aid of the party,* in a second line, and so on. If he completes the second line before the first is cast, he lifts it to the upper position, and it moves to a halfway point and hangs there momentarily; this is the "hanging of the machine" feature previously mentioned. While one line is being cast, the operator is composing the next.

Now back to the first line. When it enters what is called the first elevator, in the casting area, it triggers a clutch that puts the heavy-duty part of the machine into operation. A new set of sounds joins the others; the metallic thud of a controlled drop is followed by the creaks and clicks of squeezing, adjusting, and aligning as the line is pressed firmly against the front of a mold. The mouthpiece of the pot of molten lead alloy is thrust snugly against the back of the mold, so that everything is perfectly aligned, with no chance for leaks or spatters, or, as we called them, "squirts." Who wants hot metal spattered over the landscape? Then the firm thud of a plunger indicates that the mold is being filled with hot lead flowing into the characters carved into the back of each individual matrix. Now the newly cast slug bears the words, *Now is the time for all good men to come.* This custom-minted line hardens at once; the next sounds are those of the metal pot backing away and the line of matrices being lifted up, to be transferred to a long arm called the second elevator, which has swooped down with its own clatter. The second elevator then rises, like a heron that dips its beak into the water, seizes a fish, and lifts it into the air.

Meanwhile the newly molded line has been ejected into a stick, or holder, where a collection of lines will eventually form a galley, and the first elevator has returned to its starting position, ready to receive the second line that has been hanging around waiting for it. The process of casting a line has taken less than ten seconds.

Now a third set of sounds joins the machine's counterpoint. The matrices that spelled out *Now is the time for all good men to come* are dropped in each one's individual storage channel. There are ninety channels, one for each key, and the four *e*'s in our line will, in turn, be sorted out and each dropped into the *e* channel. Other matrices also find their separate ways home, announcing their arrival with little clicks. So the Linotype's orchestra now has, all going at once, assembling sounds, casting sounds, and distributing sounds: clicks, clacks, taps, creaks, swishes, whirrs, clashes. Subconsciously the operator hears these sounds, and if there is any that does not belong, he will react, either by pushing the stopping lever, or by taking some other action, such as muttering, "Dammit, the distributor has jammed again," and walking to the back of the machine to unjam it.

In short, the operator conducts his own complex symphony and keeps each separate instrument on the score. Any driver knows the music of his own auto and can react to strange squeaking, knowing

This picture, with the caption, "The Hand That Keeps the World Informed," was for many years a trademark of the Mergenthaler Linotype Company. In its own field it is as famous as the dog listening to "His Master's Voice" on a Victrola. It frequently appeared in *The Linotype Bulletin*, a house organ for advertising Linotype models, advantages of machine-set over hand-set composition, suggestions for the ad or book designer, helpful hints for the machinist. I read it faithfully for years.

whether he needs to pull to the side of the highway and investigate, or whether he is hearing a harmless sound that can be repaired later. The housewife identifies noises that tell her the bag of her vacuum cleaner is full or that a belt has stuck. As a people we are sensitive to the sounds of the machines around us, just as our forebears were sensitive to the grunts and whinnies of farm animals.

Smells assailed us as well as sounds. Composing room air was a compound of gas-burner fumes, molten lead smells, and at times the stench of the oily additive employed in refining used slugs. In a back corner—as far away as you could put it—was a cast-iron pot in which to remelt used lines of type and recast them into pigs. In going through the press, the lines, of course, had been inked, so a strong odor of ink, plus the oil stirred into the molten metal, enhanced the overall smell, which reached even the editor's sanctum.

Decades later, when the machines were hauled out the back door to be traded off or junked and replaced by cameras and computers, the newspaper shop became as quiet as a jewelry store with no more smell than an insurance office. You would hardly know what was going on if you hadn't read the sign out front. The composing room is—I choke to say it—*carpeted*.

So I offer my brief tribute not only to yesterday's newspaper sights but also to its vanished sounds and smells. And especially to the intricate harmonics of the linecasting machine.

30

Two operators, 29 and 13, whom I learned to call by their real names, Sonntag and Smith, lived at the YMCA, a few blocks beyond the White House. They urged me to get a room there, so I went to the Y and inquired about moving in.

No single was available. One of the clerks speculated: "We might put him in with Barker." After hesitating the other replied, "Yes, Barker has been wanting a roommate."

For a moment the two held my future in their hands. I didn't give much of a hoot who my roommate was. In three years of dormitory living I had already met most kinds. Then the first clerk said in positive tones: "Barker is out of town for several days. You can move right in and get settled. It's Room 606."

We grinned. "606" was the well-known brand of the then-current remedy for syphilis, a form of arsenic that was supposed to kill the spirochete but spare the patient. The treatment was rugged, but for long the best available. Even I had heard barroom stories about 606. So I was taken upstairs to look over my new quarters. I found a plain room, cheaply furnished with two beds, two tables, and two dressers. Lavatories and other plumbing were down the hall. The general tone was durability, not charm or grace. In a few hours I had moved in.

I liked the surroundings. Through 29 and 13 I made the acquaintance of other young men—Jack Paisley in the chief clerk's office, Paul Oehser, manuscript editor at the Department of Agriculture. Number 13 also had a new Model T Ford coupe that occasionally he let me drive. This was the last year that Ford built the Model T. Gradually I forgot about Barker.

Then one night, just as I had gone to bed, I heard a key in the lock and a slender, lean-faced figure, my height, a little older and sturdier of build, entered. "I'm Barker," he thundered.

In my normal, subdued voice, I replied, "I'm Reid."

I stood up to shake hands. "They told me downstairs you had moved in," he boomed.

As he undressed, we exchanged references, so to speak. He was employed by the then-new Veterans Administration. He came from Kentucky mountain country; I judged he had developed his voice by constant shouting across the valleys. He said he was a Republican and let pass my statement that I was a Democrat. He was currently taking night courses to get a diploma and, at the moment, was sweating out an English survey course, starting with Chaucer. He seemed curious about what I was doing but was mainly impressed by the fact that I had already survived not only Chaucer, but Spenser, Shakespeare, Milton, and Browning.

Through the walls our conversation must have sounded like long rolls of a bass drum interspersed with short bursts from the snare. Yet I was gradually feeling that we would get along famously.

He put on his pajamas, sat on the edge of the bed facing me, reached in his suitcase, and pulled out a .38 revolver. He broke it to make sure it was loaded. I could see it was. He checked the safety, put this weapon, this cannon, under his pillow, and turned out the light.

I lay there in a swivet. As a boy I had had the usual arsenal of rifles and shotguns—.22 repeater, 12-gauge, even a 10-gauge—but had never known anyone who carried a revolver, much less slept with one. Still, I did not think it would do any good to get up and leave.

Next morning I was awakened by a loud, colorful exchange. Barker had been awakened by the Chinese laundryman, tapping at each door on his usual rounds and chiming, "Laundlee, laundlee." "I've told that fellow not to collect here," Barker roared, not only to me, but to the whole floor.

A few mornings later I was suddenly awakened by an explosion. Barker was sitting up in bed, holding the revolver. The room was filled with gunsmoke. Plaster dust was falling from what looked like a fresh hole above the transom.

"Well, I guess that laundryman will not be back soon," he muttered, grimly. We never heard him again.

By now I was beyond being amazed. Principally I thought of him as a hardworking government employee, struggling to get a diploma so he could move up the VA's ladder. I also learned that he had joined the Masons and was working on various degrees in the York, or maybe it was the Scottish, rite. Often he read a few lines from a selection in his literature text in his own epic voice. "Now what does that mean, Reid?" he would demand.

Sometimes I ate breakfast with Sonntag and Smith, sometimes all of us with Paisley and Oehser. In a typical breakfast with Barker, he and I would ponder the menu while the waitress stood by for our decisions.

"What're you going to have, Reid?" he would thunder. I felt that the whole restaurant full of people had halted their own eating to hear precisely what Reid was going to have.

"I'll take a bowl of Shredded Wheat," I would suggest, gently.

"Shredded Wheat? That's no kind of breakfast. Know what I'm ordering? Ham and three eggs, hashed browns, toast, and coffee." The other diners could settle back to their own breakfasts, now knowing what Reid and whoever-the-other-person-is were going to have.

Before coming to Washington, Barker had spent years in Kentucky lumber camps. Here, he once said, he had learned to carry a gun as a matter of self-defense, since many others, often inclined to be pugnacious, also carried guns. So there is a reason for everything, and if one is patient it will come out. In the nation's capital he now missed the vigorous physical exercise of his younger days, so when he learned that a severe blight had swept the eastern seaboard, destroying hundreds of chestnut trees, he secured the permission of the superintendent of Rock Creek Park to cut down dead trees. He proposed that I join him one Sunday morning on a tree-chopping expedition. With some hesitation, I agreed.

I suppose I should explain that Rock Creek Park was mostly forest, with Rock Creek meandering through it, a beautiful place for strolling, fishing, picnicking, with ample room for everybody. I do not recall any stands or stores, though there may have been a few. And no asphalt parking lots. We went there by streetcar.

At Park headquarters we borrowed a long, double-handled saw, two axes, a sledge, and three wedges. Father, who had grown up on a farm at a time when every boy had to learn to use an axe, was adept with it. Often I had seen him cut through six or eight inches of hickory firewood, each blow biting deeply into the notch left by the previous blow. I had often tried it, but found it difficult to land two blows in the same place. Barker was superb; I was no better then than I had been earlier.

Barker's mode of operation was to select a dead chestnut, study the size and distribution of its limbs, and pick out a spot on the ground where it could fall without damaging live trees. Felling it was a combination of cutting notches with an axe and sawing partway through with the giant saw. In moments I was ready to give up my claim to a handle. Barker, however, was the most patient of instructors. Pull, don't push. Get the rhythm. Take it easy. Work with your body; don't do it all with your arms. When we had sawed into the trunk far enough, he drove wedges into the cut at strategic places.

After chopping and sawing and wedging we began to hear creakings and to note the first signs that the trunk was leaning. Barker, glancing back and forth between the spot where the tree should fall and the increasing slant of the trunk, gave the wedges their final blows—the last chance a woodsman has of adjusting the direction of the crash. If I were using the sledge at that critical moment, he shouted directions: "Hit the far one! Slam it! Slam into it! Hit the near one! No, dammit, the one next to you!" Soon the fate of the tree was beyond control. "Stand back!" And then: "Tim-m-ber-r-r!! Ball Hoot!!" in a cry that could be heard to the Lincoln Memorial.

The chestnut crashed to the ground, limbs bouncing and breaking, twigs snapping, trunk landing nearly always on the intended spot. As the superintendent did not require that we trim the trees, we gathered our tools, spotted another chestnut, and proceeded to chop and saw away at it.

Gradually I became not proficient but at least useful in the operation. One's big muscles strengthen rapidly; moreover, one gains the skill to use them efficiently. I looked forward to the Sunday sessions, a relief from the confining labors of typesetting. In turn the sessions got longer and longer. Well before noon I was ready to stop, but he pleaded, no insisted, "Just one more tree," and then "Just this little one" so that when we did finish I was thoroughly done in.

We ate Sunday dinner at Mrs. Scott's famous boardinghouse at 20th and P streets. Her sixty-five-cent price seemed extravagant, but her country-style fried-chicken dinner, with mashed potatoes, gravy, three vegetables, and other trimmings, ending with choices of pie, cake, ice cream, and watermelon, was irresistible. Mrs. Scott insisted that guests arrive on time and, moreover, be properly dressed. In his persuasive way, however, Barker had got permission for us to eat in the kitchen—an awesome concession, and one I would never have dreamed of seeking—not only long after the other guests had been served, but in our working clothes. Cooks, however, like to see their food appreciated, and the calls of the two of us, obviously starved, for seconds and thirds, delighted them. Then, too, we feasted on the choices that others had left behind and thus, like hungry goats, eliminated waste. The ecstasy of dining at 20th and P elevated my interest in the Sunday workouts.

The YMCA was occupied partly by regulars and partly by transients, some of them seedy-looking down-and-outers. Room drawings at 4:00 o'clock every afternoon made it possible for a few to have beds for the night at a minimum rate.

One night I was so bitten by bugs that I woke myself up from scratching. Soon Barker was awake and when I complained that the room was alive with mosquitoes he said, "No, they're bedbugs." In the dark he outlined a plan: at his signal he would suddenly turn on the light and we would pull back the covers, and if we were quick enough we could see our tormentors before they skittered out of sight. In seconds we could tell that we had been invaded by bedbugs, courtesy of the transients appearing at the 4:00 drawing.

Next morning we complained. As the clerk considered the problem routine, he did nothing and we suffered again that night. Thoroughly aroused, Barker proposed that we catch samples. Between us we collected ten or fifteen lively specimens and put them in a tumbler.

We waited until the 4:00 drawing when the lobby was full.

We strode to the main desk, this time armed with evidence. "I told you we had bedbugs in 606," Barker roared. This statement riveted the complete attention of the clerk and of everybody else. "And here you are," he continued, holding the tumbler aloft, then upending it so a few samples could spill out. "We'll attend to them," the clerk replied, glumly.

When we returned to our rooms late that afternoon, we saw that he had indeed attended to them. Baseboards, bed frames and legs, doorsills, and window ledges had been heavily sprayed with creosote dip. We might not be able to breathe but we would not be bitten. From that time on the bedbugs stayed below the sixth floor, and the mosquitoes, if there were any, chose not to fly into an atmosphere so overpowering.

So the weeks went by. Each of us had his own work and outside interests and his own circle of friends but we had mutual acquaintances at the Y to join at evening mealtime. And there were other ventures that I will describe later.

31

The mail brought word from my Syndicate brothers that I had had a letter published in the *Des Moines Register*.

This fact was startling, since I had never, never written the *Register*. Shortly before I had left Grinnell, however, The Syndicate had contrived that a letter to Mother Bluebird, ostensibly from me, should appear in the Sunday "Junior Register" for small boys and girls who had joined the Bluebirds. This was it:

LET'S ALL WRITE TO LOREN

Dear Mother Bluebird: I am only six years old and am in the first grade. I would like to join the Bluebirds and am sending ten cents for a pin. I have broken my leg and wish that some good Bluebirds would write to me. My mother is writing this letter for me and says she will be

glad to answer any letter. I hope you will print this letter so other
Bluebirds will write. Good-bye.

It was signed by me, from my Smith Hall address. The editor,
reading a note like that from a college town, might have smelled a
rat, judging by the comment that he printed:

Dear Loren: It is tough to have a broken leg, isn't it? We are sure that
a lot of the Bluebirds will write to you and that will help some, won't it?
Can't you send your picture so that we can print it in the Sunday *Register*? We hope you will be well soon.

In a few days, after I had left for Washington, letters from
Bluebirds began to arrive in Grinnell, a circumstance that con-
founded the perpetrators of this wicked deed. When my roommate,
Alden Greene, showed them to Gus Towner, she was so touched by
the response of one trusting child who was in a body cast that she
undertook to reply, saying she was a big girl friend of the little boy.
Alden, of course, to be remembered as the rightful owner of the
shirt I had worn into that Chicago bank, wrote me about the
Bluebird Connection and the correspondence that he had turned
over to Gus. His letter revived the memory of the incredible bridge
party, so I wrote, thanking her for looking after my mail, adding a
few paragraphs about what her former bridge partner was doing in
Washington. In the next few months we exchanged several letters.

32

When June arrived, I decided to return to Grinnell. Maybe I was
influenced by a news item that announced that a centrally operated
keyboard had been devised so one operator could set the same copy
on a score, or a hundred, other typesetting machines, located all
over the country. Stock-market quotations or baseball boxes, for
example, both difficult kinds of composition, could be set in New
York on a master keyboard, wired to newspapers everywhere, and
their typesetting machines, controlled from a distance, could grind
out line after line, displacing home talent. Wire-service news and
features could be set through this innovation. Local news would be
set at home, but obviously the need for operators would steadily
diminish. I began to feel that linotyping was doomed as a profession.

Maybe I also recalled Ray's parting advice: don't join the ranks of full-time workers until after you get your degree. Maybe the letters from Gus had something to do with the decision to return to Grinnell. Maybe I would have returned because of a promise I had made to myself. Who knows?

At any rate, I walked to George Washington University and looked at its schedule of evening courses, designed to accommodate government employees who normally worked until 4:30. I saw that if I completed three summer courses, I could return to Grinnell in September, take eighteen hours each semester, and be graduated with the Class of '27. I enrolled in Chaucer, American Literature, and Logic.

Suddenly the weeks became filled: tennis in the early morning on the Washington Monument courts, then work, then school. That summer Washington endured one record-breaking heat wave after another. Most evenings, when I returned to the Y after my last class, the weather was so sultry, and our room so stifling, that Barker and I rented a canoe and paddled up and down the cool Potomac. We seemed to have endless energy. We walked the streets at night entirely relaxed; if we were accosted, it was only by someone meekly seeking a nickel for a cup of coffee.

I had fallen in love with Washington as soon as I had arrived. The mild winter meant that the Japanese cherry trees had erupted in gorgeous splendor. The mood of the city was slow and creaking as compared with Chicago but its physical layout was entrancing. Its wide avenues, bearing names such as Pennsylvania, Massachusetts, and Connecticut, cut across a grid of numbered and lettered streets, creating everywhere circles, triangles, and squares that harbored statues, fountains, and ornamental benches. The landscape was dominated by the Capitol, the White House, the Washington Monument, and the new Lincoln Memorial. Banana carts and popcorn wagons were at every corner. Long rows of wooden barracks, relics of World War I, were now occupied by rapidly expanding government offices. Public transportation was by streetcar and, to outlying districts, by electric interurban.

I undertook to see all of the city's historical sights. I read in the Library of Congress, listened to debates in the House and Senate, climbed the Monument, wandered endlessly through the Smithsonian and the Old and New Museums. Occasionally I went to the

Keith, Rialto, and Earle theaters to enjoy their fascinating array of full-length movies plus vaudeville numbers, a combination I had enjoyed in Chicago. The luxurious seating and the rococo decoration made patrons feel like princes and princesses, and the ventilation system that blew air through ice-filled compartments was supposed to make the interior twenty degrees cooler than the streets. We saw a choice selection of magicians, acrobats, novelty dancers, performing dogs and ponies, comedians, Indian violinists, Irish lyric tenors, along with Pathé News, Aesop's Fables, and an Our Gang comedy, plus the main feature: Lon Chaney in "The Trap," for example. One way or another I immersed myself in Washington atmosphere.

Moreover, Government Printing Office employees sponsored Saturday evening parties at which refreshments were served and records played for dancing. These occasions overflowed into individual dates or into Sunday afternoon gatherings at the home of one of the men or women. After the shop gossip, the men talked baseball and the women marriage. I overheard an earnest conversation about the proper kind of diamond for an engagement ring; the women agreed that a one-carat diamond would be an acceptable size, provided that it was a blue-white diamond and not a yellow. As the prices for this size and quality of stone opened at $150, I suddenly realized that marriage was not a gate to be unlocked recklessly. The diamond talk overflowed into fur-coat talk—strange for Washington's torrid summer but understandable considering that August sales were booming. These young government employees decided that a sable-dyed squirrel, a Canadian beaver, or even a Hudson seal, the trade term for dyed muskrat, would go nicely with a one-carat-blue-white diamond. To fulfill this second dream, a young man contemplating marriage would realize that some day he would have to fork over $200 or $300, a month's salary or more. You would have thought that in a city where single females far outnumbered single males, the women would not want to breathe a single word that might frighten a prospect.

From one of these afternoon dream-$e$$ion$ I lured an attractive, slender, brown-eyed Virginia girl into going with me to a movie at the Palace. The show was so entertaining and the long ride afterward on the streetcar so pleasant that when she invited me into her parlor for a sit I happily accepted. We had hardly settled when, to my stark amazement, she began to blubber. Not having the faintest idea of what I had done or had failed to do, I implored her to tell me what the trouble was. Through her sobs and tears she finally managed to say: "I'm afraid . . . I'll never . . . get married." I comforted her as much as I knew how, but as soon as I decently could I fled to the nearby corner to catch the owl car home. On the ride back to the Y I had rich opportunity to reflect on the evening but could not figure out a reason for its strange conclusion. I decided, however, that I did not at that point want to join the diamond-fur-coat set but would remain content with the relaxed environment of the Y.

Sometimes Barker and I took a nighttime saunter up Pennsylvania Avenue past the White House. By then the streets had few strollers. The house itself was dark except for a few rooms; the nation's nerve center was no more active than the home of the average citizen. A few guards were on duty at the door of the presidential mansion and at the gate. They paid little attention to us or to the other groups that paused to see what, if anything, was happening at the White House. Its tempo was like that of the whole country—quiet, placid, uneventful. The great Teapot Dome scandal had vanished into the background. Coolidge, the current occupant of the White House, had probably already gone to bed, his mind free from worry. And he was not one to ferret out worrisome details in advance; in fact he had once declared, "If ten problems are coming down the road, nine of them will run into a ditch before they get to you."

In its way, the Government Printing Office was as quiet and uneventful as the White House. The pace was efficient but leisurely. The shop was well ordered, clean; its ventilation system carried off metal fumes; it provided competent medical service, adequate food in the cafeteria, duck pins for luncheon hours and evenings, and Saturday night dances.

My output was good enough so I could squander occasional minutes wandering about the place, just gawking. I was curious to see how the parts fit together. How could the *Congressional Record*, which might run 12 pages one day and 320 the next, get published on time every morning, along with a torrent of bulletins, patents, bills, and acts? Part of the answer was that foreman Bill Skeen could put a big crew on any one rush job and set aside, for the moment, less urgent items like Army manuals. Copy editing, proofreading,

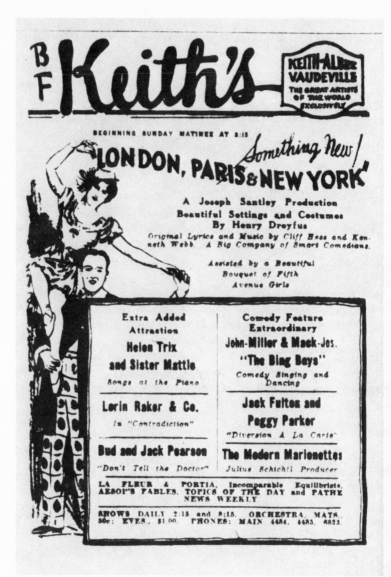

The Keith-Albee vaudeville circuit was one of the best known of the day. For 50 cents afternoon, $1.00 evening, you could see the main feature, six added attractions, Pathé News, and a couple of movie shorts like Aesop's Fables or Topics of the Day. (*Washington Post*, 1 August 1926.)

printing, and binding were equally flexible. Each section had a staff of workers who could be shifted to a rush job when needed. If the proofreaders fell behind, a detail of printers or operators would be assigned to help out. I did several stints as a proofreader. Printers, and the foreman also, got used to seeing 49 bob up at unexpected places, just looking on. One day an apprentice spilled a galley of slugs. Horrified, he went to Skeen and asked him what to do. "Oh," said Skeen, "show it to 49 and then throw it away."

During off-duty hours I sometimes listened to the debates in the House and Senate and then read that day's report in the *Congressional Record*. I saw firsthand what was achieved by the custom that each representative or senator could revise his speech before it appeared in print. In fact, I could see on sheets of copy that whole sentences or paragraphs had been deleted or rewritten after the speech was delivered. Once when I was in the gallery, I heard a congressman criticizing the commissioner of the District of Columbia and in the course of the debate, a second congressman insulted a third; the insultee hurled an ink bottle at the head of the insulter, at which the insulter became indignant and started after the insultee, overturning a table that got in his way, and hurling a glass tumbler to clear his path further. Spectators got excited, a one-legged Civil War veteran entering the fracas with his cane. A reporter had his notes knocked out of his hand. The morning papers had a full account of the incident.

I decided to locate the copy for the *Record* version to see how it had been purified, as obviously these details would not be printed. The best I could do was to locate the galley containing the type. I took it to the proof printer and asked him to pull a proof of it for me as a souvenir; he declined, saying it would cost him his job if he got caught. Once, he informed me, someone had taken an extra proof of one of Harding's speeches a few hours before it was delivered. The proof got to the newspapers, which printed it; the president was embarrassed because this version contained notions that he decided afterwards not to express; and in the investigation that followed some GPO employees lost their jobs.

Though I argued that this galley was merely a debate on an ordinary hearing, he wouldn't be persuaded. So, as lunch hour was approaching, I asked him if he had washed up yet, and he said no; I reminded him that if he waited much longer he might get stuck with a bunch of rush proofs; he said maybe that was right, gave me a big wink, and left. So I took the proof myself. As you can imagine, the *Record* omitted altogether any account of the scuffle.

On another occasion, a senator got into a debate with Missouri's orator, Sen. James A. Reed. The other senator used the "revision of remarks" privilege to delete the part of his argument that Senator Reed had devastated in his scorching manner. The revision made Reed appear as if he had refuted an argument that had never been made. On the Senate floor, Reed protested that kind of wholesale revision. Yet the system went unchanged. So one way or another I learned what nearly everybody knows, that the *Record* prints what congressmen and senators wished they had said, not what they actually said.

An underlying reason for my enjoying Washington was that it was a revisit from the days when I saw it in 1912 at the age of seven. Father was Congressman Joshua W. (Judge) Alexander's personal secretary, and as we lived in an apartment near the Capitol, life was safe and easy. In that era, all congressmen officed in the House Office Building and all senators in the Senate Office Building. Among the great names were Champ Clark, Speaker of the House; William J. Stone and James A. Reed, Missouri's senators; Robert La Follette of Wisconsin; blind Sen. Thomas P. Gore of Oklahoma; and President Taft in the White House. Often I spent a day in the Capitol, wandering from one end of the vast building to the other, cheerily greeting the great and the near-great, and talking with anyone who would stop to chat; and when everything else bored, playing on the giant tiers of steps that led to the main entrance. Father, certain that his seven-year-old towhead knew his way around, felt no cause to worry at my long absences.

I know that in Lincoln's day access to the nation's president was so casual that senators, representatives, cabinet members, and others could drop in almost without appointment, either on urgent business or to share a joke or a letter. That same ease of official living had still existed in 1912 in the House Office Building. The Judge operated with a staff of only three—in the 1980s a congressman had a dozen or more—and took care of his constituents, plus presiding over the important Committee on Merchant Marine and Fisheries. Sometimes I think I have always known that in the governmental structure was an important group with the lilting name, Committee on Merchant Marine and Fisheries. Father was continually transacting business with the Speaker and with a host of congressmen and senators, as the Judge's representative—or if not transacting business, was just visiting or talking politics, invariably finding them readily available for back-home talk, or to argue on one side or another about the upcoming Democratic convention at Baltimore. No one seemed to think it necessary to be protected and fenced in by corps of office functionaries.

That was the spring the colossal *Titanic* sank. This unbelievable tragedy to Britain's proudest liner cost fifteen hundred lives, equal to forty or fifty train wrecks, and rocked the civilized world from one end to the other. Memories still haunt me of Washington newsboys shouting the grim headlines, and of Father and Mother explaining what had happened. I read the news stories, tried to get from the maps and pictures some notion of what a disaster at sea was like—not easy for an inland youngster—and shuddered at the "artist's conceptions" of a doomed ship, with people struggling in the water, clinging to bits of floating wreckage or trying to make it to a lifeboat, gradually being overcome by the icy water.

As chairman of the Committee on Merchant Marine and Fisheries, the Judge was suddenly drawn into the controversy that followed. By the bushel, postcards, letters, and telegrams poured in—some curious, some angry, some indignant—and he, Father, and the other two secretaries were swamped, composing and typing letters. Was it true that the *Titanic* did not have enough lifeboats? And why hadn't there been lifesaving drills? Should the size of ocean liners be limited? Are American ships better run than British ships? Hearings were held, committees of inquiry appointed. After the long days of writing about the *Titanic* to the Judge's constituents, Father probably felt he never wanted to hear the name again.

That summer the Democratic convention met in Baltimore, the chief contenders for the presidential nomination being Woodrow Wilson and Missouri Congressman Champ Clark, who had recently been elected Speaker of the House. When Bryan threw his support to Wilson, Father also supported Wilson, even though the Judge and other members of the Missouri delegation supported Clark. Father was delighted when Wilson got the nomination and later won the election.

Saturdays and Sundays, Father, Mother, Don, and I saw all the sights: those I have already mentioned, plus Washington's home at Mount Vernon, the national cemetery at Arlington, and the home of General Lee. There was the all-day interurban ride and visit to Chevy Chase, the frequent Sunday afternoons strolling along Rock Creek, the tour of the Bureau of Engraving and Printing where they printed dollar bills instead of sale bills. We never patronized the tourist guides who guaranteed to show you Washington in an hour; instead, Father got volumes from the Library of Congress about the city, and I would spread them on the floor, study the maps, and read how a Frenchman, Pierre L'Enfant, designed Washington's gridiron of broad streets, slashed by broad avenues that converged at the Capitol, the Executive Mansion, and elsewhere.

Long after I had left my parental home and was established in my own, I would often find, during a visit, that we had run out of things to say to each other. They would talk about newspapering, and I would talk about professoring, and both of us about friends and kinfolk—then would come a long silence. How sad! If I had them back, I would ask a hundred questions about Washington alone. How well did you know Missouri senators Bill Stone (sometimes called "Gumshoe Bill") and Jim Reed? What kind of people were Bob La Follette, the Wisconsin orator, and Henry Cabot Lodge? He had seen them, heard them, was in and out of their offices.

. . . Now I was back in Washington after a lapse of fourteen years. Although I enjoyed the excitement of new experiences with GPO and YMCA friends, liked to listen to the debates in Congress, and wander around the Capitol and Washington's other majestic buildings, now and then I would have the strong feeling, "I have been here before and it is still much as I remembered it." Life now, as then, marched by at a stately pace and though we were vaguely aware of change, for the most part we felt that tomorrow would be pretty much like today.

33

For a month the Philadelphia Rapid Transit Company had been carrying mail by air between Washington and Philadelphia, spurred by the well-publicized Sesquicentennial World Fair celebrating the 150th anniversary of the signing of the Declaration of Independence.

Using two Ford trimotor all-metal monoplanes and flying two round trips a day, this new airline that gave itself the strange name of a "rapid transit company" now proposed to carry passengers as well as mail.

Bob and I were instantly curious. We went to the company's ticket office in the Hotel Washington to find out more about the enterprise. "How safe are these dad-burned planes?" demanded Bob. The clerk replied: "Well, here's one of the pilots; I'll let him tell you."

"We've eliminated 98 percent of the danger," said the pilot. These two aircraft, the Vare and the Kendrick, are as safe as planes can be made. They are exact duplicates of the aircraft Fokker made for Byrd's trip over the North Pole. They have three Wright whirlwind motors, any one of which can prevent a forced landing. In the whole history of aviation, no airplane has ever had more than two engines fail at any one time."

"What about the other 2 percent?" I countered. "And what about parachutes?"

"Well, the other 2 percent is dead sure against you. In case the wings drop off, the plane will head for the ground in a nose dive, the passengers will pile up among the chairs in the front end, and there won't be a ghost of a chance to use a parachute."

The planes carried eight passengers and two pilots; one was Alton Parker, who had alternated with Byrd and Bennett on the polar flight. The trimotor was currently used in Europe, the only difference being that this model was smaller. It was fully equipped for deluxe passenger service. By that I mean that although there were no hostesses or served meals, in the event of air sickness or other need there was a toilet in the rear. To add class to the enterprise, the planes were given names, like Pullman cars; these craft were named after the mayors of Philadelphia and Washington.

The distance was 150 miles; flight time was an hour and a half. The fare was $15, or $25 for the round trip. Though the flight had been advertised for days, seats were still available for the Saturday we wished. Obviously the public was not thrilled about airplane transportation.

After brief discussion, we bought a round-trip plane ticket and later a round-trip train ticket. Bob would fly to Philadelphia and I would go by the Baltimore & Ohio. We would stay at the Y. Next day I would fly back and he would return by train. Thus we could each have a plane ride, see the fair for two half-days, and not miss any work.

The next Saturday we put this daring plan into execution, each of us going his separate way to Philadelphia. When we met that night at the Philadelphia Y, after each of us had covered twenty or thirty miles of the exposition, even bigger than the Iowa State Fair, Bob exclaimed: "I'm flying back with you. There's nothing like flying."

The bedbugs were fierce that night, but nothing could be done except to lie there and suffer. I told Bob we ought to take the issue to the Bureau of Entomology, but Bob declared it was a case for the Bureau of Animal Husbandry, the critters were so large. None of this talk was really funny, but we were so exhausted we went back to sleep regardless. Still, I hate to record that my last encounter ever with bedbugs was in the City of Brotherly Love.

Despite Bob's enthusiasm for flying, I was privately worried. The papers had carried occasional reports of airplane crashes in various parts of the country, usually with one or more fatalities. And, at the ticket counter, we had to sign forms indicating who was to be notified in case of an accident. I could imagine my family's complete and utter shock to get a telegram: REGRET TO SAY YOUR SON WITH NINE OTHERS INSTANTLY KILLED TWO PM TODAY IN AIRPLANE CRASH STOP ACCIDENT OCCURRED WEST OF NORFOLK DELAWARE STOP PLEASE ADVISE. As they had no idea I had concocted this adventure, every single, startling word would need an explanation.

Bob had no trouble getting one of the eight available seats, even at the last minute, on the return flight, showing further that air travel had not yet caught the public's fancy. Promptly at 1:45 we clambered aboard the Vare, put a wad of cotton in our ears, and in a few minutes after takeoff we were so high that Philadelphia looked no larger than Osceola. We circled the Sesqui grounds; then the captain turned the plane's nose south and away we went. We were soon a mile high, speeding ninety-five to a hundred miles per hour. We wore regular street clothes, as did the other passengers, and felt just a bit cool.

In minutes I had forgotten my worries. Nothing in this world can be like your first airplane flight, especially at the dawn of civil aviation when only the brave, or the foolhardy and reckless, were

"GO by AIR" to PHILADELPHIA
The Sesquicentennial City

THE Philadelphia Rapid Transit Company has inaugurated the first regular passenger air service in America, between Washington and the Sesquicentennial in Philadelphia. Flying time one hour and a half each way. Two round trips are made every day including Sunday. Charge is $15.00 one way and $25.00 for a 15-day round trip ticket. These charges are made so low in order that as many as possible may learn the comfort, safety and speed of this latest method of transportation.

Main 3393
P.R.T. AIR SERVICE

"First regular passenger air service in America" was the proud claim of the Philadelphia Rapid Transit Company. The low fares were designed to show the public the safety and speed of this latest method of transportation.

Prospective passengers were assured that only ordinary street clothing was required. And it was comforting to read that even though air travel was the fastest known method of transportation, the average speed being ninety miles an hour, "yet to the passenger there is no sensation whatever of rapid flight." (*Washington Post,* 10 August 1926.)

feeling their way into the air. You look down and see whole slabs o
brushland, and your reason tells you it is timber; you see square:
and rectangles the size of handkerchiefs carved out of the forest
some yellowish, which are plowed fields, and some green, which are
meadow or corn. You see winding strings running along the field
for yards and yards—they are roads; and the little insect thing
buzzing along them are automobiles. Sometimes these insects find
amusement in passing one another. You see parallel threads, which
are railroads, though they may be interurban lines; only wide read
ing and long experience enables one to tell the distinction from up
in the air, though there is said to be one. You fly over a body o
water and your map tells you it is the Chesapeake, though it look:
no larger than the Osceola city reservoir; and its surface is like
pebble-grain leather, which means white caps. And you see the
Susquehanna, with boats plying up and down like water beetles; you
look down on towns and cities and wonder where the people are.

Mostly I realized that the eastern seaboard was not originally
prairie, on which people built cities and planted trees, but heavy
forest, out of which cities were carved and fields cleared. As soon as
a city's outreach ended, the forest staunchly claimed its own.

Everywhere you see motion. Cars on the highway were going at
35, a sort of unwritten maximum on eastern roads; the trains tore
along about 50 and 60, as fast as the mainline Burlington and considerably faster than the branch line. Our own speedometer on the
pilot's dashboard hovered between 90 and 100, an astonishing
speed, and sometimes went as high as 120. We could see the
speedometer because we were all in the same cabin, pilots in their
two seats, and passengers each in a wicker chair.

To us, however, there was no sensation of motion. The big wing
hung in the air; the propellors whirled so fast that they long since
had become invisible; we could count every spoke in the landing
wheel hanging down from our corner of the plane. Each of us will
carry a picture of that quiet landing wheel as long as we live; it
seemed unreal. Our plane simply hung motionless in space. When
the copilot came down the aisle toward us, much as a conductor
walks through a train, I shouted at him, above the roar of the mighty
whirlwind engines, "Will we ever get to Washington?" "Yes, of
course," he shouted back, "the reason we seem to move so slowly is
because we are so high." Now the question seems stupid, but he

1ad heard it before and knew it deserved an answer. "Look at the
ground; you can see the plane's shadow scooting along." And sure
enough, it was. I was convinced.

Twice we tore into clouds, which seemed to run away from us,
but it wasn't long before the pilot called out, "We are now just
eleven minutes from Washington." In the distance we could see
patches of red-roofed houses, the blazing golden dome of the Library of Congress, the Capitol, the gray-white shaft of the
Washington Monument, and even the Government Printing Office.
Our North Pole pilot made a perfect spiral landing; we had no
sensation of falling; and our flight was over.

Paul Oehser, our friend at the Y, who later went with the Smithsonian, met us at the field and took our pictures. And well he might.
A few days after our flight a government report proudly said that
America's airlines had flown 200,000 passengers. So Bob and I were
among the first quarter-million to fly by commercial air. I was at last
a full-fledged member of the air age. To put this fact in relation to
other famous events that summer, I need only mention Tunney
defeating Dempsey for the heavyweight championship, Bobby
Jones winning the U.S. Open again, Helen Wills winning one tennis
tournament after another, and Gertrude Ederle swimming the English Channel (the accompanying tugboat cheered her along by playing "Yes, We Have No Bananas" and "Sweet Rosie O'Grady").

Aviation continued to develop rapidly. A year later, Lindbergh
flew the Atlantic. The Ford all-metal trimotor was still in service half
a century later in northern Canada, supplying the distant fringes of
civilization. So it endured longer than the O.K. railroad that
nourished Gilman City. And if you visit the National Air and Space
Museum you can see an all-metal trimotor like mine, and also two
other famous craft: Lindbergh's single-engined *Spirit of St. Louis*
and a space module that carried Americans to the moon.

My summer was coming to an end. I had saved enough to finance
my last year at Grinnell. More than ever I wanted to see Gus. Over
the months our correspondence had accelerated.

At the GPO I told Skeen I was resigning and going back to school.
"I figured you would," he grunted, fished around his desk, and
came up with a resignation form. I quit three days earlier than I
actually had to leave, in order to catch up on my sightseeing. I
wanted to see the Bureau of Engraving and Printing, and to steam

Robert Barker (with hat) and Loren Reid, at journey's end. "Air transport is here to stay," they declared, to anybody who would listen.

up the Potomac in the good ship *Charles Macalester* to visit Washington's tomb, just as we had done years before. I took advantage of the summer sales to buy two new $40 Kuppenheimer suits at half-price, each with two pairs of pants; one suit had a double-breasted vest.

The last afternoon I packed and settled down for a final visit with Barker. We discussed his plan to form a partnership and buy land in Florida to raise cucumbers. At the moment he was struggling with Milton, frequently interrupting our conversation to read a few lines, now and then with a mild oath, which, I thought, added to the sense without especially disturbing the rhythm. It was a varied conversation, what with the cucumber talk, the stately lines from Milton, the advice to watch out for bedbugs, the casual promises to keep in touch. The beds were still unmade, and if I had bothered to lift Bob's pillow I would have found the .38 under it. The room still had a faint odor of creosote. So my final memory is that of seeing him in a chair, studying. I waved, closed the door behind me, and removed my name card, just under the notorious "606." I recalled the grins of various people to whom, for one reason or another, I had given my address. As I went down the hall, I heard the muted rumble of lines from *Paradise Lost*.

I regret that I never saw him again, and after a round of letters our correspondence withered away. A price of American mobility is that we form cherished friendships, rich in experiences, then we move. Memories are buried under new activities, and our enthusiastic resolutions to write are forgotten. Europeans and others who spend lifetimes in the same communities find it difficult to understand why Americans shift from one set of friends to another.

Late that evening the Baltimore & Ohio pulled out of Union Station for Chicago, with me aboard, not on a coach seat this time, but in my first Pullman. I wore my new pearl-gray suit, the one with a double-breasted vest; its big-city high style would be a knockout on campus. I could have had a choice of twenty fast trains to Chicago, but I knew the B. & O.'s tracks lay through the rugged mountain scenery that I was eager to see. I weaved my way to the rear platform of the lounge car and stood there to enjoy the view. The track wound in and around the forests and streams of the Shenandoah range and the Alleghenies. Occasionally the train disappeared into a tunnel, smoke from the locomotive getting so dense and so acrid that I had to retreat inside the lounge car. I did not return to my Pullman seat, however, until long after dark. Only then did I notice that my new light suit was covered with ash and grainy clinker dust. A trifle.

Riding in the Pullman was sheer magnificence, with its fresh, clean seats, upholstered in green plush, arranged in pairs European style with the upper-berth occupant riding backwards, facing the occupant of the lower berth. After dinner the porter let down the shelf that became the floor of my upper berth and hung the curtains that guaranteed privacy. He offered to bring a ladder so I could climb to my upstairs bed, but I waved it off and half-bounded, half-crawled into it. The light in the far corner revealed a hammock, obviously for valuables and small articles, and also hangers for coats and trousers. The porter took my shoes to shine, explaining that he would return them in the morning. I was hesitant to yield my only pair but his manner inspired confidence. I undressed, slipped under the covers, and read the evening paper. Though I could not sleep soundly, what with the train's frequent stopping and starting, it was considerably better than spending the night curled up on a coach seat with a two-bit rented pillow.

At Chicago I changed to the Burlington, arriving in Osceola late in the afternoon. Father, Mother, and Don met me at the station in a new Oakland landau sedan. Nobody had written me about this splendid acquisition. Don surrendered the keys so I could drive home in this superb, wheeled palace.

The Oakland symbolized the vast changes in automobile manufacture since Old Betsy first ventured over Missouri dirt roads in 1914. Our new car sprouted all sorts of innovations: four-wheel brakes, balloon tires, oil filter, air cleaner, starter, lights, even bumpers. Moreover, it possessed features that reduced vibration, the tireless enemy of older models: balanced wheels, rubber engine mounts, counterpoised crankshaft, torsion balancer. The gradual elimination of vibration impressed me as much as any other single feature of automotive engineering. The Oakland was a popular make, a couple of hundred dollars more expensive than the newly introduced Pontiac, a couple of hundred dollars less than a Buick; I was saddened when General Motors shortly abandoned it.

The Oakland was also a symbol of Father's and Mother's growing success in the Battle of the Boolge. The year 1925 had been a slow

Father and Mother and their newest acquisition, a 1926 Oakland landau sedan, with bumpers, running board, one-piece shaded windshield, electric lights, wooden-spoke wheels. The spare tire could be mounted on the rear, since the trunk was not generally available as a built-in feature.

one, scarred by a disastrous fire at the *Tribune* that caused extensive water damage to wooden typecases, paper stocks, and even printing machinery. But after the bust had come the boom, to last three more years. Father could not drive a car, and Mother was long out of practice, but they took immense pride in the Oakland. Father believed that once a man got a good car he should house it, feed it, and care for it as he would a good horse. In another two years they were able to pay off the last $500 note on the mortgage and buy one of the best homes in town.

At home Mother prepared a supper equal to anything at 20th and P. In the average lifetime a young man is not often made to feel like a returning hero, but this was one of those rare occasions. Next morning they showed me the *Tribune*'s recent acquisitions—bought since the fire—new type and cases, a new caster that would handle advertising mats.

Busy as I was, I found myself thinking of the girl on the station platform, chatting with her friends; at the bridge table, happily adjusting rules to fit necessities; writing a letter to the little Bluebird who lay in a cast. At most I would have only a few days at Osceola. Don and I would then return to Grinnell, he to begin his sophomore year and I, with nine hours of credit from George Washington University, to be a senior.

IV. The Best Part Up to Now

34

When I returned to campus, I no longer felt overwhelmed and frustrated but was in high spirits. I was now a person of substance; I could walk into the treasurer's office and devour his huge bill in one gulp. Never before, in grade school or college, had I had the chance to be a full-time student. I could spend evenings with books and people instead of with a machine.

Paul Spencer Wood, still head of the English department, asked me in a conference whether I had considered being a teacher. I told him no; I planned to follow the family publishing tradition. He disclosed that if I included only three required courses I could qualify for a teaching certificate. He argued that since I could so easily annex a second career, to fall back on if I liked, I should seize the opportunity.

My already complex schedule would be further complicated if I added courses for the certificate. Yet he patiently explored every alternative, telephoning for special permissions, carefully checking what I had already done against what I needed to do. At one stage I suggested he abandon the idea, as I was so positive I would not teach, but he persisted.

On my tentative list I had included no English courses, since I had already taken so many, and wanted to explore new fields, for instance, astronomy. "Oh," he scoffed, "you'll find a pretty girl who'll teach you all you need to know about the stars." So the astronomy disappeared, and seminars in English were inserted. He was pleased with his labors and told me that I could now receive not only a bachelor's degree but also a first-class teaching certificate. I could visualize this neatly framed document hanging in the office of a future newspaper publisher, alongside membership cards in the International Typographical Union and the Iowa Press Association.

Although I was glad to be back on campus, I found I missed Washington. Grinnell was not entirely a substitute. For the Capitol it offered Chicago Hall, the administration building, a red-brick structure that dated back to the great cyclone of 1882. For the Lincoln Memorial it offered Blair Hall, a gray-stone building of ancient origin, with wood floors and creaking stairways. For the White House it offered the campus home of President Main, a relatively unimpressive brick residence. But actually we care little about buildings unless our own lives touch them in a special way. We design our own structures, carve our own sculptures, blueprint our own visions.

I had always known that classes started at 8:00; for the first time I realized that social life began minutes later. Early in the day the announcement was made that the women's halls were holding open house. During previous autumns I had ignored such trifles. Now I sought further information.

What I learned was that on the chosen evening, the men migrated en masse to the Quadrangle. The women, dressed up, assembled in their club rooms, and the men, groomed to the teeth, prowled from cottage to cottage, introducing themselves to new freshmen and transfers and greeting friends from last season. We were told that after the open-house ceremonial, any man could consider that he had been formally presented to any woman. The ball was in his court. This procedure was a radical departure from the times when no lady would accept an invitation from any gentleman unless he had been formally presented. After open house, a Grinnell gentleman could escort a Grinnell lady anywhere, without a chaperone.

These were days when many of the old rules fell crashing to the ground. Girls bobbed their hair. Skirts climbed higher and higher and now were at the knee. One could speak of a girl's legs, not her limbs. At dances, couples held each other close, cheek to cheek. Older folks viewed these goings-on first with alarm but eventually with amused tolerance.

Most males buzzed a beeline to the freshman cottages, to preview the new crop of females. Others went directly to a specific cottage to locate a specific girl. As scores of rumors were floating around about once-devoted couples who had drifted apart during the summer, scores of possibilities existed for new alignments. One might date a girl for the balance of the evening; arrange to meet her during the chapel period the next morning; or negotiate a date for the upcoming Saturday dance.

My private beeline led to Cottage V (later named Loose Hall) to see Gus. I found her talking to other friends. Sorry, I learned when I finally reached the head of the line, she had a date for the evening. Sorry, she also had a date for Saturday. Still, we talked as much as we could before her companion for the evening came to claim her. As he must be given a name, I will call him Walter. I did, before leaving, manage to salvage a date for the second Saturday dance and then headed for the other cottages to see what they were offering in the way of girls that season. The lounges were filled with boys who had had the same idea earlier. In general, as I measured the distance to Saturday-after-next, things were not working out as I had dreamed them.

I became more aware of other kinds of student happenings than before. For example, at times we carried on an ink-bottle fight with the occupants of neighboring Langan Hall. Normally the two buildings were at peace; then a fractious group in one hall bounced a few bottles off the near wall of the other; these indignities were returned, with interest; the house chairmen met and arranged a cease-fire. (Sixty years later men and women could get a college education without even owning an ink bottle.)

Short-sheeting a bed was commonplace. Many things can happen to beds; once an epidemic of trickery strikes a building, a wise student systematically pulls back the covers before inserting his or her tender body between the sheets. One hall had a notoriously sound sleeper; on a balmy night his fellows carried him, bed and all, to the yard in front of the women's cottages. Next they returned for his study table, lamp, dresser, and rug. Anyone coming home from a late date saw a student at his slumbers, dresser and study table nearby, a rug on the grass. On the table a study lamp cast its shaded glow over texts and notebooks. Groups up and down the line of men's halls were quietly told of the escapade; they had to see for themselves. So did the early risers next morning among the women.

One blizzardy Sunday we congregated in our lounge. Somebody thought it would be a prime idea to strip and roll outdoors in the snow; instantly we started shedding our clothes. The hardy ones rushed immediately into the storm, scrubbed themselves with snow, and wrestled one another in the drifts; others either had to follow or renounce forever their claims to being men. Soon all of us were outside. Then came an agonized voice: "My God! We forgot about Miss Barnett!" The house mother would skin us alive if she discovered us. Immediately all of us "men" dashed to our rooms, snatching our clothes on the way. If she had indeed seen us, she had been too overcome to interfere. This may or may not be the spot to say that we were considered the scholarly group of the campus.

What we should have done was to send the incident out over AP wires: "Twenty Grinnell Students Face 30° Weather to Roll in Snow." For then, immediately around the nation, inmates of dormitories and fraternities would have set out to beat our record: "Twenty-Five Naked Carleton Students Brave 20° Storm to Burrow in Drifts." And: "Thirty-Eight Dartmouth Students Strip to Hold Mass Wrestling Contest in 18° Blizzard." By comparison, the later waves of goldfish swallowing, marathon dancing, and telephone-booth stuffing would have seemed trifling. And when streakers made news in the seventies, readers would have yawned and reflected: "Shucks, Smith Hall men *invented* streaking half a century ago."

On each floor was a telephone in the hallway; most buildings also had a phone in a private booth for sensitive calls. The popular number, the one no one had to look up, was 156, which connected with the Quadrangle operator, who then rang the girl desired. On days preceding a rec hour, phones were in continual use. Girls liked to be asked well in advance; a girl interpreted a last-minute call as meaning she was second or third choice. Arriving at the Quadrangle at the agreed hour one would collect her at the Central lounge ("Miss Hanky?" purred the operator, "you have a caller in Central") or, in the instance of upperclass girls, one could go directly to their cottage and yell up the stairway. You could hear your call being relayed (Brown!... Brown!... Your date's here...).

At the opening dance, which I viewed from the balcony, I could easily see that Gus was having a great time with Walter. Too great a time, I thought. He was a graceful dancer; he had traded dances with other wholly desirable partners. And on the campus during the days that followed I could see she was well acquainted. She had had two full years to cement her own circle of friends—in addition to the Des Moines high-school group she already knew. Still, as the second week of school got under way, my thoughts turned to my own upcoming Saturday date with her. The custom of The Syndicate to trade dances with each other took care of part of the program, and I scouted around to make desirable trades for other numbers.

That eventful evening, after I had scrubbed and scoured, thinking of my good fortune in being able to go to a dance instead of dining on roast beef at the Poweshiek and then running a typesetting machine, I started to the Quadrangle, feeling the whole campus was watching. I called up the stairway of Cottage V and heard my message relayed to a voice that replied from down the hall. Three or four other scrubbed and scoured young men were also standing by. Whenever we heard a step on the stone treads we each turned and looked. A lovely young lady appeared, was claimed by her escort; the rest of us waited expectantly. Before long, I was standing there by myself. In a way this was an advantage. Then I heard steps—quick, light, sure. I looked up and saw a bright smile. "Hello," it said. "Hello," I answered.

We started talking at once as we walked to the gym. I remember no empty spaces. Silences are awkward on a first date. We started with the Bluebird letters, her summer in Des Moines, my summer in Washington, our mutual friends, our common major in English.

We arrived as the music was beginning. At first my tactic was to continue the conversation while we were dancing, partly to keep her diverted in case I made an awkward step. But the music of the Mississippi Six caught up both of us, and the successive dances with each other and with other partners made the evening fly.

She reminded me that we should speak to the chaperones, a formidable array of faculty seated on the handball court at the side of the gym floor. Here were Mr. and Mrs. Intellectual History, Mr. and Mrs. Organic Chemistry, Mr. and Mrs. Teachings of Jesus, Mr. and Mrs. Dean of the Faculty. We started a conversation with each. Some we managed gracefully; others bumbled along and hung in midair. She found something to say to everybody, and especially to teachers with whom she had studied. Most couples were relieved when the chaperone obligation was fulfilled; a few avoided it altogether.

I could see small connection between what I had been taught in that Chicago dance studio and what we were doing, but in a dim way I was beginning to collect dividends on that investment. The music finally stopped, the couples began to leave, the boys of the Mississippi Six gathered their instruments, and we joined the parade of couples strolling to Candyland. Here I would cheerfully have bought her the thirty-five-cent Parthenon Jumbo, but she selected the most inexpensive sundae on the menu—the popular fifteen-cent Candyland Special—chocolate and vanilla ice cream, topped with chocolate-marshmallow sauce, sprinkled with peanuts. Any Grinnellian from the Roaring Twenties remembers it and the Greek owners of Candyland who originated it. In these days a superb creation like the Candyland would be franchised and merchandised from coast to coast under giant arches: "90 Billion Sold."

Well, I thought to myself, aiming to get her to Cottage V by 11:00 so she and her sisters could be properly bolted in for the night, this evening has worked out so well I will ask her for the next Saturday rec hour. "I'm sorry, I already have a date," she said. I did not need to ask—I knew it was with Walter. But she smiled as she said good-bye and thanked me for the evening. The language provides so few good ways to say no; we do what we can with words and hope that tones, glances, and gestures will carry the main burden. So I was not wholly discouraged. Walter got the third Saturday, but I got the fourth; he beat me to the fifth, but I annexed the sixth; and at that point he gave up.

Of course there were other activities. Occasionally the football games played away from home were displayed in the Alumni Recitation Hall auditorium on the Grid-Graph, a large board ten feet long and six feet wide, with a glass center displaying the vertical lines that represented a football field. Behind it, an electric light moved back and forth to represent the position of the ball. At the side was a list of situations, with lights to flash to show whether run, pass, punt, or penalty was involved. Other lights could be flashed to indicate names of players. The Grid-Graph was operated by an unseen hand at a control board, relaying information that came by telegraph from the playing field.

Suppose Grinnell, with the ball on her forty-yard line, makes a forward pass, Wing to Sweet, who runs for a touchdown. You see the light move across the glass; you see another light opposite "Pass"; other lights indicate the names of passer and receiver. As every imaginable situation could be spelled out with lights, the Grid-Graph was unbelievably exciting. What difference does it make whether you hear a voice over a radio or see a light on a glass screen, if your team executes a forward pass for a touchdown? I recall the game with giant Minnesota, there, with an immense crowd watching the screen in Grinnell as if everything near and dear depended upon the result. The light was positioned for the kickoff; another light indicated the Minnesota kicker, Cooper; the ball traveled to our twenty-yard line; our flashy halfback, "Hap" Moran, caught it; then, fantastically, unbelievably, the light wiggled to our thirty, then on to their thirty, and still on, across the goal; another light flashed "Touchdown!" and still another opposite the figure "6." Minnesota overwhelmed us, 34 to 6, I have to add, but only because, we told ourselves, they had too many reserves and we had too many injuries. Who needed color TV and the instant replay? Who needed computer games? We had the Grid-Graph.

If I write little about sports, it is because the main facts are recorded in college annuals, and because after many decades one event fades into another.

But not all has faded, even in the mind of this bystander. No one can forget Morgan Taylor, champion Olympic 400-meter hurdler, or Harris Coggeshall, nationally ranked tennis star, or colorful football coach Mike Hyland. Our class was almost the last to play for Grinnell in the Missouri Valley Conference, which was broken up when schools like Missouri, Kansas, Oklahoma, and Iowa State entered the new Big Six, predecessor of the fierce Big Eight.

Years later Ossie Solem and Bill Bolter, who had given us fits when Solem coached at Drake and Bolter was a star halfback, dined in our home. Solem remembered everything; he reviewed games and plays long forgotten and barely remembered. He retold Drake 7, Grinnell 6, when, in the closing moments, Drake, ahead, yielded three safeties, under the rules then prevailing, netting us 6 points, as a way of protecting the lead.

We did only fairly well in basketball, but we jammed our small gymnasium to capacity and yelled our heads off. The bleachers were so close to the court that front-row occupants had to keep their feet tucked under. At the end bleachers upperclass girls took over, despite the fact that a wild throw would send a basketball into their midst; or a player, unable to stop, would find himself on the laps of one or more girls. They quickly evolved a method of scoring: a girl who caught a basketball chalked up a point; if a player landed in her lap, five points; if handsome captain Sonny Davis came her way, ten points. No spectator sports for them.

Occasionally we saw Ernest C. Quigley referee. Quigley, the greatest official that ever lived, and the most dynamic, will ever be remembered for his indignant roar, "You can't *do* that," whenever a player committed a foul. First we'd notice the momentary pileup of players; then the accusing finger pointing to the offender; then the

"You can't do-o-o that" in thunderous tones that not only filled but overwhelmed the gym; and, simultaneously, the slap on the back, so scorekeeper and spectators would know the offender.

Once a visiting player, hearing the whistle and seeing the finger pointed right at him, started to run off the floor; Quigley overtook him, whacked him across the backside, and thus properly called the foul. We were ecstatic. We stood, gave both a standing ovation, and yelled delightedly: "You can't do-o-o-o that!" Quigley took our cheer as a matter of course, and the player grinned as happily as if he'd scored the winning basket.

Quigley treated home team and visitors with equal firmness. Local fans quickly learned to respect his decisions. If the crowd became unruly, he called a technical on it, giving the ball to a visiting player and bellowing, "Shoot one!" And if necessary, "Shoot two!" And even, "Shoot three!" The crowd would get the message.

For half a century Quigley was a year-round official. For twenty-five years he was a National League umpire, and after that, supervisor of its umpires. At Grinnell one night, at halftime, he demonstrated how he opened a game: "Battery: For New York, Mathewson and Meyers; for Pittsburgh, Adams and Gibson. P-l-a-y b-a-l-l!!" His thunderous voice could have been heard as far as Candyland, which is to say, all over the Polo Grounds.

Sportswriter Grantland Rice called him one of the best of the major-league umpires. Quigley told Rice that baseball called for split-second, split-inch decisions, but that basketball was the fastest game to handle because the action is almost continuous. He knew both games well; the statisticians recorded that he had officiated at 5,400 major-league games, including world-series contests, and 1,500 basketball games, including one Olympic final. The short interval between the end of baseball and the beginning of basketball found him refereeing football.

Quigley was a featured speaker on the spring chicken-croquette awards circuit, reassuring thousands of high-school stars and their friends that sportsmanship was a virtue to be prized a lifetime. His standards for officiating, he liked to say, were lofty: complete familiarity with the rules, mental alertness, physical fitness, knowledge of handling men and boys, and well-shined black shoes.

Our old gym has been torn down many years, but we can still visualize it: worn maple floors, temporary bleachers strung around the sides, a tiny three-wall handball court on one side, wrestling mats hung from the walls, parallel bars and an old leather vaulting horse stashed in the corner, oval, padded, mezzanine running track overhead, air made steamy by basement shower stalls, persistent odor of sweat shirts and sneakers. We have our individual memories of pickup, intramural, and varsity games, but also of the muscular, stern-faced man, then in his late forties, and his imperial roar: "You can't do-o-o that!"

35

Don, now a sophomore, set type and ran presses at the *Herald*, but still found time to try out for the Pioneers, and, as he survived the squad cut, became a regular in the backfield. The coach was experimenting with silk pants for his running backs, the thought being that runners clad in slippery silk would be hard to bring down. As the college could not afford these, the players were urged to furnish their own. Don did not want to waste his hard-earned funds on a luxury item like silk backfield pants, so he fired off a letter to Father for the necessary $35.

At the same time, surveying my social future, I concluded that it would be fitting to own my own tuxedo, boiled shirt, stiff collar, black tie, studs, and links, instead of having to borrow an outfit for every formal dance and major debate. I could have financed these, but instead wrote Father and pointed out that since he would want to buy me a Christmas present, a tuxedo would be welcome, and that if it were all the same to him, I could use it now. I figured that $50 would be about right.

Father received these letters in the same mail. If you had asked every business and professional man in Osceola to make a list of twenty items that a young college man needed, no list would contain a tuxedo, and certainly not silk backfield pants. Father could not possibly have underwritten such expenditures in his Missouri days, nor even in his early Iowa years, but business at the *Tribune* had so improved that his income was better, despite the loss of his good, cheap help. He mailed the checks promptly. He even wrote an article for the *Tribune* so that its twenty-five hundred loyal readers would know that the town's representatives at Grinnell had every-thing they needed, down to tuxedos and silk backfield pants.

Those days Father and Mother were working harder than at any other time in their lives, if such a thing were measureable. Mother was setting type for an 8-column paper that now often went to ten or more pages. Because she especially wanted to get rid of the long night sessions on press day, she launched a one-woman campaign to get news and ad copy in earlier. She started with the preachers, declaring that if they didn't get their church schedules in on Monday morning, she wouldn't print them. To a man they began to show up promptly with copy in hand, which meant they had to pick their sermon topics earlier, in itself a prime idea. She next moved in on the county correspondents, offering them the same deadline. Finally she tackled the advertisers, offering them Tuesday noon. On her part she stayed at the machine as long as necessary on Tuesday to put everything in type, occasionally working all night to keep her own deadline. Before long, the labors of press day were regularly completed well before six o'clock.

Father had hired a man to help with ads and news, but still did much of the reporting and ad selling. And he had other projects. In a previous election year he had had a high-level strategy meeting with the chairman of the county Democratic committee. For generations nearly every county officeholder in Iowa had been a Republican; often the Democrats did not even put a full ticket in the field. For the upcoming election, they decided, they would get out not only a full ticket, but one of high caliber. The *Tribune* put its complete resources behind the ticket; a Democrat agreeing to run would know in advance that he could count on ample publicity. Father and the chairman also convinced their candidates to get out and meet the voters personally.

That summer, Don and I had printed thousands of candidates' cards and posters. Father wrote, and Mother set, scores of columns about the qualifications of the candidates. When the votes were counted that November, the year of the Coolidge landslide, four Democrats made it to the courthouse, including the sheriff (sheriff's sales), auditor (board proceedings), clerk (court docket and ballots), and attorney (legal notices). Thus much legal printing and advertising, placed by these officials, deserted the *Sentinel* and came to the *Tribune*. The *Tribune*'s image began to perk up over the county. At the next election these Democrats were reelected. Though Don and I were financing by far the greater part of our education, the change in the political scene indirectly had contributed to our being able to stay in school.

36

After the spring holiday, Sunday dates and student cars suddenly became legal, so Don and I drove the Oakland back to Grinnell. In two months he would finish his second year and I would be graduated. I was, in fact, president of the Class of '27 for the second semester. At a sparsely attended meeting, my Syndicate roommate, Wendell Metcalf, had nominated me; another roommate, Alden Greene, had moved to close the nominations. The vote was taken and I was handed the gavel. It was a gratifying show of power politics.

Gus and I were now spending more time together. There had been a time, weeks back, when she felt we should take a vacation from each other. As I had found this verdict difficult to understand, I took it to The Syndicate. They agreed there was no appeal from it and prevailed upon me not only not to contest it, but to live with it. Wendell, who had a sister, reassured me that girls were impossible to live with. Alden heartily agreed and argued that I should date other girls. "You know she'll date around," he insisted. Between them they convinced me the future was not so bleak as I feared.

Unattached girls are difficult to find in midyear, since most are already paired off, and the unwritten code ordinarily keeps a man from breaking in on the promising romance of a fellow. In the next few weeks I went out with three girls but my heart was not in it. Then came an evening when Gus and I met casually, incidentally, at the library. I sat beside her and we had small, whispered conversations as we each studied our own assignments. I asked her if I could walk home with her and she smiled and said yes. We seemed to pick up where we had left off. When I got back to the study room the other members of The Syndicate were bent over their books. They looked up, grinning, and broke the iron-clad rule of silence. "Tell us about it," they said. On a small campus, news travels fast.

Iowa in springtime is delightful; days are warm and nights are cool. There was that evening when we were walking on the golf course, a favorite retreat of Grinnell couples. In those nonpolluted days the sky was closer and the stars loomed larger.

We walked in silence, no longer feeling the need for steady talk. I looked up at the sky. "The moon is lovely," I said.
"Yes, it is lovely."
More strolling. "And there is the Big Dipper."
"Yes."
"And there's the North Star."
"Uh-huh."
Long pause. I had told all I knew.
She picked up the thread, such as it was, of the conversation. "Over there is Orion." I looked in wonder, as she pointed out his belt. "There is Cassiopeia's chair. And the square of Andromeda." And so on.
What was it my English professor had said? "You'll meet a girl who will teach you all about the stars that you'll ever need to know."
Our romance also touched geography; we covered most of Grinnell's. We hiked up the M. & St. L. tracks; we strolled to Arbor Lake; we parked on lonely country roads—decades later a dangerous and foolhardy act. Occasionally we went to movies at the Strand or Colonial: the big names were Clara Bow, Gloria Swanson, Thomas Meighan, Charles Ray, Mae Murray, Norma Talmadge, Buster Keaton, Richard Barthelmas, Mary Pickford, Charles Chaplin, Douglas Fairbanks. We played tennis and were fairly evenly matched. As she was a varsity swimmer, I faithfully attended the meets in the new swimming pool. We heard the visiting lecturers.
We attended concerts: the famed Minneapolis Symphony, with Henri Verbruggen, was an annual visitor. She had studied piano, had a lifelong interest in music, and this year was librarian for the music department. My background, though lacking in depth, was powerful on variety. I grew up with a Victor phonograph on which was mounted a large, red horn, with scalloped edges like a morning glory blossom. The Victor played cylindrical records, the titles being announced in a baritone voice at the start of each selection. For sentimental occasions we chose "Hello Central, Give Me Heaven, For My Mother's There." For lighter moments we chose between "The Preacher and the Bear" and "Girl Wanted." The first narrated the scrape a preacher got into when he went hunting on Sunday instead of going to church. The latter described a family that had troubles with domestic help: "The next girl was a country lass /

Her face would give you fright / She almost lost her breath / Blowing out the electric light / One day she tried to make a fire / The wood was very green / To make the flame burn higher / She poured on kerosene!" The big red horn then emitted an explosion that made its diaphragm rattle, followed by: "Girl wanted! / Girl wanted! / Next day the sign appeared upon the door / Girl wanted! Girl wanted! / That country girl's not working any more / For now she's living up a little higher / No more she'll ever monkey with the fire / And so at break of day / Those who chanced to pass that way / Saw the sign, Girl Wanted."

Later the family graduated to a console Edison, the horn of which doubled around under the turntable and was concealed in the cabinet. Volume was regulated, not electronically, but by moving a lever that moved a large felt ball in and out of the throat of the horn. This equipment was positively deluxe. To go with it, we had "Overture to Tannhäuser," "Stars and Stripes Forever," and a selection of Sir Harry Lauder's Scottish ballads. I also had had a year's spasmodic violin lessons.

So my preparation for the Minneapolis Symphony was not exhaustive, but it had to serve. To be with Gus I would have gone to a string quartet. I did not fully realize that I was adding whole new fields of interest to those I already had, and, moreover, to those I was acquiring in the classroom. In short, the college environment—the jargon term is "the resident-campus experience"—was working its spell in more ways than one.

37

I received a phone call from Daniel B. Heller, my Osceola superintendent, now at Vermillion, South Dakota.

"I'm selecting my faculty for next year," he said. "I need someone to sponsor the school paper, *The Vermillionaire*. I remembered you and wondered if you would be available. Could you join our staff next year and direct the school paper?"

"I might be interested. Actually, that would be right down my line." And actually, I had given thought to being a teacher, at least to the extent of filing papers in the college placement office and of applying for a $1,400 instructorship in a Texas college, though as yet I had heard nothing from my application.

"For a few years we won first for being the best high-school paper in the state," he continued. "Recently we haven't even placed. We'd like to get on top again." The world loves a winner.

I hardly knew what to say. Despite my flash of interest in the Texas college, I had always planned to return to Osceola and enter newspaper publishing. More than once Father had declared that when his sons got out of school he would buy a daily.

"We could start you at $1,550," Heller added. A linotype operator could earn more.

Suddenly I had the fleeting thought that I would give teaching a whirl for one, single year. I made the decision instantly, over the phone, in the hall of the men's dorm. The newspaper could wait. "I'll do it," I said.

"We'll consider it settled." A pause. "By the way, can you teach English?"

"Yes. That happens to be my major."

I hung up the phone, excited, thrilled, awed, 90 percent of me confident I had made a good decision, 10 percent of me dazed and doubtful. Immediately I sought out Gus.

We were sitting under a maple on the south campus. Behind us were Goodnow Hall (mathematics), Blair Hall (zoology). Farther back were the Y building (bridge party), the gymnasium (rec hours), the Alumni Recitation Hall (Lavell, Wood, Ryan, debating, Grid-Graph), Herrick Chapel (lectures, concerts, chapel, vespers). To the left were the M. & St. L. tracks and beyond them the long spread of Quadrangle cottages. In front, blocks away were the Hotel Monroe (first night in Grinnell), Candyland (refreshments), the *Herald* (don't forget your pay). In a week I would be a college graduate.

"I'm going to be a teacher," I announced, and told her what had happened.

She smiled her incandescent smile and her eyes danced. "That will be nice." Four simple words, but they reassured me mightily. She put her hand on mine. Something told me that if it had been dark she would have given me a big hug and kiss, but in the olden times couples did not display affection in public. Oh well, in war-time maybe, on station platforms, when you were seeing your sweetheart off to battle. Some couples, it was alleged, visited station platforms at train time for a bit of hugging and kissing even though neither one was going to war.

Graduation activities were hectic, especially for a class officer. I needed to conduct the poll to determine the six honored, senior chapel speakers. On those last six Fridays, the seniors, led by class president and vice-president, marched to chapel in a body, wearing caps and gowns; we took our graduation events seriously. I delivered the class oration, presenting a mantle to the juniors along with exhortations to carry on our good work.

Then, too, our class needed to rehearse the commencement ceremony. We had to be shown how to line up, where to sit, when to walk up for our diplomas. One slip and a dozen people would get the wrong sheepskins. As an innovation, I scheduled a final, midnight, senior chapel. Our class had a gifted organist, Loren Adair, and talented singers from our award-winning glee club; around them I wrote a simple ceremony. I gave a brief talk, ending with the benediction that President Main used at vespers: "The Lord bless you and keep you. The Lord make his face to shine upon you and be gracious unto you. The Lord lift up his countenance upon you, and give you peace . . . this night and evermore." The building was fuller than usual for the first, and probably the last, midnight chapel.

To be a senior was to attain the heights. Only an urgent reason could tear us away from commencement. Not to get the final, public confirmation of our labors was hardly to be graduated at all.

The commencement formal was the swishiest of the year, Gus in a striking white gown, I in my tuxedo. The Quadrangle dining room with its cathedral ceiling was a glamorous setting. The men could hardly be handsomer, the girls lovelier. Our red hot mammas who usually wore short skirts now were attired in long, flowing dresses. You could hardly glimpse an ankle, much less a knee. Both of us were aware that a time of our lives that had meant so much was about to end.

At commencement, 125 diplomas were awarded. The president reminded us that ideas were the vitalizing power in the making of the world. Virtue, righteousness, and truth enter our lives and express themselves in our human relations. The Greeks truly knew that the things that are seen are temporal, the things unseen are eternal. Did he reflect, as he stood before us, that in his early days as a professor of Greek all seniors could read the *Iliad*, the *Odyssey*, the great tragedies, in the original? And that, since we could not, he would give us a final glimpse of Greek thought? We can never know.

Lavell would have made the ideas soar, but Prexy did well enough, in his dignified, majestic, distant manner. Nevertheless, at the planned moment, each of us filed past him on the platform, receiving a handshake and a diploma with the proper name on it; everything had worked out exactly as we had rehearsed. For an immortal instant each of us stood alone, in front of our teachers and our peers, enjoying the glory of it all. We got our sheepskin, in person, on the spot, not later, from a harried subaltern.

Noon brought the Alumni-Senior luncheon; we were formally welcomed into the society of Grinnell alumni. We had made the transition. Now we could smoke, drink, eat supper in our shirtsleeves, drive automobiles the year around, get married, anything.

Together Gus and I filled the Oakland with all my possessions and most of hers. Our first stop was at her home, where her parents helped us unload. They were becoming accustomed to see me come up Harwood Drive. I stayed a short time and then drove to Osceola.

I was as weary as if I had spent three successive days chopping chestnuts in Rock Creek Park. The winding, hilly road to Osceola seemed endless. I got home at 6:00; Don, as an underclassman, had been set free days earlier. Gallantly, he had come home by train so I could have the car. The family was together during the supper hour, then he drifted off to see his steady, Dorothy. I immediately announced that I was going to bed. Father wryly said that it was great to have the boys home because we had had such a good, long visit. I tumbled into bed and slept completely around the clock, not appearing again until the next supper hour.

And not until then did I unpack. I emptied my pockets to see that I had a single $10 bill, the sum I had had that first day at Grinnell.

As Grinnell deserves more space than I have given her, I will add a few lines that will parallel anyone's college days in the twenties:

The beanie-burning bonfire, signifying that even freshmen were accepted as people.

The football games: our stadium occupied only a part of one side of the field. The basketball games: scores were small, like 35–27, 28–22; a game's high scorer was elated to make as many as ten points, often most of them with free throws.

Homecoming, with raucous thirty- and forty-year-old alums,

laughing, making silly jokes that only they thought were funny, and commandeering our beds, compelling us to sleep on the floor.

Chapel and vespers, and the time it was drizzling and Henry Matlack, the college organist, played softly, during the benediction, instead of a classical excerpt, a new song; "Let a smile be your umbrella on a rainy, rainy day."

The short skirts that the girls, our version of flappers, wore. When a girl danced with a tall guy and put her arm over his shoulder, thus displaying a segment of bloomer or leg, other couples, to be helpful, yelled "Fire!"

The strict segregation of the women. If a man, for example, a janitor, came upstairs, the first woman to see him called out "Man on second!" One woman, surprised by the laundry collector as she stepped from the shower, covered her front with the towel, then turned and fled. Later she moaned: "He saw me in my curlers!"

The spring romances that seemed made in heaven, for eternity; then came the summer separation; next fall most people started dating someone else.

The long hours at the library. Twenty students trying to share two reserve books to meet an assignment due the next morning. How we would have prized a copying machine! The endless term papers, book reports, laboratory experiments, math problems. The hours spent in translating French, German, Spanish, Latin, or Greek. The makeup assignments if you missed something. Tests, quizzes, examinations.

The simple fact of going to college when there was no beer. No Bud. No Schlitz. No Miller. No Michelob. Nobody would have know what "six-pack" meant.

The sudden appearance of cars driven by parents to see their young ones at the end of the school year. Packards, Cadillacs, and Buicks stirred in with Fords, Chevies, and Overlands. Until then, who knew or cared who came from rich homes and who from poor!

The chaperones at the dances. We really should offer to trade a dance with them. Well, at least let's go say hello. Well, after the next dance; right now they seem busy. Well, next week for sure.

Trying out for plays and for John McGee's *Malteaser Scandals*. ("Malteaser scandals, like fairy-story vandals, will steal your heart away...").

The sigh of relief when each new Friday arrived.

College was not the best part of life, Prexy had said, but it was the best part up to now.

38

One morning in Osceola while at the keyboard I was intrigued by a War Department publicity handout. It invited young men of the nation, those in top physical splendor, to spend August at a Citizens' Military Training Camp. Cadets who spent four Augusts plus additional duty could be commissioned as second lieutenants. I readily saw myself in uniform, a gold bar on each shoulder, an officer in the United States Army.

I decided to enlist in the artillery at Fort Snelling, near Minnesota's twin cities. College days were over; Vermillion High School would not open until after Labor Day; CMTC seemed a good way to spend a month.

On arrival, I joined the long line of men who were being given a medical examination. At one point I simultaneously got shots in each arm. At another I traded my basket of clothes for a uniform, including a pair of the heaviest shoes ever designed, and was directed to report to Battery A. Though Fort Snelling was a long-established camp with an attractively landscaped residential area for officers, and permanent buildings to house the supporting services, I found myself in wooden barracks left over from World War I. Inside were rows of bunks made up with olive drab blankets. (Millions of young Americans had faced this routine the previous decade, and other millions would the next.)

I joined forty others, many from the Deep South—the army did not operate a summer camp in that torrid part of the country. A few men, wearing "red" or "white" insignia indicating that they were in their second or third summers, became the battery's corporals and sergeants. One young man, wearing "blue" insignia, was student captain. In command was a reserve army captain named Ringe, plus a regular-army sergeant. Ringe was an inspiring commander, combining a businesslike attitude with a sense of humor. Though he leaned heavily on the sergeant for technical details, such as how to pitch a tent, fold a sheet, or exhibit equipment on inspection days, he had the qualities of a natural leader.

Our day opened with 6:00 reveille, followed by a march to the drill field for calisthenics. After breakfast came the cleaning or "policing" of the barracks area; we then made up our bunks. Later we were lectured on how to care for a rifle and other vital topics. We had a review of close-order drill: squads right, squads left, and the lot. All in all we welcomed the morning break with its issue of half a pint of cold milk.

I enjoyed the rifle drill: taking the weapon apart, cleaning it, and assembling it. Some of my skills as a linotype machinist could come into play. Eventually came the morning when we were marched to the range, issued live ammunition, and allowed to shoot at standard targets. Most of us won "marksman" or even "sharpshooter" medals. Grandfather Tarwater, the onetime army scout, would have been proud of me. These activities, however, were but a short refresher; we were eager to start fieldwork with the big guns.

Our battery had a dozen French 75 field pieces—the famous weapon of World War I. Each piece was mounted on wooden, iron-rimmed wheels, pulled by six horses harnessed in pairs. The first pair, relatively light horses, were the "lead" team. An artilleryman rode one but controlled both. The middle pair, the "swing" team, also had a rider. Finally came two massive "wheel horses," which actually did most of the work, with a third rider. Thus I learned what the term *wheel horse* actually meant.

Lead-team riders had to know the captain's arm signals that ordered the starting, stopping, and wheeling movements necessary for artillery warfare. Each rider had to keep the harness taut so that his team did a fair share of the pulling. I was pleased to be designated a lead-team driver; this distinctive honor probably came because I was the only college graduate in the battery.

We had vast areas on which to drill, with an abundance of streams, gullies, and other natural obstacles. We began by going full speed, single file, each caisson rattling like a wagon going over a bridge; then, on signal, swinging right or left to form twos or fours; speeding up, slowing down, or halting altogether. First came the signal indicating the maneuver; then, after a pause, the signal to execute it. If, however, a lead-team rider confused either the signal, or executed it too soon, complete and utter chaos resulted, part of the battery going one way and part another. Captain, sergeant, and their red, white, and blue helpers then stopped the maneuver, reassembled teams and caissons, reviewed the signals with copious editorial comment, and repeated the operation. We learned rapidly, however, and often a whole morning went by without a major blunder: horses, riders, and caissons wheeling and turning, bouncing over streams, up and down hills; sometimes narrowly avoiding collisions, sometimes creating uneven spacing, all to a backdrop of rattling, rumbling, neighing, snorting, shouting, yelling.

Wellington, surveying his men before Waterloo, exclaimed: "I don't know whether these troops will frighten the French, but by God they frighten me." I don't know whether our outfit would have frightened the enemy, but we terrified each other. To me the situation got fearful whenever I found myself in the middle of a solid acre of thundering horses and heavy guns moving at top speed, hoping fervently, dear heaven, that I didn't miss the signal and pull my caisson over the teams on the left or right, and also that some other lead-team rider didn't miss the signal and drag his cannon over me. Eventually, wondrously, we got the signals properly so that we could unwind our massive firepower and trot away from the melee in orderly single file.

We arrived for our noon meal minutes after the infantry companies had completed their morning's labors and were already in the mess hall. Even then, however, we could not eat until we had cared for the horses. We must not only unharness them and lead them to their stalls, but we must closely inspect them—lifting each foot, picking out small stones or bits of gravel that might, if neglected, be driven deep into the hoof and possibly lame the animal. Not until each hoof was inspected and cleaned, and each horse has four, could we leave the stable area, scrub ourselves, and walk to the mess hall.

I say *walk*, although that is not a precise term. A morning spent straddling a wide horse, with tender bottom exposed to the pounding of the saddle, inevitably affects the gait. As you never entirely recover from one day's bruises by the following morning, your situation steadily deteriorates. Even though you twist and turn in the saddle in order to expose fresh tissue to its blows, you get little real relief. Mercifully, however, your system adapts to these insults and you become able to take the worst the saddle can offer.

Afternoons we were on our own. We could swim in the river or venture into the Twin Cities. Actually, after we got toughened up, many of us went horseback riding, selecting the best of the lead horses. At 5:00 on specified days we assembled on Fort Snelling's vast parade area. Infantry companies lined up for inspection, and Battery A, with teams and caissons, joined the group. For once it was pleasant to ride to work when others had to walk. When roll was taken, the calls of "present or accounted for" could be heard up and down the line; the band played, the bugle sounded, the flag was lowered. I recalled the Decoration Day ceremonies in Gilman City and the Armistice Day celebrations in Osceola but a Fort Snelling parade was all these and more. The worst feature was standing at attention a full twenty minutes, cadet lieutenants and sergeants ready to bark at you if you wiggled a muscle. Once in a while a brave trooper collapsed from the heat, but mainly we stood firm.

By suppertime we could easily devour table, food, and all. Afterwards came boxing in the open-air arena, and then a movie.

If we had considered the enemy we were preparing to fight, we would have visualized Japan rather than Germany. Germany was shackled by the terms of the armistice, but occasionally we read analyses by military experts about the grave danger from the Far East. The yellow peril was described as a fanatic enemy whose troops were prepared to make any sacrifice. Japan's naval strength was rapidly growing; in fact, Japan had been a major participant at the naval disarmament conference.

The Citizens' Military Training program, in its seventh year when I participated, continued until 1940. Artillerymen who successfully completed the course and received commissions in the Officers' Reserve Corps gradually realized that the first blows would come not from Asia but from Europe. What they did not realize was that the horse-drawn field piece would never fight anybody at all.

The mustering-out process was simple; we checked in our gear, marched past the paymaster to collect our mileage, reclaimed our civilian clothes, and fanned out in various directions. Most of the way I hitchhiked in a white Marmon that rode like a dream, especially when compared to a lead horse. Two men were in the car, bleary-eyed as if they had been driving all night, and after we had speeded southward an hour the driver asked how far we were from the Canadian border. I gave him an estimate, and after another hour he again asked how far I thought we were from the border. Something nudged me to question him, "Are you trying to get to Canada?" and when he said he was, I had to tell him he was going in exactly the wrong direction. He slammed on the brakes, let me out, made a U-turn that fogged the air with gravelly dust, and headed north at a mile a minute. As I stood there waiting for the next ride I decided the men had stolen the car and were trying to beat the sheriff to the border.

I guess you know that although our generation did not invent hitchhiking, we perfected the art.

I stopped in Des Moines to see Gus. The house was empty; I suspected she was still at her playground job. I prepared to wait, but saw that the front screen door was not working any better than it had when I was there previously. For a long time everybody had had to give it extra pushes and jiggles to get it latched. With time on my hands, I removed the door, tightened the hinges, squared top, bottom, and sides, readjusted the latch, reset the spring; when I rehung it, it clicked into place with a precision that old Mergenthaler himself would have applauded.

Gus's father, mother, sister, she herself—one by one, as they returned home—noticed the change. At supper table the question arose: "Who fixed the screen door?" As nobody knew the answer, I modestly took all credit. From that moment onward I was regarded as worthy husband-material; good, solid-citizen type; responsible, capable of taking initiative, and doing something without being told. No talent I had previously shown was as impressive as fixing the screen door. Later everybody denied attaching any importance to the incident; long before, they insisted, they had perceived my innate virtues. I can only set down my own smug recollection.

V. I Join the Second Oldest Profession

39

Artillery training was fine preparation for starting a career as a high-school teacher. A teacher, like a lead-team driver, has to be able to interpret signals, manage headstrong creatures, live with both praise and blame, keep one's bottom unbruised, and avoid advancing in directions that will never be of any use to anybody.

Arriving in Vermillion, I reported to Superintendent Heller's office. He was startled: "You look so much younger than I remembered." Though I was twenty-two, and could vote in the next year's election, I looked like a high-school senior. Heller gave me a syllabus, a grade book, and showed me where my five English classes would meet, but he was simply going through the motions; he had a deep-seated worry that I would not be able to manage high-school students. His concern eroded my own self-assurance.

I found a room in the most famous boardinghouse north of Lincoln and west of Lake Michigan, run by Anne Vaith. Anne, of Bohemian ancestry, had come to the University of South Dakota years previously; to help finance her education she worked for Thomas Sterling, dean of the law school. When eventually Sterling went to Washington as senator, he left his house in Anne's care, giving her permission to take in boarders. She rented the upstairs rooms, turned the downstairs parlor, sitting room, library, and dining room into a large dining area plus a smaller dining room. Out of her earnings she was eventually able to buy the house. At the time I was there she was feeding from sixty to a hundred people.

I shared an upstairs two-room suite with Raleigh Baldwin, from the university registrar's office; two female teachers and two downtown employees lived in the remaining four bedrooms; a common bathroom was at the end of the hall. We regularly ate in the small dining area with eight others, all teachers. The university and townspeople who took over the large dining room were a world apart from our group.

Over the years Anne had established distinctive routines. You took a plate from your table, went to the kitchen, and helped yourself from steaming pots and giant skillets on the big wood-burning range. We could predict the menus of the noon meal: roast beef on Mondays, meat loaf on Thursdays, fish on Fridays, chicken on Sundays. Along with the entree were fresh vegetables, mashed or scalloped or new potatoes, beets or asparagus, a variety of salads, biscuits, homemade jellies and jams, and at least three kinds of pie.

Anne loved people with hearty appetites. She was eager for her patrons to go back for seconds. Over and above the standard menu she often introduced a specialty. Once she served steamed pudding, thick with raisins, topped with hard sauce; we raved; she served it several days in a row. Often our second-floor roomers went downstairs for a late-night snack, filling up, perhaps, on oranges; she was proud of us.

Sunday's fried chicken was served at the table; the white cloth and the fine china and silver gleamed more than usual. At the signal we rushed to our places, passed the platter of crisply fried chicken, helped ourselves to mashed potatoes and to a huge portion of her special salad, a mix of celery and apples, nuts and pineapple, dates and marshmallows, along with whipped cream. Dessert was ice cream, made that morning by two high-school boys who turned the crank until it would turn no longer. As part of their reward they got to scrape the dasher, first repacking the tank in ice and salt and allowing the ice cream to set until its texture was firm. Anne's ice cream was so delicious that hardly anyone was satisfied with a single dish.

Whether you paid by the single meal or by the month, you left your money in a teapot on the mantel. You didn't say to Anne, "I'm leaving the money on the mantel"; you settled with the teapot. I paid $30 a month for the room, three meals a day, and midnight oranges. Rumor said that Anne instinctively knew who paid and who didn't, or who was slow about it, but if she ever dunned anyone, that fact never got out.

She did have kitchen help—I remember the Koster brothers, Al and Max—but was up early every morning preparing breakfast, her day not ending until long after the last dinner table was cleared and the huge stack of dishes and pans washed and put away. Even today when former Vermillionites of a certain age meet, they are not likely to say, "Were you a teacher (or a student) at the university?" but "Did you eat at Anne Vaith's?" The boardinghouse on Forrest Avenue had hundreds of loyal patrons. It was my Vermillion home for two years.

40

At the teachers' meeting held the Saturday before school opened, I learned about attendance and record keeping, and met Vermillion High School's dozen other teachers, who would be in charge of her three hundred students. If Heller had more than usual to say about the importance of classroom discipline and especially of being stern at the outset so pupils will be overawed, it was because he had a young-looking, inexperienced teacher in his midst—charged with teaching two classes of sophomores and three of seniors.

When I awoke Monday, I kept repeating to myself: "This is your first day; you may teach two or three hundred days, if you are not thrown out at the end of the week, but this is Number One."

I could have cut through the ravine but I purposely walked to school the long way round, trying to glue each moment in my memory. I entered the building in a first-day mood and sought out my classroom.

I wanted to be there early. If the students arrived at the room before I got there, they would likely tear it apart.

When the bell rang, I could hear a mob scampering down the hall, not overly noisily, since other teachers were on patrol. Heller believed that if students were muzzled in the halls, they would be more manageable in the classrooms. In fact, students were monitored at all times. An individual student could not move between classrooms, except when classes were changing, without a piece of paper in his hand stating whence he came and whither he was bound. Heller had been brought to Vermillion the previous year, in fact, to introduce a measure of discipline into the system. Under his strict rules, school life became better; the good students saw that orderliness gave them a better chance to get on with an education, and the others fell in line. The reasoning is still valid.

Thirty sophomores entered my room and filled the seats, which, of course, were bolted to the floor. A moment later Heller strode in and stood at the back. I was not prepared for an official visitor. He had been more alarmed than I had thought.

I forgot all about what he had said about being stern and ominous at the outset. I began by telling a few stories. I made remarks on what English II was about. I suggested activities we would pursue together. I told them that as I had grown up in a newspaper office, I had learned firsthand the importance of spelling and grammar. I mentioned instances when newspapers had been embarrassed because of poorly arranged sentences that put the modifier next to the wrong noun. Gradually I relaxed and the superintendent did also.

I still had a hurdle. I could get pupils to smile, but could I get them to work? What if I asked them to go to the board and do exercises and drills? Would they actually obey me or just sit there in defiance? I had never had any experience in ordering people about. I gave the order and held my breath. Without delay they quietly went to the board, and the superintendent departed.

Then and there I realized that every new teacher owes a debt to those who preceded him and who had taught pupils the elements of classroom behavior: to hold up a hand if they wanted to recite, to listen when the teacher or other students were talking, to remain in their seats unless they were told to stand or move about. Pupils are not born knowing these customs. I also realized that it was my class, that I was in charge, and that everything would be all right. I had an advantage in that I could draw heavily upon speaking and debating experience. Every young person who wants to teach should take high-school and college speech courses.

Working with the *Vermillionaire* staff brought me in contact with the bright and active boys and girls in the school. Many had already had a year's experience on the paper; what I could do was give them professional direction. We worked after school and on press days at the *Vermillion Plain Talk*, one of the town's two weeklies, and our printer that year.

Outside activities were then an assignment laid atop a regular teaching schedule, without extra compensation. In addition to teaching five courses, each teacher did a combination of hall or cafeteria duty, or supervised a study hall. Many teachers left the building at the end of their last class, but I had a school paper to publish biweekly. In addition, I coached the debate team, which meant tryouts, discussions with the squad about good arguments for either side, rehearsals, and practice debates with other schools before tournament competition began. Every evening I seemed to reach the boardinghouse front door just as the supper line was forming in the kitchen.

As South Dakota's salary schedule was among the better ones, my own $1,550 stipend being $300 higher than that paid by comparable

Iowa schools, Heller had been able to assemble a young, competent staff. Most of us would cast our first vote for president in the next election. Our group at Anne Vaith's kept up a steady stream of small talk about school life. If I needed information about a student, I could collect expert opinions in a hurry. Teachers in small schools can readily help each other when one has a puzzling problem that involves motivation or discipline. Teachers love to brag about a good student. They talk about a good theme, an unusual classroom speech, an achievement in music, mathematics, or physical education.

We did not spend all our time in shoptalk. Coach George Deklotz had a new Ford—the speedy, dependable Model A had just come out—and sometimes took us for a drive, filling both front seat and rumble seat. He could easily do 60 miles an hour on South Dakota's gravel roads, a step ahead of Iowa's clay and dirt. Once he drove 120 miles to a teachers' meeting in 120 minutes. Baldy and I invested in a radio—a used Freed-Eiseman, if any experts are listening—with storage battery and recharger; after a night of listening, we recharged the battery for the next day. We paid $25 each for this set, including the big loudspeaker that sat on top. On a winter night we could bring in signals from hundreds of miles but our best programs came from a powerful Yankton station that featured a young band leader named Lawrence Welk.

During the cold winter nights, and South Dakota nights are often irrationally cold, we went ice-skating on the Missouri River. River skating is not the world's most elegant, since you are always likely to hit a twig imbedded in the ice, but each night we skated a few miles, built a fire out of brush and branches, sat around and rested, and then skated home.

Meanwhile, Gus and I managed a weekly exchange of letters. We levied no restrictions on each other's social activities; the topic, in fact, had never come up. She briefly mentioned dating a fellow to whom I will give the name of Walter II, but I got a fuller account from the lone survivor of The Syndicate. "Walter II took Gus to the homecoming game," he wrote; I was not disturbed. Later: "Gus is going to the basketball games with Walter II." The information seemed trifling. More important was the news that she had won an Honor G letter and had been elected to Phi Beta Kappa. Still later: "I just saw Gus and Walter II sitting under a willow

Breakfast, luncheon, and dinner companions at Anne Vaith's; what we didn't know was hardly worth knowing. *Left to right:* George Deklotz, coach; Harold Smith, banker; Charlotte Benbow, home economics; Helen Justus, art; Loren Reid; Violet Greene, grade-school teacher; Hazel Bremmer, grade-school principal; Charlotte Coffin, girls' physical education; Illa Ludeman, grade-school teacher; Raleigh Baldwin, university registrar's office.

tree, reading poetry to each other." That news was alarming. My heart suddenly froze. I cussed Walter II out, anapestically and trochaically. That Friday afternoon I took the train for Grinnell, to rebuild my fences as necessary. But everything seemed immediately right. Before I left, we made plans to go to her commencement dance.

At 5:00 the evening of the dance, I arrived in Osceola. Father and Mother, eager to see me, sat down for what they expected would be a long visit. In the back of my mind was the thought that the dance began at 8:00 and here I was, 110 miles away. I blush to think that I had been home hardly ten minutes before I asked for the car to drive to Grinnell. Father was about to hit the ceiling but Mother squelched him with a glance and a gesture. "Of course you can, son," she said. I dressed hurriedly and rushed to the car with the scantiest of good-byes. I know now that they were saddened to give me up right then; I could think only of the long drive between me and Cottage V, and that at best I would arrive long after the dance had started. The narrow road seemed more than usually clogged with slow-moving vehicles. I arrived long after 8:00.

I parked the car and headed for her cottage. That whole side of the campus was deserted. As I neared the window I could hear the sound of a piano. I entered the club room and saw her sitting at the keyboard—blonde hair, strong, slender arms and shoulders, a radiance about her face. She saw me and leaped across the room in two squeals and a bound. Over the years I have treasured this imperishable moment.

Although my own class had graduated, I found that I knew most of the seniors and juniors and their dates. Her class, notable among other reasons for a cluster of bright, animated, fun-loving girls, was among the great ones.

Next morning, after her commencement, we drove to Des Moines, bringing her four-year collection of college stuff, and I returned to Osceola. I began to realize that I had had an extremely brief visit with my own family; that I had given no advance notice that I was going on to Grinnell; that the car, in fact, might have been in the shop, undergoing repairs. Luck and the understanding of my parents had ridden with me all the way. When I observe a young person doing a thoughtless deed, I have to reflect that nobody could top the record I set in that category at the ripe age of twenty-three.

Back at Vermillion, I was caught up in the plans of the seniors for their annual party. Serving as their adviser led me to draw heavily on my own college experiences. To decorate the gym, we put a large, round tank in the center of the floor, rigging a garden hose so it would throw a spray of water into the air, falling back into the tank. By adjusting the nozzle and the force of the flow, we could simulate a fountain and make it elegant with colored spotlights. Overhead we mounted a plywood medallion, decorated with crepe paper in school colors; wide streamers from the medallion to the walls and continuing down the sides created a false ceiling and sidewalls that transformed the gym completely. We worked steadily until 6:00; by then we were worn out, wondering if we could pull ourselves together to enjoy our own dance, starting in a couple of hours.

Superintendent Heller had had a meeting after school with two patrons and decided to show them our handiwork. His guests were astounded; people are often amazed to realize that young folks can accomplish anything at all. To astonish his visitors further, he turned on the fountain. Not knowing its secrets, he turned it on too strong. The stream hit the crepe-paper streamers, and in seconds the whole ceiling lay on the floor. The three were horrified at what they saw; the work of hours was undone in a minute. Luckily or unluckily, some of us had not yet left the building; tired as we were, we started to rebuild the ceiling by cutting out the wet, weakened places and splicing in new lengths of crepe paper. We finished the job only a few minutes before the party was scheduled to begin.

That evening the gym was filled with couples looking as happy and refreshed as if they had napped all afternoon. Such is the energy of youth.

Our debate squad of novices got to the regional in a state that had an extraordinary tradition of speaking and debating. The *Vermillionaire* did not win first, but it placed. I was offered a contract for another year.

Sometime those last few months I passed the point of no return so far as becoming a newspaper publisher was concerned. I had been so involved with publishing's editorial and mechanical aspects for so many years that I had become overly saturated. Meanwhile, my enthusiasm for teaching increased. For this I have to thank the 125 South Dakota youngsters I taught that first year. Most of them I have since forgotten, but I can still construct a long list, each name calling up incidents, happenings. The teachers were a congenial group, and the superintendent and principal stood solidly behind us when difficulties arose, a priceless aid, not always recognized. We did not have to contend with drugs, alcohol, racial strife, violence, or the variety of anti-intellectualism that sometimes creeps into high-school groups and undermines them.

Not only did I decide to become a teacher, but in the back of my mind was the thought that I should prepare for college teaching. I would start that very summer by attending graduate school and

enrolling in advanced courses in English. I would return to Chicago.
Where else?

41

The University of Chicago would not be ready to receive Robert
Maynard Hutchins for another year, but it had already received
generous Rockefeller support and had a strong Department of English.

I knew the famous textbook by John M. Manly, head of the department, and his colleague, Edith Rickert, and had heard of their
monumental scholarship in Chaucer. I did not know then, but
learned later, that they, along with Thomas Knott, editor of Webster's dictionaries, had won the respect of the profession of crypt-
analysis because of their ingenuity in cracking enemy codes during
World War I. Nobody was overly amazed that people who worked
with words, and who could collate a dozen medieval manuscripts in
order to decipher what Chaucer really wrote, could readily get the
hang of code breaking.

Other professors of English at Chicago were then analyzing literary style, sorting out the minute features of each author's writing as
a kind of literary fingerprinting. After studying, for example, samples of Jane Austen's writing and subjecting them to detailed inspection, they claimed that, given a stack of unidentified specimens,
they could select the one by Austen. Or, given a suspected forgery,
they could determine whether or not it was written by the supposed
author. In all, Chicago seemed a lively place to study.

On registration day I found myself at the end of a long queue.
After a wait, I saw a staff member start at the head of the line, asking
everyone a question. When he got closer, I could overhear him:
"Where did you do your undergraduate study?" When he asked me,
I replied: "Grinnell College, Grinnell, Iowa."

"Oh," he said. "You don't belong here—you belong over there,"
indicating a much shorter line. I was surprised and pleased that
Grinnell wrought such an effect. In minutes I was enrolled and
relieved of my tuition, while the long line I had abandoned was still
inching forward. I have no idea why I received preferential treatment, but few privileges are more gratifying than to be shifted from

the end of a long line to a short one. And eventually I learned that I could answer a certain question by saying only, "Grinnell," no adding the name of the town.

I enrolled in American Literature, Shakespeare, and Anglo Saxon. The first was taught by a visiting professor who should have stayed home. The second was taught by an outstanding Shakespearean scholar, Charles Read Baskervill, then in his sixties. He limited the discussion to Shakespeare's tragedies, and further limited it to sources from which Shakespeare borrowed, but his command of that specialized range of material was unquestioned. As he himself was reasearching the Elizabethan jig, he commented freely on dance and musical features as they bobbed up in various plays. He was so enthusiastic about the sources of Shakespeare's plots that we overlooked his failure to say much about the sparkling aspects of Shakespeare's genius. Those who live amongst the footnotes miss the grand poetry. On the whole, however, I felt the course was a fair warning about the nature of graduate research, which tends to plunge deeper and deeper and emerge with less and less. Baskervill was the first true specialist with whom I had ever studied. Moreover, in later years I could say, when talking to young professors of Elizabethan literature, "I studied at Chicago with Charles Read Baskervill," and if I uttered those words in just the right tones, I could bring the average conversation to a halt.

Anglo-Saxon was taught by Henning Larsen, an absolute star in the classroom. Larsen, then on the staff of the University of Iowa, was that summer a visiting professor. He was not colorful, but he had a surpassing ability to be both clear and interesting. We reviewed an Anglo-Saxon grammar and read parts of Beowulf and the Anglo-Saxon *Old Testament*, but I particularly recall how he could trace the origins of a particular word through Old French, Old High German, Old Norse, Sanskrit, and the like, going back and forth, up and down, displaying the word's parents, cousins, and in-laws, and the kinship among languages and cultures. At first I was overwhelmed, but he filled the blackboard with such a variety of concrete examples that I began to see reasons for the connections. Without hesitation he repeated a given principle as many times as seemed necessary. If a student raised a question on Wednesday that Larsen had already thoroughly covered, he treated the question as if it were both original and penetrating, and had never come up

before, going back to the blackboard and rediagramming the answer, with new examples. Day by day most of his enthusiasm and
part of his competence rubbed off on us.

Of this class of thirty, twenty-five were advanced Ph.D. candidates, either in English or a foreign language, as I learned from
conversations before and after class. In the group, however, was
another poor wretch, who, like me, was only beginning graduate
study. Between us we knew a bit of modern French and German,
but not Old French, Gothic, and the like. We did not ask the
informed questions that came naturally to the others, but we did
spend a solid four hours every afternoon going over our notes. With
that kind of labor, something had to give, and after a few weeks we
felt we would survive.

The university's giant library was an exciting place in which to
study. Grinnell's holdings totalled 80,000 items; Chicago's, 660,000.
As an undergraduate writing term papers I had often discovered
that the library lacked many promising books or journals. By contrast, at Chicago I could secure in minutes almost anything I
wanted. Here were, for example, every conceivable edition of and
commentary on any given Shakespeare play, a situation to warm the
blood of a graduate student writing his first term paper.

Chicago was then experimenting with the grading system. The
graduate school had decided to abolish letter grades except P and F;
a student either Passed or Failed. After a time, the professors had
decided they needed to recognize and reward the superior student,
so they added H (High). Even that did not suffice, so they added (+)
and (−) to indicate other gradations. I received the full range of this
advanced thinking, getting a P, a P+, and an H. Summer sessions
those years were lengthy, and after twelve weeks I was ready to go
back to my own teaching, having picked up twelve hours toward a
higher degree, and, what proved to be more important, having had
my first experience in writing detailed, technical papers using the
resources of a giant library.

That fall I would have another new experience, that of casting my
first vote in a presidential election. I naturally leaned to the Democratic candidate, Al Smith, four-time governor of New York and an
Irish Catholic, who was generally liberal in his views. In a nomination speech, young Franklin Roosevelt had called him "The Happy
Warrior," and the slogan stuck. Al Smith could have had a career on

the stage if he had not chosen politics instead. In the campaign he traveled widely and spoke frequently, and his cigar, brown derby, and theme song, "The Sidewalks of New York," became immediate trademarks. So also did his Brooklyn accent and manner and his pronunciation of *radio* as "raddio," indicating that the medium was still new enough that even a governor of a big eastern state had not become familiar with the prevailing pronunciation and thought it unimportant to change his own, despite all the jokes and jibes about it. His opponent, Herbert Hoover, was as dull a candidate as I had ever heard, but was able to capitalize on Smith's unpopularity in the West and South, plus the prosperity of the country that made voters unwilling to change the politics in the White House, and swept to a landslide.

The election itself, of course, would not be along for several weeks; right now I was looking forward to September and my second year as a teacher.

42

Back at Vermillion, I found a note in my box: "See Mr. Heller at once." It did not say, "Please see Mr. Heller at once," or "Mr. Heller would like to see you when you are free."

I entered his office almost before the ink was dry. He was standing and looking out a front window, maybe at the flagpole in the grassy yard. He waved me to a seat and continued to stare at the flagpole.

A grim message was in store; I wondered what. As the *Vermillionaire* had not won the state competition, perhaps he was going to assign it to someone else. The silence deepened. My new speech class had enrolled fifteen, half the size of the usual class; perhaps he was going to cancel it.

Normally, he was not so grim. Maybe he was going to tell me this would have to be my last year on the faculty . . . maybe the last semester . . . maybe less than that. Were teachers like printers? People who could be fired on two weeks' notice? I had never investigated this point.

Finally he came to his desk, sat down, looked directly at me, and said: "The school has a chance this year to graduate an even one hundred seniors. We have never had so many."

Part of my fear vanished. Yet I was not wholly at ease; more like a patient whose surgeon had said, "I guess we're not going to have to take your leg off—*above* the knee."

"We cannot achieve this goal unless we can give special assignments in English to two people not now in school who need to remove a deficiency."

So this is it; I would have a monumental amount of extra work to do.

"Moreover, among the remaining 98 is one boy so notoriously poor in English that he can't possibly graduate unless you give him special attention." When he mentioned Joe C*** (name, initial, and asterisks all ingeniously invented), I understood the full sweep of the challenge. Often Joe's name had intruded into the back-room conversations at Anne's, in connection with missed work. His potential had been smothered under years of indifference.

Already I was teaching five classes a day; the empty spaces were filled with school paper, debate, hall and cafeteria duty, plus taking tickets at athletic events. I did, however, catch some of Heller's interest and told him I would help try for the one hundred.

"We have still another problem. We send a greater percentage of our graduates across town to the university than any other high school does. The word has come back that they are notoriously poor in freshman English. Whatever they are teaching, we obviously are not preparing for it."

I agreed to visit the university's English department and investigate. So I started my second year with two special assignments.

Every teacher knows about Joe—or Josephine—the student who is poorly motivated. Or lacking in background. Or is a slow learner. Our Joe had all these difficulties.

I resolved to try to make my instruction clear; to use probing questions; to summarize, review, and repeat; to try various approaches, since some pupils are eye-minded and some are ear-minded. Maybe I had Henning Larsen's skill in exposition at the back of my mind. Whenever I saw a student outside of class, I struck up a conversation about his work. Accordingly, few could have noticed that Joe was getting special attention. He was encouraged by his progress, slight as it was, and began to see that he might get a diploma after all.

As for the two former students who had met qualifications for graduation except the incomplete in English, I encouraged them to write their missing term papers. Once the school showed an interest, they responded and did the long-postponed work.

My visit to the university's English department was illuminating. Yes, the chairman was positive that Vermillion students did worse than average. No, he had not pinpointed the specific problem. Yes, he'll consult the staff; come back and see us again. Yes, you can look over the class rolls and see how Vermillion students had fared. Yes, here's the current syllabus.

The difficulty proved to be that their course was heavily slanted toward formal grammar, whereas our students had studied much literature and little grammar since their sophomore year. The grammar I taught my sophomores had to endure until they entered the university. Since I also taught the seniors, I proposed to Heller that we end their year with six weeks of grammar review. The result was striking; next fall our graduates led the parade in freshman English. This was my first experience in Adjusting the Curriculum to Meet the Needs of Society.

The last two months of the year were full. Our debaters won various individual tournaments and made it to the state finals. The *Vermillionaire* won first in the state competition. And I must also mention that Vermillion had by far the best high-school music program I had yet encountered. When young musicians from all over South Dakota flooded the university campus that spring, VHS's talented boys and girls ranked high in several vocal and instrumental solo events. Most of the performers in the high-school orchestra were students of mine in either English or speech. I attended the contest, and when various soloists and the orchestra won first place, I was as proud as if I had coached them myself.

During the year I had had to answer a further question: Now that I wanted to be a teacher, should I choose English or speech? Here I was at a time when communication in writing and speaking was becoming increasingly vital—the population was growing, society was becoming more complex, families were more mobile, technology was exploding—and I had a background that would let me move in either direction. As I reflect on the factors entering into this decision, I realize that that spring perhaps two hundred young men and women were also standing at the crossroads between English and speech. Some would get their advanced degrees a summer at a

ime; some would stop at a master's degree; a few would go all the
way to the doctorate.

Though I enjoyed teaching in both fields, I was beginning to
weary of correcting the hundreds of themes that were a by-product
of large English classes. Most of the corrections dealt with elemen-
tary problems that made the high-school teacher say, "Why didn't
the grade-school teacher cover this?" and that made the grade-
school teacher exclaim, "Why didn't this child learn these things at
home?" A colleague got so far behind that he had to stay after school
one late afternoon after another, working through his heap of
themes. Late one afternoon, having finished my own labors, I halted
at his doorway to say a few words of commiseration. "We're just like
prostitutes," he moaned; "they'll never invent a machine to do this."
If his allusion is to the world's oldest profession, surely teaching is
the second oldest. Human creatures could never have come down
from the trees, survived the perils of the broad savannas, and finally
learned to live in communities, sharing each other's special talents,
unless each generation could teach its accumulated experience,
tinged with warning, to the next.

A positive reason tilting my decision toward speech was that as a
discipline it was being revitalized. It has always had a distinguished
heritage: its great teachers included Plato, Aristotle, Cicero, St.
Augustine. Each had written about the spoken word. During the
nineteenth century, however, the practitioners of elocution had lost
interest in the communication of ideas and had overstressed vocal
and bodily techniques. In the last fifteen years, starting about the
time I was in fifth grade, it had shifted its focus to the critical and
historical study of public address, to rhetorical theory, and to experimental investigation.

And then I must not forget my own years on this planet. I had
grown up in a family that made its livelihood through the newspaper. It had long had a keen interest in political speaking; not only
Bryan's but also that of innumerable congressmen, senators, and
governors. Politics, and anything else that happened in the community, was thought of as something to be investigated and reported. I
had written hundreds of columns of news stories, starting about
eighth grade. My college major was English, and I had a graduate
summer from the University of Chicago behind me. But, like many
of the two hundred others who stood at this particular crossroad, I

had participated year after year in high school and college speaking and debating contests and had studied and taught public speaking as well as English. This decade of the twenties had seen the coming of radio, which added a vast dimension to the effectiveness of the spoken word. If I had come along even three years earlier, I might have stayed with English, but now my own preference, perhaps swayed by the turn that communication was taking, led me to decide to be a teacher in this new field.

Six universities then offered a Ph.D. in speech, among them Iowa, Michigan, and Cornell. I liked Iowa: it had a good faculty headed by Woolbert, who had spoken to our debate club at Grinnell, and A. Craig Baird, author of the first discussion-and-debate textbook. Its course offerings included rhetoric, British and American public address, debate and discussion, interpretation, theater, radio, speech pathology, phonetics. It was close to Gus, now planning to teach in central Iowa. What better reasons were there?

If I were to study for the doctorate, I realized I must leave my teaching position altogether and give full time to being a graduate student. In three years I could get further than by going to summer schools stretched out over a dozen years. That much I had learned at Chicago. I had an earnest conversation with Heller about my future. Neither of us wanted to sever our relationship, but he cordially endorsed the move and I prepared to leave.

At commencement we did graduate a hundred seniors. I felt proud because each of them had studied with me. After the ceremony, several of the new members of the Class of '29 came to my room to help me finish packing so I could catch the late night train. They went with me to the station; I still see their small cluster on the platform. I hated to leave the students, the other teachers, Anne Vaith's, the town on the bluffs of the Missouri River. It had been a rewarding two years. I boarded one of the yellow coaches of the Chicago, Milwaukee, & St. Paul, curled up on a seat, and headed back to Iowa.

VI. Great Crash, Great Depression

43

Seven years had passed since I had come to the University of Iowa to participate in the state extemporaneous speaking contest. Now I was here to study for the doctorate in speech. I had had no correspondence with the Department of Speech and Dramatic Art. I have since met graduate students in speech and history who were preceded to Iowa by glowing letters from presidents and deans, who were warmly received by their department heads, taken to see the graduate dean and other luminaries, and cordially welcomed into the company of scholars.

At the University of Chicago, the admissions officer had moved me from the end of a long line to a short one. Right away I had felt like a special person. Here my experience was to be different. Here I was given the impression that only after careful scrutiny would I be allowed to join any line at all.

I was a real walk-on.

Now, in June 1929, I found myself in the office of E. C. Mabie, head of the department, to register for summer school. Mabie, short, stout, and volatile, whose disposition is better described by adjectives such as stormy, hard-driving, temperamental, and impatient, than by sweet and docile, lost no time coming to the point when I told him I was there to study for a Ph.D.

"How long are you going to stay?" he demanded.

"Until I get the degree. Three years or whatever."

"What speech courses do you plan to take?"

"Sooner or later, all of them."

"What is your main interest?"

"Debate and public speaking."

I had the feeling that one wrong answer, and I would be out in the hall. So far I had survived, simply because, in my own mind, my purpose was clear. Debate and public speaking, plus dramatics, were certainly the core of speech, and here was where I proposed to study.

Actually the word *speech*, in this sense, was new. Only a few years previously Ryan had written an article urging departments to call themselves by that name instead of by *oratory* or *elocution*. Most departments had done so. This plain fact shows the new direction the discipline was taking.

The inquisition continued. "Well, then, what courses do you plan to start with?"

Would there be an end to this barrage? this show of firepower? I had, however, studied the summer schedule. "Teaching of Speech, Advanced Public Speaking, and Discussion and Debate," I offered. I wondered from what direction the next shot would come. I did not have long to wait.

"Instead of Teaching of Speech," he said, "take Phonetics. Instead of Advanced Public Speaking, take Anatomy of the Vocal Mechanism. You can keep Discussion and Debate."

I was Number 49, going to the copydesk, receiving a two-page take marked "Fol. Lit.," and returning to my machine.

As Mabie's eyes turned to the next student in line, I departed. My mind was in a whirl. I barely knew what *phonetics* meant. I saw that Anatomy of the Vocal Mechanism was being given in the School of Medicine building, a fact that in itself was ominous. In minutes my concept of graduate study in my new, chosen field was broadened.

Fully a hundred students gathered at the physics building for the first phonetics class to meet with the professor, Stephen Jones of the University of London. He began by describing the International Phonetic Alphabet as a way of recording pronunciation by using one symbol for each sound, comparing and contrasting this system with the more awkward use of diacritical marks found in most dictionaries. Jones covered the blackboard with illustrations from many languages, his procedure reminding me of Larsen's.

For the opening assignment he asked us to prepare a list of ten words illustrating a variety of spellings for the sound of *ee* as in *feet* such as *heat* and *police*. "Can you do it?" he asked, solicitously. "Is it too much?" "No," we replied, in concert, "it is not too much." Five minutes, we said to ourselves, will be ample. The previous summer I had spent hours on Anglo-Saxon and the accompanying linguistics. Jones's daily assignments were ingenuous. "Can you do it? Is it too much?"

One day he discussed the *s* sound, contrasting it with *z*. Some foreign-born speakers of English have difficulty distinguishing between *seal-zeal, rice-rise*.

"To show the difference," he explained, "I have prepared a sensitive flame." He exhibited what looked like an ordinary Bunsen burner, connected its long hose to a gas outlet, turned the valve, lit the burner, and adjusted it so we saw a tall, blue flame. "When I say s-s-s-s," he demonstrated, "the sensitive flame burns steadily. But when I say z-z-z-z, you see what happens." The flame flickered noticeably.

"Suppose the foreign-born speaker tries to say *raze* but it comes out *race*." We saw the flame bobble on *raze* but not on *race*. "You can use this device, asking your student to try to say *raze* until he gets it right and the flame wavers."

We were astonished. We had worked with Bunsen burners and were unaware that they had this characteristic. Like Mark Twain's jumping frog that looked just like any other frog, this burner looked like any other Bunsen burner. When we questioned him, he said blandly that he had specially adjusted the flame.

"Here, it will work for you." He pointed to a woman in the front row. "Say *maze*," he asked. She did, and the flame ducked. "Say *mace*," he said to another student. He did, and the flame burned steadily.

Eventually we realized that our professor had, in fact, unknown to us, pinched the hose when he wanted the flame to flicker. We had been taken in. That moment of enlightenment led to another: he knew that he was giving us minimum assignments. Nevertheless the flow of information and the good humor were so stimulating that we enjoyed our daily meetings. He opened new fields of observation. He taught us to listen. Gradually I became aware that only a small group of speech students were in the course; phonetics was also invaluable in music, education, and foreign language.

The next class lay across the Iowa River, in the amphitheater of the anatomy department. Thirty of us sat in circular tiers of seats, overlooking a pit in which the lecturer stood. On his table were a huge model of the larynx and three jars, each containing an actual larynx in a preservative fluid. Colored chunks of modeling clay were alongside. At the rear was a chart showing the section of the head visible when the left half was removed, and another showing the section visible when the front half was taken away. You could thus see the relationships among teeth, tongue, head, and throat cavities. This was the setting for Anatomy of the Vocal Mechanism.

Soon a man in his early sixties entered the room and, holding to the rail, gingerly made his way to the arena. "My name is Prentiss," he trumpeted. His frailties of age did not affect his voice. With him was an assistant, a slight, bent man named Paul, who stood quietly at one side, available for various kinds of assistance.

Prentiss went around the circle, asking names and major fields. We came from speech, music, psychology, physiology. He pointed to a sheaf of charts. "I have just finished giving a short course to a group of physicians," he announced. "I am going to give you the same course."

A fact of campus life is that students are seldom aware of the professional achievements of their teachers. They may be vaguely aware that a professor is nationally or even internationally known, but they seldom know for what he is famous. Henry James Prentiss never told us, "I am a recognized authority on the sinuses of the head." He never revealed, "I have been chairman of the department of histology and embryology for twenty-one years." We never heard an aside such as, "Incidentally, I have been chairman of the athletic board." Even though he told us he was giving us "the same course" he had offered to a group of physicians, he did not add, "I have given short courses on anatomical subjects to medical associations, dental associations, and hospital staffs, all over the United States."

Professors as a group are reticent, seldom discussing their specialties outside of their immediate departments. I know Professor A only as a gracious and charming host; Professor B as an expert bridge player; Professor C as an avid reader of contemporary literature; Professor D as a dangerous opponent in draw poker; Professor E as one who has traveled almost everywhere and can name the best restaurants in half a dozen overseas capitals. Only incidentally do I know about their awards, prizes, grants, offices in learned societies, participation in international congresses, honorary degrees, if these are in fields other than my own. What a strange business professors are in.

Prentiss did not need to tell us much about himself; we could see his competency at work. He had no syllabus. No textbook. No class roll. He made no assignments. We came and he lectured.

But what lectures. In a highly technical field, he had the enormous virtue of being clear. He demonstrated that if you knew your stuff you can present your ideas in simple language. He proposed to describe and explain the function of every bone, cartilage, muscle,

nd nerve that has a role in the production of vocal sounds. He
picked up the large model of the larynx and pointed to the cartilage
that contains the vocal cords, the front edge of which is called the
Adam's apple. "This is the thyroid cartilage," he boomed. "Paul," he
commanded, "hand me that jar." He opened the jar, dipped his
fingers in the solution, and pulled out a prepared section of unusual
size. "This is the larynx of a bull." He walked around, holding it so
all could see. "This is the thyroid," he indicated. From another jar
he extracted a second specimen. "This is a human larynx—this is the
thyroid." We stared as attentively as if he were holding a golden
double-eagle.

Prentiss (medical students, we learned later, irreverently called
him "Prent," but they uttered the word as they might have that of
another great name in medicine, Luke) played on his console of
visual aids like a concert artist. He turned to one of the charts. "We
call this a sagittal section," he explained. We could identify tongue
and teeth, and the distant half of a nose. "Here's the thyroid." He
drew it on the board in colored chalk. He modeled it in pink clay.
He tilted his head and pointed to his own. "Locate your thyroid," he
said. "Feel it with your fingers. No, your own—not that of the
pretty girl next to you."

"*Thyroid* comes from a Greek word meaning *shield*. The early
anatomists, trained in the classics, thought it looked like a pair of
shields joined at an angle." He illustrated with his own prominent
Adam's apple. No one could possibly think of calling it anything but
a pair of shields.

By the end of the hour we knew full well what a thyroid cartilage
was. Prentiss's information was never dim or doubtful.

So it was, day after day. The tiny muscles that operate the tiny
cartilages within the thyroid. The sinuses and other cavities that
give the voice richness. The great muscles of chest and abdomen
that regulate air supply. Prentiss was an artist with his colored
chalks. When drawing symmetrical figures, he drew with both
hands at once—one hand shaping, for example, the left side of the
rib cage, the other its mirrored counterpart.

Midway through the first week he announced: "This class is
scheduled to meet five days a week, but I'm going to come over
Saturdays. If any of you feel like it, you may join me." We were
there.

In the class were W. Norwood Brigance and George R. R
Pflaum, names of teachers of speech that later became known to
many. Often we saw each other in the medical library, reading and
sketching, on our own, choice plates from Gray's *Anatomy*. Nobody
said we had to do this.

Occasionally Paul wheeled in a specially prepared cadaver, so that
Prentiss could demonstrate a further point. Seeing a cadaver for the
first time gave me an eerie feeling as I looked at the relic of what
once had been a person. Once when it slipped off the table and fell
to the floor, Prentiss picked it up gently and laid it on the table. "We
must not forget that this was once a human being," he said with
feeling, "having hopes and dreams like our own. I have often wondered who he was in real life, and what he did." A moment later
Prentiss was the professional lecturer, sounding the virtues of the
abdominal muscles, indicating each on the cadaver by pulling back
layers of skin that had previously been partly cut away. "Now this
large muscle," he declared, "is used in childbirth." He approached a
woman in the front row. "Did you ever have a baby?" he demanded.

"No, doctor, I never did." She blushed like the pink chalk in the
tray.

"How about you? you? you?" He went down the line. The women
giggled, but had not had any babies.

He queried a slightly older woman. "Yes, Dr. Prentiss," she said
completely self-possessed. "I have a daughter."

"Well, mother," he went on, the class chuckling, "do you remember when . . ." She did remember the stage when, the moment
at which the mother makes a powerful effort with her abdominal
muscles to expel the new life. Thus the point was nailed down.

We had no final examination. The grades were capricious, but
that attitude is often a part of genius. As I received no grade at all, I
complained to the registrar. He had heard the story before, so he
wrote a note, explaining that I had been properly registered and had
completed all my other courses. I took the note to Prentiss, who,
sitting in his office, talked, somewhat to my surprise, in normal
conversational tones. I showed him my notebook and the sketches I
had copied out of Gray as well as those I had made in class. He
seemed convinced and, eventually, sent along a grade.

I may be giving the impression that Prentiss was wholly strong
and vigorous; actually, he was pouring his available energy for the

lay into our class. His powerful voice belied the fact that he was desperately ill. Once he stopped his lecture and bellowed to his assistant, "Paul, bring me my powders." Paul handed him the medicine, which he dissolved in a tumbler of water and gulped down. He wiped the white froth from his lips and muttered something about the stupidity of the doctors who were trying to cure him. Shortly after our class he suffered a heart attack, taught his next classes from a wheelchair, and died almost two years from the day he first met our group. We had taken his last "short course."

My third class was with A. Craig Baird, an energetic, handsome man in his mid-forties. He had been an undergraduate at Wabash, had studied at Union Theological Seminary with, among others, Harry Emerson Fosdick, had taken a master's degree at Columbia with such greats as Brander Matthews, John Erskine, and Charles Sears Baldwin. He had directed debate at Dartmouth and Bates, introducing international debating, and had joined the department at Iowa about the time I was leaving high school. Seeing him in action reminded me of Wood, in that he was widely read, and of Lavell, in that his riches were not mobilized like a string of beads but were displayed unstrung and unmounted.

I was never exactly sure what any of his assignments were, since so much latitude was given; but I could see that the scope of discussion and debate was steadily being broadened. He linked it to logic, argumentation, political science, psychology, and philosophy. He greeted our efforts with enthusiasm, and when he was especially pleased, his face lit up and he rubbed his hands together excitedly in keen appreciation. He was one of the two or three people I have known who could pay you a compliment in such luminous, star-studded, boldface-italic terms that you could chop it into a thousand bits, and glow over each bit. Baird's ideas had a delayed impact. So casually was a Baird notion expressed that it entered your mind quietly, not elbowing away any of the stuff that was already there, but gently adapting itself to your inner furnishings. Only later would you hear yourself reflecting, "That was quite an idea."

My own thought was to select a field and a man; study one and work with the other. Not long afterwards, I decided that Baird was the man I wanted to be associated with.

My second-term summer courses were all with one instructor: Harry G. Barnes. Barnes, also a former student of Ryan's, consti-

H. C. Harshbarger (*top left*); A. C. Baird (*top right*); and Henry J. Prentiss (*lower right*). (Special Collections, University of Iowa.)

tuted the whole staff those five weeks; I took his Advanced Public Speaking, Teaching Speech, and Play Directing. The course in Directing opened a new area: to study a play from the director's point of view. I had always liked the theater, and after Barnes's instruction, when seeing a play, became able to spot the director's talents as well as the actor's and writer's. That insight was quite a bit to get in a brief course. Though Barnes's career was shortened by illness, hundreds of students cherish him as one of their outstanding teachers.

Ironically, Woolbert had died a few days before I arrived in Iowa City. He was one of the founding fathers of the discipline in its new form, and in the eyes of his Iowa students, like Brigance, Lester Thonssen, and Elwood Murray, he had fully lived up to his nation-wide stature.

About midsummer I realized that graduate-school expenses were heavier than I had anticipated, and more than ever I did not want to leave school until I had completely finished. I sought out the composing room of the *Daily Iowan*, which a few years previously had offered Don a job and then had snatched it away. The chief operator and machinist, Fred Flack, in charge of the battery of four machines, was eager to talk when I told him I was looking for a position and became even more so when I told him I was machinist as well as operator. He hired me immediately to work on the night shift. "I get tired," he confessed, "of having to come over in the middle of the night to look at a darn-fool trifling thing that anybody ought to be able to fix." That night I joined a force of eight, normally working until 2:00 A.M.

In those days Prohibition ruled the land. A near beer called Bevo—said to come from discontented horses, a play on the Carnation Milk claim that it came from contented cows—was popular with the printers. They bought it, fortified it with raw alcohol, and then put the bottles in the water cooler. The glue that soaked off the labels made the water unfit to drink, and I did not care to trifle with Bevo. Stories abounded about people drinking, not grain alcohol, but wood alcohol, by mistake, which often caused blindness. Others claimed that even much of the grain alcohol was drained from the cadaver storage tanks of the medical school. Good beer is an acquired taste, and one I had not acquired. Bevo was far from good beer; it was atrocious.

The printers also discussed their experiences with homemade wine. One could buy a pressed-grape brick at the grocery store, with a caution on the label not to soak this choice brick in a mixture of sugar and water plus a little yeast and allow it to stand in a warm place more than twenty-four hours or it would ferment. The end result was that a printer seldom lacked a bottle of either spiked beer or homemade wine at his elbow, though I never saw one too unsteady to work. I would not dream of calling them boozers.

Outside of having no suitable drinking water, I found working conditions agreeable. The friendliness of the group was heartwarming. At times after the paper was out we started a penny-ante game that lasted until eight in the morning, carefully breaking up just before the day shift came to work. We went to nearby Smith's Cafe for breakfast before proceeding to classes. Suddenly my days were filled. One way or another, the first summer came to an end.

44

That year Gus and I had seen each other only a few days at a time, during vacations. By all the rules we should have drifted apart. Ours was the most scattered, distributed courtship two people ever had, short of the long separations forced on couples during the war years.

She had wanted to teach after graduation. Already she had had a year at Stuart, near Des Moines, behind her and was now looking forward to Emmetsburg, near the Minnesota line. At Stuart she had taught general science, world history, physiology, and coached girls' basketball—the kinds of odds and ends that fall to the new teacher because nobody else wants them. At Emmetsburg she would be a full-time teacher of English, her major field.

I shared with her the dream that graduate students were imagining at the opening of school in the fall of 1929. When I got my Ph.D., which would be in two years, I would get a post as assistant professor in a good university department at $3,500 a year. I had taught in high school for less than half of that. I told her my plan was to finish my degree, get a good job, and save $1,000. We could then get married. She wanted to teach a longer period but finally was persuaded. I won my most important debate.

I had never actually proposed, and she had never actually accepted. We talked very little about our future married life. We did not speculate upon having few children, or many children, or no children at all. Talk about finances, religion, in-laws, separate careers was incidental. We entered into none of the agreements or understandings which everybody says is essential. We were too full of the present to worry about the future. Intuitively we knew we would walk the same lane, or boulevard, whichever it proved to be.

Well, I do remember one issue we explored, two or three weeks before we were married. I had been sorting my clothes and came upon thirty pairs of socks, each needing darning. I had kept them for no good reason and now had to make a decision. One night I brought the subject up: should they be saved, or pitched? "Better save them," she advised. So it turned out that when she started her married life she had more of a backlog of mending than a future mother of four should have had.

Times were getting better; closing-out sales and bank failures now seemed a thing of the past. Everybody was rejoicing in boom times. I sensed the prosperity at Smith's Cafe, a few steps from the *Iowan*, where our group of printers ate because we could get swift attention during our brief break for refreshments. The Smiths were doing a rushing business. As their prices were higher than those of many, they served a desirable clientele, offsetting the price by outstanding service. "Keep the water glasses filled," Smith reminded his staff, "Don't keep a customer waiting. See that he gets everything he needs before you leave him." A waiter who neglected these courtesies soon found himself fired; working at Smith's was not easy. "The little things bring the customers back," he told us. The Smiths developed fast-food service long before it became franchised.

Here was ambience, of a sort. And we liked the talk, these days, about the stock market. Smith's customers echoed the stories we ran in the *Iowan* about the nation's economy. One could hardly buy wrong; stocks were going up, up, up. Even when the Dow Jones took a dip, the prevailing optimism was not altered; the opportunity to buy was that much better. Customers talked about their gains. Cities Service. American Can. RCA. New York Central. Buy on margin. "How did your GM do today," our senior pressman might ask the cashier as he paid his check. "Up five points," or "up seven points," or whatever, she would beam, as she rang up the sale. Customers glowed over their own profits. Buy, buy; hard to go wrong.

None of this seemed to have anything to do with a graduate student in speech. No autumn could open with greater promise.

45

After the summer session, most graduate students returned to their teaching positions; others remained for the fall term. In the late twenties it did not seem adventuresome to resign altogether and enter graduate school and be reasonably sure that you would find a new job when you received your degree. In that category were Thonssen, Murray, Floyd Lambertson, and Dina Rees Evans, who had cut loose from jobs to begin graduate study. Others, like Brigance, were on leave. Barnes, on the university teaching staff, was planning a research program. These were those most advanced toward the hoped-for doctorate in speech.

When I registered in the fall of 1929, Mabie talked seriously about my Ph.D. program. After setting down Rhetorical Theory, British and American Oratory, and Speech Pathology, he asked: "What had you planned to minor in?"

"History and English." These, my undergraduate majors, were the preferred supporting areas for one who wanted to write a dissertation in, and later teach in, the area of rhetoric and public address.

"You'll have to minor in psychology," he ruled. "Have you had any?"

"Three hours."

"Well, you'll have to start with seminars. You can't waste time taking beginning courses." He added Systematic Psychology, a seminar about psychological *systems;* I had had only a brief exposure to *principles*. He annexed a laboratory course in experimental psychology, saying that I should study the experimental method. I emerged with a fifteen-hour schedule.

Since Mabie's interests were in theater, especially directing, and more especially directing original scripts, he had vague notions of what a dissertation in public address should be. In fact, no one in the department had had experience in planning a complete doctoral program and seeing it to a conclusion, although the faculty had supervised numerous M.A. theses. Fifteen people were enrolled who hoped to get Ph.D.'s in speech pathology, speech science, speech education, theater, and public address. Several of them were not even so far along as I was.

The department had not yet turned out a Ph.D.; moreover, the dean of the graduate school, C. E. Seashore, once had indicated that the department should not be allowed to give the degree "in its own right." Professors in other departments should share the supervision to assure that we candidates would be properly exposed to research methods. But the other departments, for example, the history department, did not entirely welcome us; it felt that speech students who wrote on historical figures such as Woodrow Wilson or Edmund Burke would be trampling on its domain. It was, however, almost as suspicious of political-science students. Brigance had a running scrap with it over his study of the famous jurist, Jeremiah Sullivan Black. Professors in psychology and English also zealously guarded their long-staked-out territories. And, internally, the head of our own department had little appreciation of, or enthusiasm for, studies in rhetoric and public address.

So the decision to require me to minor in psychology was burdensome. Three or four courses in psychology would have immense value; not only because a little psychology is "good for" anybody but also because a course such as social psychology is directly related to public speaking, and the study of psychological systems overlapped and reinforced the study of rhetorical theory. These, however, I could have taken without the load of a formal minor that I was now asked to shoulder.

All this was in addition to the requirement of a heavy load of courses within the department. One characteristic of the doctoral programs that were slowly emerging was that a Ph.D. candidate should gain a broad view of the field. In its pioneer days, a discipline cannot afford to train specialists. Our group of candidates took courses in phonetics, speech pathology, speech science, and, occasionally, in theater or oral interpretation, as well as in our own specialty.

We slowly became aware also of political reasons for being prepared in psychology. By "political," I mean campus or departmental politics. If the doctorate in speech fell through, we could shift to psychology, become experimentalists, and survive. The dean, an experimental psychologist, would not disfavor such a shift.

These internal and external factors introduced a certain disquietude into our study. Here we were, struggling in a field the boundaries of which were not defined, even within the department itself, under a faculty that was was learning about Ph.D. programs along with its students, under a dean who had reservations about the whole process. At times we felt that we were carrying the department, and, in fact, the discipline, on our backs. How different it would have been if our administrators had said: "We welcome you young men and women, pioneers in this field, and will give you every conceivable help with your writing and research. Your discipline has an ancient, distinguished history, going back to the great thinkers among the Greeks and Romans, and we think it is just dandy that you are picking up the torch, ready to carry it to new heights." What encouragement we got came from our teachers and from each other.

Later I figured these matters out for myself; about ten years later. An extra touch of the spur was that we were told we must not only seek out courses taught by tough-grading professors in other departments, but that we must get the top grades. We must try to be outstanding, since a reputation for attracting first-rate students enhances a department's campus standing almost more than any other single factor.

Our group of hopeful aspirants did well with these courses. As former debaters, we had sharpened our research skills preparing to argue controversial issues. We more than held our own in oral reports or term papers, crucial points at which a student must demonstrate his capacity for original thinking. In courses like Systematic Psychology we found that we had more background than we had realized; names like Plato, Aristotle, Hobbes, Locke, and William James were familiar to us as students of rhetorical theory.

We also learned that the field of psychology was itself fighting for a place in the sun. As late as the first decade of the century, departments of psychology were beginning to break away from departments of philosophy. As long as fifteen years after I left Iowa I saw the struggle of a department of psychology to get itself recognized as a legitimate natural science instead of as some kind of humanistic or social study.

That fall I took two courses in speech that proved central to my lifelong research interest.

Clay Harshbarger, a Grinnell graduate and student of Ryan's, came to Iowa the fall of 1929 to offer the department's first full-fledged course in rhetorical theory. He was a brand-new Ph.D. in speech from Cornell—that pioneer department had already awarded five Ph.D.'s in the field—had been an instructor in the department and had written a study of Edmund Burke's speeches on the American colonies. He had studied with famous Cornell professors in speech and the classics, including H. A. Wichelns, and to that background added his own clearheaded good sense and ever-present willingness to lay his mind alongside that of a student in the pursuit of a problem. Qualities like these were invaluable when, years later, he became head of the department.

We evolved a concept of rhetoric that linked it firmly with the effective communication of ideas, not with the older notion of flamboyant language or flowing gesture. We thus broke with the nineteenth-century elocutionary tradition, to which most of us had been exposed beginning with our high-school days. We studied Plato—the *Phaedrus,* the *Gorgias,* most of *The Republic*—applauding his insistence that truth itself could not prevail unless convincingly presented. We noted that he denounced those orators who talked first on one side of a question and then on the other. Public address was not to be thought of as a demonstration, a display, but as a way of explaining and persuading. We applauded Plato's conviction that a speech was more than rambling talk, but should have organization—a beginning, a middle, and an end.

We read Aristotle's *Rhetoric,* one of his three or four most influential works, chapter by chapter. Here at the height of Greek glory, four centuries before the opening of the Christian era, Aristotle examined the hard, specific problems that confront every speaker: how to analyze an audience, how to appreciate the necessity for good content, such as specific instances, how to organize the speech. Over and above that, Aristotle tackled the broader, philosophical issues: the persuasive impact of a speaker's character—his good sense, high moral standards, good will; ways of heightening the impact of an argument; how a speaker, for example, a statesman, could reason about what was *likely* to happen in the future when no one could be certain. On this last point, for example, the editorial writers and the Sunday supplement feature writers were beginning to note the tensions between Japan and China—the "yellow peril"—and speculate upon what Japan would likely do, and upon what China would likely do, and what would be the probable effect on us if these fanatical warriors turned their attention in our direction.

Aristotle's *Rhetoric* made me realize more clearly than I had before that rhetoric is the art of talking sensibly about matters involving contingency, probability, and judgment. This notion was a contrast from my high-school debating days, which had quite an air of "Now I have absolutely proved" about them. It was also a contrast from the notion that rhetoric is a frothy thing, a substitute for wisdom, a smokescreen to cover inaction, an outpouring of fancy language, a devious tool of self-serving politicians.

After Aristotle, Harshbarger directed our attention to Cicero—not only the best speaker among the Romans, but the most talented, with his interests in politics, law, philosophy, and, in fact, the art of living. Cicero, who wrote more about the art of public speaking than any orator of any century, had something to say about every conceivable problem that confronted a speaker. His influence was enormous: great eighteenth- and nineteenth-century orators in Britain and America read his speeches diligently. Woodrow Wilson and Harry Truman were ardent readers of Cicero.

We then spent a long time with Quintilian—the distinguished Roman teacher of oratory—whose *Institutes* addressed the career of the orator, beginning with the selection of a nurse (engage one who can speak distinctly), and ending with a statement about the proper time to retire (well before being done in). Ryan, of course, was an admirer of Quintilian, making his presidential address, when he was elected to head the national speech association, on the modernity of Quintilian's message.

One day Harshbarger suggested that we might take a look at Longinus's *On the Sublime*. I decided to go to the library at 7:00 that evening and read until 9:00, then go to a movie; for some reason I was not on duty at the *Iowan* that night. I secured the book, picked it up for a moderately quick skim, but found that once in it, I could not put it down. Nine o'clock came and went, and I was still buried in it.

Longinus not only discussed the arts of speaking (and writing) as useful or practical arts, but cited passages that rose to sublime heights in literature, drama, and oratory. Audiences and readers

ould not only be entertained or persuaded, but *transported* by the
true sublime. To attain these heights, the speaker or writer must
draw richly from lofty thoughts, deep feeling, figures of speech,
noble diction. He must also be aware of selection, arrangement,
word order, and other details. To illustrate sublimity, Longinus
drew perceptively from Homer, Plato, Demosthenes, Euripides,
Sophocles, the Bible, and other sources. He formulated the now-
classic test of sublimity: an idea so expressed that it would grip the
imagination not only of the writer's or speaker's own generation, but
of generations to come. He reached for new, higher standards. An
ironical fact was that nobody knew who Longinus himself really was;
here was an inspiring treatise without a known author, and even
part of the treatise had been lost.

I was stirred by *On the Sublime,* and still am. If Longinus were
alive in the early 1980s, he would deplore the lack of great oratory,
as he did in his own day, but would find passages in Shakespeare,
Milton, Webster, Lincoln, and Churchill that would have delighted
him.

We uncovered these and other notions in that long-ago class in
rhetorical theory. We felt pride in discovering that these subtle and
penetrating thinkers were, in a real sense, teachers of speech.

The second course, with Baird, was a survey of British and
American public address. Names of great speakers passed in review:
from England, Chatham, Burke, Fox, Pitt, Sheridan, Erskine; from
America, Clay, Webster, Calhoun, Lincoln. I will not comment on
his stimulating seminar in detail except to note that each name was
associated with controversial issues. We read, discussed, dug into
original sources, presented papers. We speedily discovered that
conventional biographers had little to say, and often nothing to say,
about speakers as speakers. As to the occasional judgments and
appraisals expressed by these biographers, Wichelns of Cornell had
described them as "the literary criticism of oratory." I do not make
these statements idly. Years later, before undertaking to read several hundred volumes of Gladstone's letters and papers, I wrote a
British historian who had just gone through the lot, if I could expect
to find much about Gladstone as a speaker. He wrote that such a
search would not be worthwhile, adding the old, glib saying, "Great
speakers are born, not made." Quintilian and Cicero could have told
him that great speakers, like great people in any walk of life, are the

result of natural gifts plus unbelievably hard work. I determined to inspect every Gladstone volume; I found dozens of speech outlines and related materials, and even a lengthy essay that Gladstone had written detailing his own theory of public speaking. He worked as diligently to improve his speechmaking as any man that ever lived.

So we learned in Baird's class that what we wanted to know about themes, sources of argument, use of language, audience response, influence, preparation, delivery, we had to dig for ourselves in diaries, correspondence, newspapers. We got little help from secondary sources. Baird questioned, probed, speculated. He came at us from unexpected directions.

I asked him about writing a master's thesis. "Why don't you study Charles James Fox?" he suggested. Fox was an outstanding parliamentary debater, an advocate for American independence, a believer in free speech, an opponent of the slave trade, and so on, little has been written about him this century, et cetera, you are just the one to do it, et cetera.

The idea seemed promising and I departed. I had heard little of Fox, except, in a shadowy way, as being linked with Burke. I hurried to the library and fingered the card catalogue. Before I appeared at the *Iowan* that evening I knew much of what had been written about his career.

A few weeks' research showed me that no one had undertaken to describe the ways in which Fox had educated himself to be such a superb speaker. How could a young man enter the House of Commons at the age of twenty and within a few months establish himself as its most brilliant speaker? What did he do during his school years to prepare him for parliamentary debate? What was there in his politically oriented family to acquaint him, at an early age, with controversial issues? Whence came his extraordinary poise, self-assurance, and fluency? How did he develop his phenomenal ability in the art of argumentative discourse, both to support his own point of view, or to refute an opponent's? Available biographies glossed over these questions. Here was a chance for a student of rhetoric, armed with a new point of view, to offer an analysis that historians and biographers had neglected. Baird was pleased with this idea for a study and became more so as weeks went by and we reviewed the evidence I was accumulating.

So much for daytime activities. At night I lived in another world.

saw the news stories passing through the *Iowan*'s composing room listing General Motors, General Electric, American Telephone and Telegraph, and scores of others, whose stocks were fluctuating five dollars, ten dollars, fifteen dollars a share. Those swings seem unbelievable to investors of later years who rejoiced at a daily gain of even a dollar or two. That September the Dow Jones average, which earlier in the decade had sunk to 63, reached a high of 381. The market talk at Smith's Cafe continued to be full of hot tips that were certain winners. If the stock went up, the urge was to buy more of it, borrowing on margin if necessary. If a stock went down, it became an irresistible bargain. The business and professional men who lunched at Smith's talked of little else. Even their secretaries took modest plunges. The pot of gold could be moved into their own front rooms.

Then came October, with, in succession, an alarming Thursday, a dark gray Monday, and finally, Black Tuesday. As for that Thursday, the headlines shouted: 12,800,000 SHARES ARE SOLD. Police Called, Ambulances Clang as Stocks Crash. Floor traders collapsed and had to be carried from the floor. Losses totaled more than $5 billion; orders to sell came by telegraph and telephone, by overseas cable and radio; scores of stocks tumbled $15 to $70 a share. The 12,800,000 figure was ominous because it was three times the average daily volume.

As for that dark gray Monday, the headlines proclaimed: STOCKS SHRINK ANOTHER 10 BILLIONS. The subheadings amplified the disaster—that $10 billion sum was twice the cost of the Great War, the largest figure the world had ever seen.

Bleak, black Tuesday brought a drop of another $10 billion. Rallies followed on subsequent days, as buyers rushed to snap up what appeared to be bargains, but their investments, too, were swallowed up. The lofty Dow high of 381 hit a low of 41 in the next three years and did not pass 381 until 1954. The little group of speculators at Smith's saw their investments collapse, crumple, crash. Before long you could buy a hamburger and not hear any stock talk at all.

I had a bad scare one evening when I heard the rumor at Smith's that my Iowa City bank was in bad shape. As I had $38 on deposit, promptly the next morning I went to draw it out. I found the doors locked, a typewritten notice saying that the bank's condition was being reviewed by examiners. Eventually every bank in town closed its doors. If anyone had asked me at the time how much I had lost because of the stock-market crash and the dire events that followed, I would have said $38. No one could have predicted what lay ahead. At the time I was too interested in Aristotle, Longinus, Burke, Fox, Locke, Descartes, Helmholtz, and the theory that stuttering was caused by a shift of handedness in childhood, to worry about tycoons J. P. Morgan, Samuel Insull, and Charles M. Schwab, economist Irving Fisher, or even President Herbert Hoover. I also had my own problems.

46

An ominous hurdle for a graduate student in any area was to acquire a reading knowledge of two foreign languages, inevitably French and German.

To clear this hurdle meant facing professors from each department, meeting whatever standards they chose to set. So, while we were attending seminars in speech and psychology and doing research, we also had to plug away at foreign languages.

Eventually graduate schools were to offer more useful and pleasant substitutes (except in a few specialized areas), but for us there was no escape; we must demonstrate that we could read French and German, or no Ph.D. Students from other lands will smile, but we are not a bilingual people.

I expected little difficulty with French, which I had studied in high school and college, but I had had no exposure to German. I tackled French first. The examiner did not know what went on in a speech department, but thought that anything literary would be suitable. She approved my suggestion of *Le livre de mon ami* by Anatole France.

On the shelves I located not only *Le livre de mon ami* but also *My Friend's Book*. I read the two side by side; the translation made it unnecessary for me to look up continually words in a French-English dictionary. That convenience saved an immense amount of time and, what is more relevant, alerted me to idiomatic usages. A translator uses expressions that are not literal renderings but that catch the spirit as well as the meaning of the original.

The day came when I reported for the test. Although the examiner thought my translation was freewheeling, that was a merit of

orts; besides, she could always stop me in my tracks and demand a
literal meaning. After long probing, she signed my slip, which I
carried to the graduate office as tenderly as a $20 bill. Passing
French before I took my final master's degree examinations meant
that I could count those examinations not only as meeting a requirement for the M.A. but also as a qualifying examination for the
Ph.D. The net result would be to short-cut considerable red tape
and save several months' time.

Gradually my thesis entitled *Factors in the Life of Charles James
Fox Accounting for His Ability as a Parliamentary Speaker* began to
take shape. The cumbersome title was, and still is, typical of thesis
topics. Fox was an outstanding speaker almost as soon as he entered
Parliament, which is to say, before he was twenty-one; I sought to
explain why. From childhood he was in the company of sophisti-
cated adults, who, by encouraging his participation in their conversation, developed in him an immense self-confidence as well as a
facility in argument. As a young man he debated, competed in
oratorical contests, studied Greek and Latin oratory in the original,
participated in theatrical productions, and lived with a family that
breathed political discussion on every controversial issue. I found
examples and other forms of supporting evidence in journals,
diaries, correspondence, pamphlets, newspapers, and autobiog-
raphies of contemporaries. As most of these materials were not in
the university's collection, I sought out the interlibrary loan service,
bearing lists of the titles I needed, and one by one they trickled in
from the great libraries of the country. Scores of graduate students
will remember Irene Steidl, in charge of this service; she attended
to our wishes as diligently as she did those of a full professor. I also
visited the Newberry Library in Chicago to consult its indispensable
collection of eighteenth-century newspapers and pamphlets. In
short, I investigated every possible source to discover what Fox did
in boyhood and young manhood to develop his skill as a speaker.

Fox's personality was as intriguing as his speaking ability. He
could have married into a prominent family, but he chose to associate with women who hardly met the standards even of that
fast-living age. He was an obsessive gambler, drawing upon the
family fortune for vast sums to pay his debts. By "vast," I mean what
in the twentieth century would be reckoned in millions of dollars.
His passion for gambling continued even after he entered Parlia-

When the night's work at the *Daily Iowan* slackened, and the force sat around awaiting the last batch of front-page proofs, an enterprising operator could compose a letter to his girlfriend in the form of a news story. This Linotype, used for headlines as well as for straight matter, had all of the typefaces and sizes illustrated. The headline style is typical of that day—and of the next twenty years.

Seven Profs Stagger As Reid Passes French Exam

Rules Fall as Osceola Flash Attacks Ogre of Long Standing

(Special to Gus)

IOWA CITY, May 5 (AP) —Seven professors at the State University of Iowa died of heart failure today when it was announced by Pres. W. A. Jessup that Loren Reid, G of Osceola, had passed a French reading examination thus allowing him to qualify as a candidate for the degree of doctor of philosophy in speech.

Miss Knease Pays Tribute

"Of course the examination itself was merely a matter of routine," Miss Tacie Knease, department examiner, assured Associated Press reporters. "We had only to decide whether Mr. Reid was speaking the Mayonnaise dialect or that of the Rue de la Damfino. But I have only praise for his rendition. He translated so naturally and effortlessly that it seemed he had never studied the language."

Professor Baird Gasps

Just before he went under for the third time, Professor A. Craig Baird, of the department of speech, sighed: "This is too much. I never dreamed that it would take the French department so long to ascertain the exten of Mr. Reid's knowledge."

At home, lying on a sofa after his strenuous labors, Mr. Reid finally granted an interview to the besieging reporters. "Of course, I know it was a unique feat,' he said. "Naturally I am glad it is over. But—" and here his voice sank to a whisper — "please, boys, keep it out of the papers." Then he fell into a sort of stupor, muttered something, but the reporters caught only the word "June" spoke with a rising accent.

No hope is held out for the seven professors.

ment; at times he went directly from racetracks to House of Commons to gaming table. Yet seasoned politicians were immediately impressed by his effectiveness in debate; he was called "the phenomenon of the age." Young as he was, he was more than a match for his opponents, both in the ability to state an argument and to answer one. He could reason, he could use evidence, he had a sense of the humorous and also of the ridiculous, he was audacious.

During his career he was on what we would call the right side of nearly every controversial issue. He not only favored American independence, but he foresaw that an independent America would continue as a friend of Great Britain. He advocated discussion and negotiation instead of armed force as a means of settling disputes between nations. In an age when most people were arguing in support of the slave trade, using an ingenious assortment of economic and even military reasons, Fox denounced it because it was morally unjust and saw his belief enacted into legislation. He succeeded in getting the libel laws changed so that critics of the government could not be jailed or transported overseas.

Fox was one of the many who have served the public despite grievous shortcomings, even vices: partly sinner, by no means a saint, entirely human. His eloquent public speeches, in and out of Parliament, reflected his compassion for the slave, for the oppressed peoples of India, for American and French revolutionaries struggling for independence, for those who cherished religious freedom. His love of conversation led him to seek out people in all walks of life. "There isn't a man," he once said, "that I can't learn from, if he will talk to me." Edmund Burke, something of a genius himself, in his younger days called Fox "the greatest genius that ever lived." In his political campaigns, Fox was described simply as "a man for the people." When he died, in 1806, all London followed him to his grave.

What Fox achieved, he achieved through the power of the spoken word, both in large groups and small. He was an inspired choice for research by a graduate student in speech. I need to say he should not be confused with George Fox, a man of great piety, who lived two centuries earlier and who is famed as the founder of the Quaker church.

Eventually I got the thesis written and deposited in the graduate dean's office. I then spent a busy week going over in my mind

answers to questions that might be asked in an examination de
signed to meet the double purpose of approval for the M.A. and fo
the privilege of pursuing the doctorate. From my peers I had
learned that questions would not be limited to the thesis but would
roam widely over the fields of speech and psychology.

Only recently I had heard of a book called *Genetic Studies o
Genius* that had a sketch of Fox and scores of others, with estimates
of their IQ's. I well knew that committees liked to discover whether
a candidate was keeping abreast of current literature, so I decided
I must look at this study.

When the committee convened, with five members instead of the
nominal three or four, the first question was: "Have you seen Lewis
Terman's *Genetic Studies of Genius?*" I was glad to be able to say
yes, I had looked at it recently. So the ordeal got off to a good start.
When you are in a den of lions it is helpful if the lions only breathe
on you and do not take large bites. For two hours, questions were
fired at me from professors of speech, psychology, and history, on all
sorts of topics. I was grateful for every scrap of Grinnell background,
for the summer at the University of Chicago, for incessant talk with
other graduate students, for extra reading I had done to keep
abreast of seminars, for experiences in speaking and debating, for
years as a classroom teacher, for Ryan's insistence on "answering the
question that is asked." Finally the committee excused me and sent
me into the hall to await its verdict. I wondered what the decision
would be. The committee could fail me outright. It could pass me
for the M.A. but deny me the privilege to proceed to the doctorate.
It might say, "Well, you can continue for a Ph.D., but not in
speech—you'll have to begin over in another field." What it did was
to pass me for the M.A. and approve me for the Ph.D. in speech.

A few days later another committee passed Brigance in his final
oral examination, certifying that he had met every requirement for
the Ph.D. We now knew that a Ph.D. in speech was possible at
Iowa. Just because Brigance made the grade, however, did not
mean that the rest of us would. He had received his bachelor's
degree fourteen years previously; for eight years he had been a
distinguished member of the faculty of Wabash College; he had
written fifteen articles and two widely used textbooks. He was brilliant and articulate. And he was no walk-on graduate student; he had
been properly presented, to Mabie by Woolbert, the department's

most distinguished professor, and by Mabie to the graduate dean. And the same week Lambertson, also an older man with years of college-teaching experience, passed his final orals. Our small huddle of graduate students felt more optimistic, though not overly confident, about our own future.

When Gus came to Iowa City for commencement, we talked more earnestly than we had previously. She was thoroughly enjoying her second year of teaching. She was immersed in her favorite field, English. She talked of going back, so she could have another year at the same school. Yet we wanted to be together.

"You haven't finished your Ph.D.," she observed.

"No. And it may take longer than I thought. If I ever get it."

"Once you said we should wait until you got a good job."

"That's true. And right now the job market is tightening up."

"You wanted to have a thousand dollars in the bank.... How much do you have?"

"Three hundred and twenty dollars and fifty-eight cents."

She smiled. "I guess that's close enough."

The girls have more courage than the fellows. She agreed to resign her job, much as she loved it, and move in on my three hundred.

I suggested a June date. "No, I have a summer playground job. I'll need to get my clothes ready. But we can get married in August, after summer school." And then she added: "By then you'll have German out of the way."

As her offer was the best deal I was likely to make, I left it at that.

47

A man shudders to recall the perils of sailing into his first harbor and wonders how he managed to escape ripping the insides out of his craft or crashing into the dock itself.

Mornings were filled with classes; afternoons with dissertation research and studying German; nights with running the machine, setting ads and headlines, and avoiding the Bevo-label-flavored drinking water in the cooler.

Occasionally I slipped into the University Theatre, sat noiselessly in a back seat, and watched Vance Morton, Whitford Kane, or B. Iden Payne direct a play, to see how it came alive under skilled

238 Finally It's Friday

handling. I might get a job some day that required me to direct a play.

Sleep time was what I could seize between 3:00 A.M. and my first class, plus, occasionally, a nap. My fellow operators agreed that the difficulty was not in getting enough sleep, but getting it in one chunk.

I come from a line of hardworking people. I have seen Grandfather Tarwater plow corn on an August afternoon on his low-lying bottom farm near Grand River; the plot was so surrounded by trees that no breeze could penetrate the stifling humidity. He, like the team, was drenched with sweat; he stopped the horses every other row to let them get what rest they could. My Grandfather Reid, the one I never knew, spent weeks after the autumn crops were harvested chopping wood for winter's fires. At the end of the day he piled the wagon high and drove the team home, walking alongside with another piece of firewood on his shoulder. "Dan," his neighbors protested, "why do you do that?" "To save the horses." "Well, there'll be lots of horses long after you are dead and gone." People said he worked harder than the horses.

Our group of graduates also worked harder than the horses. The "dissertation credit" that supposedly gave us time to work on our writing was often only a bookkeeping entry; the list of courses was no shorter. Every area in our discipline was linked to another discipline. Psychology to back up speech pathology. History to back up public address. Dramatic literature and fine arts to back up theater. Physics to back up speech science and stage lighting. Around the cornices of the older buildings were the names of great men. ARISTOTLE. LOCKE. FARADAY. DARWIN. LEIBNITZ. SHAKESPEARE. HELMHOLTZ. A score of others. Before we had been graduated, we could identify them all. Scattered around the campus were half a dozen divisional libraries. LAW. PHYSICS. CLASSICAL LANGUAGES. EDUCATION. ENGINEERING. We pursued assignments in each; even OBSTETRICS. (Birth injuries can cause spastic speech.)

I did not dread the writing of a five-hundred-page dissertation so much as facing the German examiner. A slightly alleviating factor was his reputation for being reasonable. The preceding June, however, the graduate school had sponsored a dinner honoring the successful Ph.D. candidates of that spring. One professor had made a lighthearted after-dinner talk. The response by a selected Ph.D.

candidate had been equally lighthearted. In fact it was so light-hearted that it poked fun at the language requirement, coming down hard on the examiner in German, observing that he was so softheaded that the requirement was a cream puff. The examiner, present on that occasion, was furious.

Those of us still in the wings were horrified when we learned what had happened. The rules of the game had suddenly been stiffened. From now on the German department would be rough on us.

I would be the first of our group to face the new rules.

As material to be examined on, I selected a slender book on phonetics that described the individual sounds of speech. The vocabulary was technical but at least I knew what the German phonetician was trying to say about each sound. As Stephen Jones had surveyed the phonetic alphabet with us, and the sound systems of various languages, I was on familiar ground. My teacher of German for Ph.D. candidates had introduced us to grammar and vocabulary. I had learned that the German sentence was an awesome creation, the verb often at the end coming.

Among the available examination dates was one scheduled two days before my wedding day. "By then," Gus had said, "you'll have German out of the way."

My inquiries about tutoring led me to a student in the School of Nursing who had had a major in German. We spent many sessions on the little book. Between my knowledge of phonetics and hers of the language, we evolved a translation. She was invaluable in identifying tenses, idioms, and verb forms. As the summer wore on, the reading got easier. Yet I felt uneasy and considered postponing the examination. A candidate who failed one trial could not appear for another until after a substantial lapse of time. Even so, I decided to accept the risk. A man about to be married does not give up easily.

On the appointed afternoon I reported to the examiner. A dozen others had assembled, scattered at seats around the classroom. Each of us had brought an official slip indicating our authority to be there, with spaces for his verdict and signature.

We looked intently at him when he entered; I was surprised to see that he was not carrying a poleax. He walked to the desk at the head of the first aisle, opened the candidate's book at random, and asked her to read a passage. I could hear his questions and her answers, seldom prompt, often faltering. Without comment he moved to the next desk and then another. I was halfway down the second aisle. His questions to me were not on phonetics, where I was comfortable, but on grammar, where I was shaky. Even so, there were moments when I was sure of my ground. He moved to the others and then started around the second time.

Now came the crunch. Everything in my future seemed to be at stake. How could I be a proper bridegroom without knowing German verb forms? As he approached closer and closer, I could hear the mumbling of questions and answers. I saw him sign two slips, the lucky holders leaving the room hardly touching foot to floor. I heard him tell four others to stay for a third round. If they did not pass, they would have to wait weeks before being allowed another chance.

When he came to my desk, he flipped the book open to a place where the pages were spotless. This time the questions were on the phonetics; I supplied answers even when he asked about sounds peculiarly German. He signed my slip and I fled from the room.

Next day I wrote final examinations in three courses. The rooms were so hot—air conditioning was still decades away—that the perspiration from my hands and arms blotted the page. After the last test, I took the train to Des Moines. It was a Friday. I had a wedding rehearsal and, besides, I had my own wardrobe to get in order. On Saturday I would become a married man.

48

If you are about to undergo a trifle like having your appendix carved out, the surgeon will explain in detail what lies ahead; but if you are going to get married, a more critical operation, you are left in the dark about what is to happen. You are informed only on a "need to know" basis. Wedding preparations, being in the realm of the bride-elect and her mother, are revealed only casually to the groom. Since the groom does not need to know much, he is not told much.

The first surprise, which had come early in the summer just after we had made our big decision, was a series of parties suddenly scheduled by the friends of the bride-to-be. As a linotype operator I had set up hundreds of wedding items, never dreaming that the event itself would get closer to me than my copy tray. From time to time on my visits to Des Moines, Gus had happily displayed the loot—kitchen gadgets, mainly, like measuring spoons or flour sifters, with, occasionally, towels or a whisk broom and dustpan. Then the heavy stuff had begun to roll in: plates or cups and saucers from the pattern she had selected at Younkers, sheets and pillow-cases, pewter pitchers (six in all), a big picture two by three feet (this from my most recent competitor for her attention), knife sets, pans, skillets. I would ask, "Who gave us this silver salt and pepper shaker set," and she would reel off a name I had never heard of: a church friend, or a business associate of the family, or a neigh-bor, or parents of long-ago North High schoolmates. So my second surprise was that I was to share presents given us by strangers, people I had never met and might never see. Every young couple must feel considerable astonishment that their parents not only know a host of people, but that these same people generously come forward on wedding occasions with good wishes and presents.

Though nearly a year had passed since the great crash, one would hardly have known a depression was beginning if he had looked at the heap of gifts gradually filling an upstairs bedroom.

Our number-one gift was a set of sterling silver—a dozen five-piece place settings, with extra pieces. I had grown up in a home with no silver whatever, and here was enough to serve a football team and its coach. The benefactors were two of her aunts. I promptly dubbed them "the silver aunties" and learned to love them dearly. We later estimated that this cascade of silver cost the formidable sum of $150. Most of her friends also received that much sterling, or more, as wedding presents; yet silver was to become so prohibitive in cost that their granddaughters would receive very little. Father and Mother gave us an enormous set of china, includ-ing big plates, medium plates, small plates, cups and saucers, serv-ing dishes, a huge meat platter, and a gravy boat. The set was not fancy—I think it was the by-product of an advertising deal—but we would eat handsomely, if we could earn enough to buy the food.

We were to begin our married life with only two electric appliances—a toaster and an iron. Well, three, if you count a hair curler that she already had. The toaster had sides that when low-ered, let the bread flip over, and was a decided improvement over holding a slice of bread, speared on a long-handled fork, over a gas burner. The iron was a grim necessity for linens and clothing, in-

New Pavement Said to Cause Catastrophe

An unlooked for result of the completion of the pavement between Des Moines and Osceola was the announcement this week of the approaching marriage of Miss Augusta Towner to Mr. Loren D. Reid.

"For a long time," said Mr. H. S. J. Towner, commenting on the event, "everything was in our favor. A good rain would knock out the roads for at least a week, and thus most effectively keep the young man at a distance. And then, too, there was usually a detour or two could be depended on to keep things rosy at our house. I used to watch the road reports closer than my change at the meat market.

"Of course, there were some disadvantages in the plan, too. A light sprinkle after he got to Des Moines would keep him here at least a week. But then, about that time, the highway commission built a new bridge north of Indianola, and when I heard of the fifteen mile detour I felt quite encouraged. But at that time he went to Iowa City, and shortly after the commission announced the completion of the pavement between Iowa City and Des Moines. That was the final straw. I think I'll go Bolsheviki in the next commission election.

"However," he concluded, "I feel I've done my best in the cause, but of course you can't expect much whenever the commission keeps following the two around with paved roads."

Mr. Dudley A. Reid, father of the young man was frankly relieved. "To date I've bought 215348 gallons of gas and 4385 quarts of oil. I feel that my income will be considerably lightened. Naturally I am in better spirits than I have been for years.

"I hope their future life is just one paved road after another," he added.

Another Well-Matched Couple

Not every girl is fortunate enough to have a suitor who can compose his thoughts in hot metal. This "news story" was composed on the *Tribune's* Model 14 Linotype; the headline was hand-set in Cheltenham bold italic. The illustration is a fortuitous selection from the newspaper's extensive supply of livestock illustrations, used for sale bills and who knows what else.

After three years of courtship between towns connected by dirt roads, the couple finally saw the strategic lanes between Osceola–Des Moines and Iowa City–Des Moines paved. This personal reflection is another way of recording that the years between 1927 and 1930 were active periods of hard-surfaced construction throughout mid-America.

cluding trousers. All college men knew how to press pants, using a hot iron and a heavy, damp, pressing cloth. We and our friends did not get the big-ticket items for five or ten years or more. This rate of acquisition seemed normal.

Even the groom had preparations to make for the wedding. Following Emily Post, who also advised the Vanderbilts and Morgans, I had learned that, when making reservations at the hotel where the couple would spend its first night, the groom should candidly tell the reservation clerk: "This reservation is for a honeymooning couple, so we would like a nice room." The clerk, thus alerted, wrote Emily, would take pride in setting aside his finest accommodations; he might even add a bouquet, a basket of fruit, and a personal note of good wishes. Seeking a private phone at which I could make this delicate call, I went to the booth at the Rock Island station to call a hotel at Ames, an hour's drive when the roads were dry. The clerk assured me that a sumptuous room would be in perfect readiness for us.

Another detail that Emily assigned the groom was to offer cigars and candy to the guests. Selecting the candy was no problem—a five-pound box of Fanny Farmers would delight the females. But the cigars represented an entrance into an established male rite— the accepted way of responding to congratulations when one got married, had a baby, or got a new job. I consulted the clerk at the Union Cigar Store, who showed me a long, fat, dark beauty of the kind that one associates with the wealthy and prosperous, and who judged that a boxful would be exactly the right amount. I did not think to tell him that many of my guests were young college men for whom something thin, pale, mild, and short would be challenge enough. Chocolates and cigars took the best part of a ten-dollar bill, but I reflected that a man gets married only once and should do it right.

We had invited our psychology professor, the Reverend Doctor Stoops, to officiate. He replied with rare grace: "The man who has won the heart of Augusta Towner captures my imagination." He had reviewed the ceremony with us the afternoon before the wedding; it was partly Congregational, partly Anglican, partly John D. Stoops. He offered to jettison the line asking those who disapproved of the marriage to step forward or forever hold their peace. I was amazed that he had the authority to make this sweeping alteration, but I was glad to see it go; I had overcome too many obstacles to want to face another. He liked "love, honor, and cherish" better than "love, honor, and obey." Gus also liked it. I thought it a reasonable concession.

I spent my last night as a single man in Osceola. Next afternoon I drove to Des Moines, carefully avoiding the Towner residence, as it was bad luck to see your bride on your wedding day before the ceremony. She was, of course, fully occupied; in addition to the usual preparations she and her sister stamped out a brushfire that afternoon in the neighboring vacant lot. But for her timely exertions, her house might have been burned down, silver, pewter pitchers, gravy boat, and all.

We were married in her home in front of the living-room fireplace. The rehearsal was a simple affair; most of it was impromptu, as maid-of-honor, best man, and even the groom learned cues and duties minutes before the ceremony. ("You stand there on the porch until you get the signal from the piano player. Walk through those two doors and stand in front of the fireplace just this side of the poker. The preacher will tell you what to say and when you can kiss the bride.")

By 8:00 the house was filled. Father and Mother were there; later he wrote a piece for the *Tribune* contrasting his son's wedding with his own. He and his bride had driven in a buggy to the preacher's home, remaining sitting during the ceremony. We did not have a buggy, but I had stashed our getaway Oakland in a secret place. At the proper moment Gus's father would drive us to it, and we would leave for Ames and Lake Okoboji.

With my best man, I waited, clad in the tux I had wheedled out of Father during my senior year, until I heard the piano music begin and was flashed the signal. At the altar I met Gus, all smiles, eyes glistening, dressed in the gown her mother had worn at the dawn of the century. The Reverend Doctor Stoops was there, short, a little stout, slightly bald, hair fringed with gray, small goatee, looking at us over his glasses as he might have in psychology class. "Dearly beloved," he said, and all the rest. I summon these memories fifty years after the event.

In minutes we had promised to love, honor, and cherish. Like any bride, she spoke her lines in a clear, bell-like voice. Like any groom, I mumbled and stumbled. Our college friends, filing past us, made a big point of congratulating me vigorously, saying to her, waggishly, in tones registering heavy doubt, "I *hope* you'll be happy." In the dining room the guests enjoyed what we called, in newspaper language, "dainty refreshments."

The bride went upstairs to change; I circulated through the rooms offering cigars and chocolates; the women took Fanny Farmers and as the men liked the candy better than the dark, forbidding, El Productos, I was left with most of the cigars, and eventually threw most of them away. After I had changed clothes, I tried to act like a man who had no intention whatever of leaving the house. But when I got the high sign I dashed to the door, joining my brand-new wife to make a run for her family car. Or so we had planned; but our college friends intervened, separated her from her father, and carried her to their own car. When they tried to stuff her inside it, she stiffened like an ironing board, foiling that attempt. Her father, in hot pursuit, grabbed her, saying, in commanding tones, "Come along, gal," and succeeded in separating her from her kidnapers and getting her in his own car. The two took off at top speed; the bandits followed in their car; then came a Hollywood chase through the streets of western Des Moines. I shudder to think about what might have happened, but after a time the pursuing car dropped back and the bride and her father could proceed, more carefully, to the original rendezvous where the groom was impatiently waiting, wondering whether he would ever see his bride again or not.

In no time we passed the Des Moines city limits and seemed to have the road to Ames all to ourselves. The day, an August scorcher, had only slightly cooled, but the car whipped up its own breeze and the dust we kicked up floated behind us. Before we knew it we were in Ames and in the small town of those days had no trouble finding our hotel.

The night clerk gave us the number of our room—I am not sure there was a key—and we quickly found it, two stories up—small, hot, airless. Like most hotels of that day, ours was close to the depot and next to the tracks; our room, at the back, was on the track side. We could hear switch engines chunking back and forth—slamming single freight cars into short lines, and short lines into longer assemblies—bells ringing, engines puffing, cars banging, voices shouting. Obviously a hotel executive who would assign newlyweds to such a room had never heard of Emily Post, much less have the

Honeymooners at Lake Okoboji. Partly as a gag, this young couple decided to try for something ultra high tone and artistic in the way of photography. The generation ahead of us would have called these bathing suits daring, if not actually immoral.

race or the enterprise to think of flowers or even a welcoming note. But who really cared? It was our Day One.

In later years people grinned when I told them we heard switch engines all night long, but that's the way it was. The social historian in me says, "How lucky to have a honeymoon so typical of the age—no air conditioning, no wall-to-wall carpeting, and with beautiful background noises of trains!" I hurry to other pleasant memories: the long, quiet drive to Lake Okoboji, over roads that were now gravel surfaced everywhere, the cabin with magazines and a phonograph, a kitchenette with a range that used clean-burning coal oil. We put on our bathing togs and went for a swim in Okoboji's cool, unpolluted waters; we got out the rowboat and paddled half a mile to the next cabin and back—no outboard motors to be seen or heard anywhere; we did our first shopping in the nearby grocery store; we went to a dance that evening at the big pavilion. No German exam, no brushfires, no playground mobs; just each other.

We stayed until the morning after Labor Day. Then the pavilion closed, the grocery store locked up for the winter, the visitors slipped home by the scores. As the place got almost too quiet, we loaded the Oakland and headed for Des Moines.

All this was in 1930. Another year and I would have a Ph.D. in speech and certainly a $3,500 job. And as a final note, I will mention that the Reverend Doctor Stoops lived to be a hundred. Decades later, at class reunions, I could remind him that he had married us when he was a young man of sixty-two.

49

We settled in the best $30-a-month apartment to be had in Iowa City—Dorothea Thonssen and other veteran graduate wives claimed to know every one, and even a few at $25. We found we could transport everything we owned—wedding presents, books, clothes, my Underwood, and a floor lamp—in the Oakland, skillfully disemboweled by removing the bulky backseat cushions. In our two rooms, the kitchen table doubled as a study table; the living-room sofa could be made up into a bed; the bathroom, down the hall, was shared with the family. The house nestled against the Rock Island station, but after a time we didn't notice whistles, bells, screeching brakes.

I signed for the usual fifteen-hour block of courses. I was now a Master of Arts, getting closer to a Ph.D. Gus enrolled in dramatic literature, poetry writing, stage design, stage lighting, gradually accumulating enough hours for a master's degree. I continued to report at the night shift of the *Iowan*, starting at 5:00 P.M. Gus's day was also turned upside down; she would be waiting for me when I got home at 2:00 A.M. or later.

Though we, like our graduate colleagues, had limited finances—my $320.58 quickly vanished, as did her own savings—we had a social life of sorts. Being entertained at a Sunday evening cheese soufflé was high living. Dinner at the Harshbargers, the Barneses, and the Thonssens was an occasion. In turn they came to our abode. Once we invited the Bairds and Gus decided to serve oyster stew. It is easy to forget that oysters then were delicious, readily available, and cheap. "What if they don't like oysters?" I ventured. "Well," she reflected, "at least they'll like the crackers." Of course the Bairds, with their New England background, liked oysters. Our evenings were filled with talks about books and theater.

Occasionally we were in a home with a radio. Everybody enjoyed Baron Munchausen. His program followed an always predictable and, therefore, enormously delightful, format: first, a tall tale; next, an expression of doubt from his straight man; and finally, the clincher: "Vuz you dere, Sharlie?" Nearly everybody listened to Amos and Andy, and at the conclusion of each program the workers at the city water plant claimed they could detect a sudden drawdown of water, as a city full of listeners simultaneously rushed to the bathroom.

With other students, we incessantly talked shop. We were driven to learn everything we could. We kept abreast of journal articles and new books. As at final doctoral exams we could be quizzed on anything, we shared every idea we ran across. One psychology professor thought everybody should master not only names and contributions of psychologists but also where they were teaching: who was at Harvard, who at Cornell, who at Chicago. We quizzed each other: "Where's McDougall?" "Duke" had to be the answer.

Horror stories kept surfacing about final oral examinations. One professor was reputed to have thrust a German book at a candidate, demanding that she translate a paragraph. Another was said to have left the examining room, gone to the library, looked up a point to be

sure about it in his own mind, and returned to quiz the candidate on
it. In the middle of an oral examination faculty rivalries sometimes
bobbed up, putting the candidate squarely in the middle of their
conflicting points of view.

When the School of Medicine moved to its new home across the
Iowa River, its old quarters, East Hall, a giant of a building, were
turned over to the Graduate School. Advanced students were assigned individual offices. I found myself in splendid accommodations that had been part of the venereal-disease ward, a suitable
assignment for a former occupant of a room numbered 606. Fred
Evans, studying British homiletics, was officed in the room where
his wife had given birth to their first baby. We filled our offices with
books and research notes. We became acquainted with graduate
students in other fields.

Some of our group became famous in their specialties. One was
Wendell Johnson, whom we called Jack, after the heavyweight
champion. He became a renowned authority on stuttering, though
he himself had a severe stutter. He learned to manage his own
fluency—in later years I heard him lecture almost flawlessly. Yet at
any moment he might get tangled. He liked to tell the story about
the boy who came to the Iowa speech clinic.

"Wh-wh-what is your p-p-problem?" asked Johnson.

"I st-st-stutter," said the boy.

"How-how l-l-long have you had this p-p-p-problem?"

The boy reflected, then blurted: "D-d-do y-you st-st-stut-stutter?"

"Y–y–y–yes, a l–l–little," admitted Johnson.

"W-w-well, what in the h-h-h-hell am I do-do-doing h-h-here?"

We attended the free lecture series: Sir Hubert Wilkins, polar
explorer; Lewis Browne, author; Will Durant, philosopher and historian. For each lecture, Professor Benjamin Franklin Shambaugh,
political scientist, prepared an imaginative introduction. Shambaugh had a majestic appearance, a magnificent voice, and a dramatic style in everything he did. I never saw him walk across a
muddy farmyard and enter a privy, but if he did, he would make it
appear as if he were strolling down the velvet carpet in Westminster
Abbey at the queen's coronation. Nobody, repeat nobody, could
preside over a commencement, or introduce a speaker, as Shambaugh did. He invariably intrigued and captivated both the speaker
and the audience, and he did it time and again.

Other outstanding events we had to miss. Ethel Barrymore, in person, came to town with her repertory troupe. Tickets were $1 an extravagant price. Her one-night stand came toward the end of a month when most of us were on the tag end of our budgets. We simply did not have the money, but explained sadly to ourselves "We'll see her some other time, after we get that good job." She was then only fifty-two. We never did see her.

One morning Gus and I were sitting at the breakfast table eating our usual bowl of cornflakes: notes, books, and the Underwood pushed to one side. Suddenly she mused: "We should really have a carpet for this floor."

I choked on my cornflakes when I heard this thunderbolt. It had never occurred to me that marriage included buying a carpet. She couldn't help noticing my consternation.

"Even a piece of used carpet would do," she went on. "It doesn't need to be fancy. Something to cover the bare floor."

As no young husband could deny his wife a piece of used carpet, we visited a secondhand furniture store. We entered an appallingly dingy establishment, passing rows of battered sofas, caved-in easy chairs, floor lamps, dining-room suites, bed frames. The air smelled musty. We approached the proprietor of this emporium, who was sitting on the corner of a cluttered desk. "We would like to look at used carpets," I said.

Not moving from his perch, he motioned over his shoulder. "You'll find some stuff back there," he mumbled.

We saw a small assortment of carpets; some flat, some folded, some in rolls. All were partly soiled, as if they had just been ripped from the floors of abandoned houses. We saw nothing appealing and left.

The problem subsided, then one weekend we found ourselves in Des Moines. The morning paper had announced a sale at Davidson's, Iowa's leading furniture store. As in this depressed era people had slowed down their buying, the management needed to unload in its scramble for cash.

In moments we were on the Ingersoll car, headed downtown. The atmosphere at Davidson's was attractive. We took the elevator to the rug department on the fourth floor. Here we saw, stacked in piles four feet high, acres of rugs. We stopped to look at a few of these beauties. A man in his mid-fifties approached us.

"What can I show you?" he asked, pleasantly. "We're interested in buying a secondhand rug," I said, awed by all this splendor.

"Oh, fine. You young folks are furnishing a home."

Of course, I reflected. We are not buying a used rug, we are furnishing a home. This is real class. This salesman is indeed a perceptive gentleman. This salesman can tell quality customers. I brightened right away.

"Do you live in Des Moines?" he asked.

I found myself confiding in him fully. Her parents live here; he's an electrical contractor. My family is in the newspaper business at Osceola. We're graduate students at the state university.

"We have several nice used rugs," he went on, nodding understandingly. "I'll be glad to show them to you. While we're here, however, let me show you two or three of the lovely rugs in this stack." He pointed to the one on top, let us look at it, invited Gus to feel it, showed us the close-woven, heavy webbing on the back. Then, slowly, he began to peel back the ones under it, flopping each one over as soon as we had viewed it. Halfway down he came to one that Gus liked immensely.

"That's an Anglo-Persian," he explained. "This pattern is magnificent." He invited us to finger the thick nap and showed again the firm webbing. "We've been selling these for $124 but have a special of $89.50." Seeing my jaw sag, he continued, urbanely, "Most people buy these on terms. Eight dollars a month or whatever sum they feel comfortable with." My jaw slipped back into place. Eight dollars was ten hours' work on the *Iowan*'s number-one ad machine.

He showed us others, but Gus kept coming back to the Anglo-Persian. "Do you like it?" she asked me. I did indeed, but I also knew our bank balance. "We need to think it over," I finally said, making the last stand of a young husband who was willing to face the inevitable but not too much of it all at once. I asked the salesman:

"What's your name?"

"Rowe. This rug is as good a buy as we have on the floor. You know, a rug is the purchase a couple should make first. When people come into a room, they look immediately at the rug. Why don't you think about it and let me know what you decide?"

The long, slow ride home on the clanking, complaining Ingersoll car gave me time to agree that Mr. Rowe's Anglo-Persian was the rug for us. Next morning we were back on the sales floor as soon as the doors were open and hurried to the stack. We located our rug, but fastened to it was a red tag marked "Sold."

Gus was near tears. "Well," I said, "that's too bad. Why don't we pick out another one?" By the side of Our Rug, however, the others looked colorless, ordinary. Gus was inconsolable. "I'll go hunt up Mr. Rowe," I offered. "Maybe he has another one."

I waited while he concluded a sale, then told him we had decided we wanted that rug, but that it had been sold; we wondered if he had another just like it.

"No," he confessed, "your rug is not sold; I put the tag on it myself. I was sure you would be back." When Gus heard these words, she brightened like the rising sun. He prepared an install-ment contract and we were about to sign it.

"Now really, you don't want to put this lovely rug on the floor without a pad. Why don't you let me add another eight dollars to your bill and you pay it along with the rest?" By now I was in the mood of the big spender, the young man who was furnishing a home. "Of course," I agreed. He commented: "You and Mrs. Reid have made a great buy, and you will get years of good service from this rug."

As a student of rhetoric, I reflected that we had seen an unusual demonstration of fine salesmanship, especially as contrasted with the listless attitude of the Iowa City used-furniture dealer and his stuff in the back room. I commented on Rowe's interest in selling and asked him if some salesmen sold notably more than others, even working with the same stock. "Oh, yes," he replied, "I will sell several times as much as any beginner. You need to study human nature, you must know your merchandise, and you must assure yourself that your customer is happy with his purchase—that he hasn't bought something he will regret next day."

When we got the rug to Iowa City, we did find that visitors looked at it the first thing. Actually, it was one of the few things in the room *to* look at. Eventually four children and four German Shepherd dogs were to romp and play on that rug, without dimming its luster. When after thirty years its linen fringe was completely worn away, we gave it to the church for use in a classroom. It gave another decade of service there and was worn almost all the way down to its heavy, close backing, before it was finally abandoned.

50

The telegram on my copy pan at the *Iowan* glared at me like a danger sign. The other printers collected as I approached it and watched as I picked up its yellow envelope: a telegram meant special news, often bad. I ripped the envelope open: MOTHER SERIOUSLY HURT IN PRESS ACCIDENT COME HOME IMMEDIATELY LOVE. Ten words—the maximum length for the minimum rate. My friends could tell by watching me that the message was alarming. I read what it said; they agreed I must leave at once. Printers know what a press accident can mean.

As I hurried to our apartment I reviewed the available train schedules for the remainder of the day. Students know by heart the train times between campus and home. Together Gus and I wondered and worried about what could have happened. I telephoned both home and office but nobody was there to answer. Press accidents were rare but alarming. Was the press the small jobber that opened and closed its jaws like a vise, or the Huber with exposed belts and gears and the big cylinder that rolled over a flat bed? In either situation, fingers or even hands could be caught and mangled. Or worse.

I caught the Rock Island home in a mental fog of worry and fear. After two changes, I arrived at 3:00 A.M. and was met by one of the printers; he, too, knew departure and arrival times and had stayed up to meet me. The news was grim; Mother had caught her right arm in the Huber, and it had to be amputated. Don was out of town; Father was in a state of shock. Mother was in Dr. Sells's hospital. Only Dorothy, now Don's wife, had been available to get the word to the absent family.

At the hospital a nurse greeted me and took me to Mother's room. The air was strong with the smell of ether. Mother, white-faced, managed a smile. She put her strong left arm around me as I bent over to kiss her.

"Mother," I said, "You trying to ruin a perfectly good press?"

She grinned. "Son, they're taking me away in pieces. But there's a good deal of me left." The twinkle in her eye, slight as it was, showed she still had heart and spirit.

She was positive she would recover. Her next words were: "Since it had to be, I'm glad it was me and not one of you boys." She had

thought it all out. "I could never get over anything happening t
you or Don. And an accident like this would have killed your father.

"He was out of town when it happened, but came here as soon a
he got back and is terribly broken up. You must look after him. Do
can't get home till mid-morning. Dorothy has been with me and le
just a little while ago."

I lingered to reassure myself about her condition, but she in
sisted: "Go look after your father." The nurse entered, overhear
her, and said that I should do what I could to comfort him; Mothe
was out of danger at least for the time being. "All we can do now i
wait. I'll be right here and the doctor is sleeping in a room down th
hall where he will be available." I knew her well, of course; I ha
been a frequent visitor at the hospital and she had given me many
news item.

When I reached Father, he greeted me and broke into sobs. "If
had stayed home, this terrible accident would never have hap
pened."

I knew that what he said was true as soon as I learned the details
The foreman was printing election ballots on the big newspape
press. As the ink fountain was not correctly adjusted, it put an extr
blob of ink on a roller which in turn made a smear on each ballot
Father had always looked after ink-fountain adjustments, which re
quired a delicate touch with thumbscrews. No one else really un
derstood how the fountain worked. Mother knew that the ballot
must be printed that afternoon, to meet a deadline, so she stoo
alongside with a small rag in her hand and wiped the surplus ink o
the spinning roller at each revolution of the press. She would no
assign this dangerous task to the foreman; he must have agreed wit
reluctance even to feed the press. After a few hundred successfu
wipes, the rag caught and pulled her fingers, and then her righ
hand and arm, under the rollers, mangling her hand and most of he
arm. She screamed; the foreman instantly slammed the press int
reverse, releasing her. She fell to the floor. He rushed out the bac
door, across the alley, up the stairs, and in a minute Dr. Sells was o
the scene. Although she got instant medical attention, nothing coul
be done to save the arm.

For two hours I let Father talk himself out. What could I say
when he kept repeating the simple fact that if he had been there
the accident would not have occurred? He would have adjusted th

fountain by turning a few screws, and the ink blob would have disappeared. Now I realize, as everyone does, that an apparent immediate cause is only one in a chain of increasingly remote causes, but all I could say then was to make the observation that none of us can foresee the future; to remind him that he had left on a purely business trip with only the welfare of the family in mind; that Mother had a hundred times supervised the printing of all kinds of jobs; that she did not blame him for being away, nor did the office force, nor I, nor Don; and finally to express my faith that Mother's strength and pluck would pull her through.

That approach failing, I tried another. "When did you eat last?" "Not since yesterday noon." I persuaded him to go to Adams' Grill where we would be able to get breakfast even at this early hour. The slow, cool walk interrupted a conversation that was getting nowhere.

The leisurely breakfast also helped. One of the small, perennial jokes in our family was Father's insistence that his coffee always be steaming hot. Frequently when eating out, he had sent the coffee back to be reheated. Sometimes he sent it back a second time; this action invariably challenged the cook, who took care to return it bubbling. On this occasion the coffee was lukewarm, so he asked that it be reheated. We both had to grin; and grin again when it was returned, scalding hot. The incident might have reassured him that we were still a family and would go on as a family. The meal also refreshed him. Once back home, I persuaded him to try to sleep, which he agreed to do, being reassured that Mother was under constant watch.

In the next few days, Mother's host of friends packed her room with flowers; so many vases arrived that there was barely room to walk from the door to her bed. She knew every business and professional man and woman in town, and scores of others; they were shocked to hear of her accident. She had hordes of visitors, and, strangely enough, a little of her good temper and unwavering optimism rubbed off on each. The minister who preached a sermon about her said it as well as anybody: "I went to cheer her," he told the congregation, "and left being cheered myself."

When I saw she was out of danger, I returned to Iowa City. Father was so shattered that he could hardly bear to enter the back office. A few months later he wrote that he and Mother had decided to retire and were planning to sell the *Tribune* to its competitor, which had recently assumed new management. They had reviewed their finances and had decided they did not need to work longer.

After only a few days they could not bear the thought of being idle, so they investigated other newspaper properties. Their next letter told me they had acquired the *Booster-Express* at Valley Junction, Iowa, a suburb of Des Moines, later known as West Des Moines. I realized they were in business deeper than ever. Their retirement had lasted exactly nine days.

At Valley Junction, Mother, already crippled in one knee, now had to face the world with one arm. She tried running the machine for a while but that task was beyond her. A printing office is not made for left-handed people; job presses, for example, are designed so that the right hand does the major work of adjusting each sheet snugly against the gauges, whereas the left hand has only to snatch it out when printed. In handsetting, the agile right fingers select each character and place it properly, top side up and right side to, in the "stick," or holder; the clumsier left fingers merely hold it in place. Don, a lefty, had had to learn to perform these operations like right-handed people. Lacking her right arm, Mother took her post in the front office and became the managing director of the *Booster-Express*.

Gradually printers looked to Mother as the person who saw that work was completed on schedule. The *Booster-Express* printed not only its own paper but also two others, plus magazines and booklets. Mother waited on customers, quoted prices on small jobs, helped figure big jobs, ordered paper and other needs from suppliers, paid the bills, and collected accounts. She did the hiring, and, if necessary, the firing. She opened the office and was the last to leave.

Father and Don wanted her to get an artificial arm to attach to the stump that only partly filled the top of that empty sleeve. They persuaded her to talk to a salesman, himself an amputee, who fitted her with an arm and hand—she could not bear the thought of a hook—the fingers of which could be opened and closed by straps operated from a leather harness around her shoulders, concealed by her dress. After a few days she abandoned the contraption. "All those straps," she confided to me later, "kept cutting into my flesh."

Other one-armed salesmen, and occasionally saleswomen, appeared at intervals. "Look how I do it," they would say as they wrote with a pencil, or picked up a paper clip, or opened a ledger, or used knife and fork, but as she watched them she kept shaking her head. Occasionally she tried other appliances, but only under a strict "on approval" basis. Eventually each nearly successful one-armed salesperson returned to see the right-handed appliance he or she had hoped to sell, lying unused in its box, and regretfully, even reprovingly, carried it back to its maker. The art of prosthetics still needed many years, including those of a world war, in which to perfect itself.

Meanwhile, Mother steadily assigned new tasks to her left arm. She had her beauty operator cut off her waist-long dark brown, almost black, hair, to the now-fashionable bobbed-hair length. This hairdo she could manage by herself. At first Father helped her with corset and shoes but she eventually managed to dress herself. She located a special bit of cutlery, equipped with tines and also with a cutting edge, that served as both knife and fork. They moved to a new, downtown apartment, first checking to make sure its stairwell had rails along each side. To simplify housework, she acquired a vacuum cleaner. Father ingeniously designed handholds for her at strategic locations, as, for example, in the bathroom, so she could move about easily, although actually she was still agile and mobile. She had abandoned driving the car years before since her sons had so eagerly taken over the wheel.

Immediately she had to learn to write. Jobs had to be figured, notes taken about news stories, intrashop memos written. At first her jottings were scarcely legible, but she improved. Before long I was getting notes at school from her. Her left-handed script looked almost exactly like her right.

She demonstrated her achievements proudly. I heard no complaints or regrets; her life seemed rich and full. She did, one day, after an especially close mother-son talk, confess that in the stump of her arm she could feel discomfort that seemed to come from her missing fingers—perhaps their final sensation before being detached. If, later, I asked her, "Mother do you still feel that pain?" she would say, "Yes, son, it's there all the time." A surgeon tried to block the nerve with an injection but the relief was only temporary. Yet she never mentioned her discomfort unless I asked.

On my visits I drove her to downtown Des Moines, particularly to Younkers, its famous department store, where she bought dresses for herself and for her daughters-in-law, ending with a trip to Men's Clothing to buy shirt, shoes, or other apparel for her chauffeur. Each summer I took her to the Iowa State Fair. She headed first of all for the livestock exhibits, reliving her girlhood on the farm by admiring each horse, each mule, each cow, each hog. She patted everything in reach, calling my attention to its special virtues of size, bone structure, and trueness to breed, and to qualities of intelligence and affection. Most of all she loved horses: the saddle types, the draft types, the all-around work types; but once we stood beside the pen of a giant sow, so huge she filled the pen, hardly leaving room for her family of pigs. Surely everybody realizes that an Iowa blue-ribbon sow is the very queen of sowdom throughout the known universe. When we left, I am positive that sow felt so pleased by Mother's praise that she raised herself to her full circumference and exclaimed, "Come on, judges, I'm the champ. I'm the best there is."

I could tell that Mother was recalling all the animals she had loved and cared for, and even I thought of the horses, the cows, the hogs, the chickens, the occasional banty and guinea, on the old hill farm not far from Grand River in northwest Missouri.

Luncheon was in a big tent, served by the Methodist Ladies Aid or the Baptist Ladies Aid or some other church group—three kinds of meat, mashed potatoes and that unbelievable cream gravy, roasting ears, homemade relishes and preserves, hot biscuits, and country butter. Boys and girls of the church scampered from one customer to another, bringing anything you had forgotten or more of something you ran out of. I do not know what happened to American pie, once found at least in some barbarous form in every restaurant in the land, but at the state fair your waitress could recite the whole luscious list: cherry, raisin, mince, peach, apple, chocolate, banana, coconut, with open-face, cross-barred, meringue, or covered tops, all lovingly baked at home. And for the mature gourmet, master of exotic flavors, sure of his taste, one who had previously sat at this table and knew he was assuming no risk, there was gooseberry, with covered or cross-barred top, the extra sugar sparkling like crystals. If you had already had enough pie that week, you could have cake or watermelon.

After luncheon we made our way to the grandstand, bearing the complimentary passes to front-row boxes that were the birthright of

any Iowa editor. We viewed with trained eyes the current offering
of aerial performers, magicians, dogs or horses, high divers into
small tanks of water. Then came the races—sometimes harness but
now often automobiles, attaining speeds of ninety and a hundred
miles an hour, filling the air with the penetrating smell of burning
castor oil. If we returned for the evening show, we could see the
magnificent display of fireworks.

When I was not home, Mother could see a movie any evening.
They were, of course, black and white, but by the thirties all were
"talkies." Directors were learning to use the new medium as a way
to present dialogue throughout, instead of halting the story so that
the star vocalist could sing a whole song while his girlfriend fixedly
and adoringly listened, knowing that her turn was next. And then
there was radio, now inexpensive, run not on batteries but on ordinary house current, with local and network programs.

I said that Mother abandoned her printer-operator career for one
at the manager's desk, but that statement was not wholly correct.
On press day even front-office staff helped in the back shop, and in
that weekly reassignment of tasks someone with experience was
needed to feed the folder. Our folder, an antiquated model that
Father had salvaged from the *Osceola Tribune*, had three folding
stations, so that an eight-page issue needed two feeders, and a ten-
or twelve-page issue a third. Mother determined to be one of the
feeders for this operation.

Open your evening paper, and you will see the size of the sheet
that is to be handled. Imagine a stack of two hundred or more such
sheets, and that you are to move each sheet a few inches so that side
and top touch gauges—you wish, of course, that the machine fold
your sheet straight and in the middle. You separate a single sheet
from the top of the pile by grasping the corner nearest your right
hand, giving it a flip so that it can float through the air to its proper
position. The sheet must be exactly at the gauges when the machine
calls for it. Obviously it is a delicate maneuver even with two hands,
and impossible with a single left hand. Yet Mother did it and did it
accurately, tens of thousands of times.

I would like to think that some of the magic that she had acquired
as a feeder with two hands—the little pinch to separate the top sheet
blended into the flip that lofted it forward and to the left—simply
flowed into her stubby-fingered left hand. I used to watch her work-

ing as a team folding a thousand or more papers an hour. In fact, I used to try out my own left hand. I had to decide that her wizardry was compounded from an oak-hearted determination not only to survive, but to conquer the spirit that got her out of that flower-strewn room in Dr. Sells's hospital in the first place.

She was then forty-nine. She ran that folder every press day until she left the front office at the age of seventy-seven. Even then she occasionally returned to the office of what became the *West Des Moines Express* to run the folder.

I think Mother was slightly regretful when the firm eventually bought a new press with an attached, automatic folder. But if somewhere a *Celestial Express* is being published, I am sure Mother is not only running the folder but also probably managing the whole shebang.

51

As 1931 opened, the economic situation became increasingly desperate. Two members of our Iowa graduate group received Ph.D.'s and found teaching positions: Thonssen at the College of the City of New York and Murray at the University of Denver. Yet even as we rejoiced in their fortune—these posts were in the rapidly vanishing $3,000 to $3,500 range that young professors in the making had dreamed about—we knew that these could be the last of the good jobs and that even the mediocre positions would disappear before the rest of us entered the market.

One Friday evening the manager of the *Iowan* called me in and told me that my job was to be terminated. Advertising and subscription revenues had steadily dwindled. Somehow I persuaded him to postpone this Friday evening massacre two weeks so Gus and I could readjust our budget.

I was not overly alarmed; I was now involved in writing dissertation chapters and needed the extra time to keep to the schedule I had set for myself. I had continued my study of Fox; I had uncovered so many leads that I was eager to explore his career further. The ever-present course load plus the writing had become heavier and heavier. Our combination dining table–study table became so cluttered with notes that we started eating off our plates while sitting on the front-room sofa bed.

Early in my research I decided that a prime contribution to my discipline would be to write a different kind of study about a man who was an outstanding speaker, minimizing purely personal details and generalized political background, and focusing on the individual as a *speaker*. Charles James Fox was easily one of the best speakers in an age when parliamentary debate was brilliant; among his contemporaries were Edmund Burke, William Pitt, and Richard Brinsley Sheridan. Fox would therefore be a prime candidate for this type of study. My approach would touch only lightly on such details I have mentioned as his compulsive gambling and his life with his mistress, except as they affected his credibility as a speaker, and would stress his parliamentary career: the sources of his ideas, the way he thought out his speeches, the characteristics of his delivery, the impact on his contemporaries. Just as a biographer of Mozart should have, among the usual talents, a sensitivity to music, a study of Fox should reflect a competence about the public communication of ideas. No previous biographer of Fox had adopted this point of view; in fact, no really full biography of Fox had been written.

I was also determined to avoid stereotyped, traditional, mechanical features of dissertation writing. Most dissertations followed a set pattern: first a section on "Statement of the Problem"; then came "Previous Research"; then came an exposition of your own analysis of the problem you had stated; next a chapter headed "Conclusions," which typically ended with a few paragraphs about the problems in this field that still remained to be investigated. Many followed this form, some more rigidly than others; few liked it. Sensible people agreed that if ever you wanted to publish your study, you would need to rewrite it to remove the dissertation odor from it. I decided to develop my theme in narrative fashion, composing specific chapter headings that described the scope of the chapter.

The more I read, the more I found that supported my plan of explaining and describing a speaker as he went about his work. I decided to go back to the Newberry Library, to dig further into its collection of eighteenth-century manuscripts and printed materials. (Father got us due bills on the Sherman, so our hotel bills were offset by ads in the *Tribune*. Late New Year's Eve, after a daylong session at the Newberry, dressed in old clothes, hands and faces dusty, we returned to the Sherman, and, feeling like tramps, walked through the lobby full of men in tuxedos and women in formal gowns, assembling to dance to the music of Ben Bernie and All the Lads.)

Then came the weeks of reading, digesting, analyzing, outlining, and writing. By mid-May I sensed that the end of my graduate career was in view. I wrote and passed the final comprehensive examinations, a three-day effort. My dissertation was approved by professors in both the speech and history departments, so I proceeded to the final typing, in itself a long, arduous task. I deposited it, all 560 pages, with its array of signatures, in the office of the graduate dean. I did not yet have a job but at least I could get my degree.

In the next few days all hell broke loose. The registrar wrote that he had just discovered that I had never had an undergraduate major in speech and, therefore, was not qualified to receive the degree. The dean's office claimed that I had only seventy-eight hours instead of the required ninety. The chairman deplored that I had not taken acoustics, offered by the distinguished George Stewart, head of the physics department, and an influential voice in the graduate school.

So here I was, attempting a degree in a new discipline, in a situation in which procedures were ill-defined. A year previously Brigance had discovered, a scant week before his final examinations, that the graduate school had lost track of him entirely. Any graduate student or professor can contrast my predicament with current practice. Item: A graduate student learns at his first advising session whether his undergraduate preparation qualifies him for advanced courses. But the graduate office at Iowa had not only mis-added my Iowa courses, but had lost track of my Chicago courses. Item: Early in the program, committee and candidate prepare a list of required courses. The candidate knows in advance what is expected. But here, at the last minute, the authorities were raising the question of acoustics. No really good reason existed for requiring a candidate in rhetorical theory to take acoustics; it was simply one of the tough courses strewn in our path as a hurdle. I got out of this difficulty by offering to stand an oral examination in acoustics; I studied the course manual almost nonstop and then confronted the professor, Stewart, in his office. This was quite an experience. Baird shot down the other objections.

Then, two days after I turned in my dissertation, Seashore decided not to approve it.

I made an appointment to see why he had reached down through two administrative layers, the department head and the major adviser, to unscrew my head. I walked into his East Hall office heavyhearted: angry, fearful, apprehensive. Nothing cuts into a man's soul like injustice.

I opened with something like, "I've been told that you have disapproved my dissertation on Charles James Fox."

He looked at me like a judge who had passed sentence on a miscreant and did not have to defend it.

"Your dissertation is far too long. A dissertation should not be longer than fifty or a hundred pages. You have too much biographical information that has been covered in many other books."

I could hardly believe my ears. "The information I have included about Fox's career has been carefully selected. Biographers have been unaware of much of it. I know of only two biographies of Fox this century, and their approach is entirely different from mine. And you have already approved two other dissertations in my field which are longer than mine."

He was unimpressed. "I have conferred with Mr. Mabie and he says your dissertation lacks focus."

"I don't believe Mr. Baird would agree. I developed a detailed outline before I began writing just in order to give the study focus. I have also consulted with Mr. Plum [professor of British history]."

Already he was getting impatient. "I have been dean of the graduate school a long time and I just know"—how can I forget the "I just know"?—"I just know when a dissertation is or is not acceptable."

So the prerogative of this graduate dean included the authority to pass final judgment on a dissertation, overriding the signatures of the professors who themselves knew the field and had approved it—part of an administrative system that concentrated great power at the top. I was dismissed with a "You go talk to Mr. Mabie about this." The conference had been blunt and chilling.

A hundred other Ph.D. candidates, in twenty fields, could tell a hundred other hardship stories. A major adviser could resign or go on leave, and no one else in the department could or would take over. Professional students in law or medicine do not have to face this hazard. Or, after two or three years of courses, the department could suddenly decide that the candidate was unqualified. Eventually departments learned to forestall personal calamaties like these and others by counseling a candidate in the early stages, instead of delaying until the final month or the final week to drop a block-buster on him or her. Even so, no one ever said that attaining a Ph.D. was easy, especially when breaking ground in a new discipline.

I broke the news to Gus, just as we began our noon walk home. I will not repeat what she said, except to report that lightning flashed, thunder crackled, big branches waved in the storm, and smaller trees were uprooted altogether. We still remember meeting an older gentleman, probably forty-five, and his bug-eyed look as this tornado swept past him.

I got no help from Mabie, except his comment that he thought the study was incomplete and unfocused. I should have titled the first chapter "Statement of the Problem" and the last chapter "Summary and Conclusions" so that even those outside the field, those who made the fateful decisions, could have got the point.

Plum would have said that the sources were adequately handled, the boundaries of the study well defined, and that it illustrated originality and breadth. Baird would have been even more em-phatic. I reflect that if I had submitted my M.A. thesis for the Ph.D. dissertation, instead of the other way around, I would have avoided all my troubles. A ponderous topic like "Factors in the Life of Charles James Fox Accounting for His Ability as a Parliamentary Speaker" would have defused all objections. Its length, a hundred pages or so, would have enhanced its acceptability. But maybe not; departments then drew sharp boundaries around themselves, the better to fence in and fence out. A certain suspicion attached to anything from a new field of study.

Father was outraged and offered to write the dean and "touch him up a little." I could have transferred to another campus, but to replan and rewrite a doctoral study with a new adviser could take two years. I could have returned to high-school teaching; Heller, now superintendent at Eveleth, Minnesota, had recently written me. Gus and I banished these possibilities and decided to stick it out where we were.

For us both, it was a low point. I had moments when I felt that if that classy hearse with the walnut-lined compartment, powered by a Continental Red Seal motor and ornamented with a pair of lush, twelve-inch brass headlights, had driven up Clinton Street, I would have cheerfully boarded it.

The ringer came a few days later when I was told that Seashore had exclaimed: "Why does Reid want to study that old Quaker preacher?"

VII. Bad News, Good News

52

Here we were, no degree and no job, and in the middle of the Great Depression.

Just as the word *panic* became too frightening to utter after the financial disasters of last century, the word *depression* has been avoided after what happened in the thirties. It took on a special, bitter meaning, like *holocaust*. When later setbacks came along, they were called merely *readjustments, slumps, recessions*, not *depressions*. Economists explained that these lesser creakings of the machine were not comparable to the depression. Those who survived the depression without exception became more cautious than those who came along later. They had an entirely different way of looking at the dollar. Or at living. They scrimped, cared for, made do, mended, patched, repaired.

Historians remind us that even during the French Revolution's Reign of Terror, most ordinary activities went on as usual. So with the depression. People bowled, ran for office, visited relatives, organized skeet shoots, attended church, enjoyed ball games, won prizes, fell in love—activities that can be called good news. Yet bad news aplenty was on hand to be reported. Trains were derailed and houses burglarized. Army worms and grasshoppers threatened crops. A child fell off a horse; a train thundered around a curve and ploughed into a herd of heifers; a barn burned to the ground. All these were bad news of the common sort; though they dismayed us, we could pick up the pieces and go on about our business.

Then bad news of a more sinister sort began to drift across the copy trays at the *Iowan* and other newspapers; some of these stories were written locally, some were edited from the wire-service bulletins that appeared on the clacking, clattering teletypewriters on the second floor. One story put on our hot, shiny slugs was a small notice that the American Legion was helping unemployed men get in touch with farmers who needed hired help. Another was that a roundhouse normally employing sixty-four men was now employing seven. Corn dropped from thirty-eight cents to twenty-eight cents a bushel in six months' time. And in a single year the number of marriages decreased 40 percent.

Then came column after column of "original notices"—the first public, legal move against debtors. Their prose was ominous: "Unless you appear by stated date, default will be entered against you and judgment and decree rendered thereon"; or "Mortgage will be foreclosed on your NE ½ of SE ¼ of Sec. 24"—and more of the same. Linotype operators dislike fractions, but, more to the point, each original notice almost certainly meant that a demoralized, hardworking family was being uprooted. Occasionally an uprooting led, eventually, to happier conditions, but that did not lessen the immediate despair of losing home and possessions.

Throughout mid-America farmers were unable to repay money borrowed for land, improvements, or seed. The amount might be $10,000, $20,000, or more—with one of my relatives, a mere $300—but in each instance it was a sum impossible for the family to raise. At foreclosure sales, the farm, its implements, and its livestock went for a fraction of their worth. In some Iowa communities farmers found a way of retaliating against insurance companies, land banks, and other mortgage holders; at the foreclosure sales, neighbors agreed to make ridiculously low bids, intimidating any prospective buyer who may have wanted to go higher. They bid in a sulky plow at a nickel, a team of horses at a dime, a farm at a penny an acre. Auctioneers had to close the bidding at these prices; mortgage holders stood by helplessly; and after the sale the "buyers" returned plow, team, and farm to the owner.

The depression followed us to the movies. Pathé and Movietone News pictured the signs outside factory gates: "Employment Office Closed." We saw views of smokestacks with no smoke. We saw long lines at soup kitchens; men selling apples or pencils on the streets; panhandlers seeking nickels or dimes. We heard songs like "Brother, Can You Spare a Dime." Another took a brighter view: "Potatoes are cheaper / tomatoes are cheaper / now's the time to fall in love."

People told about the hitchhiker who stood at the roadside, alternately thumbing east and west. "I don't care which way I go," he said. "I just want to get out of here."

Two blocks from the *Tribune*, Burlington officials commented on another phase of the depression. Freight trains, they said, were alive with unemployed men shifting from place to place. Brakemen found it next to impossible to keep them off. One day they counted thirty-five bums in one car of a westbound freight and seventeen in another, and, the brakeman added, it was not an especially good day for bums, either.

A layoff brought an immediate halt to a family's income; no unemployment checks nor organized welfare was available to bridge the gap. No government agency was at hand to help, or try to help, with loans, support prices, or employment registers. The damage of droughts, floods, and tornadoes, as well as unemployment, had to be battled with a family's own resources. The *Des Moines Register* had conducted a contest to devise a slogan that would best describe the state's opportunities; the winner was, "Horace Greeley Meant Iowa." Yet by the thousands, Iowans decided that Greeley did not mean Iowa at all and struck out for the Pacific coast, where resources were greater. One year in the thirties seventy-five thousand former Iowans met at Lincoln Park in Los Angeles for a reunion celebration.

The miseries of city, town, and farm were even worse at taxpaying time. "How can I pay my taxes when the things I buy cost more, and the things I sell bring less?" cried the farmer. "Why do we spend so much money on roads when we can barely pay the wholesaler, much less the tax collector?" demanded the businessman. School boards faced dwindling revenues; some, after cutting salaries to the bone, had to pay in scrip, much of which was never redeemed. Colleges began to miss payrolls. Graduate students who planned to teach could ask themselves, "If I get a job, will my salary be paid?"

Along with my own worries, I was concerned with those of my students, who felt they were preparing for a world that had ceased to exist. Bright, competent young men and women faced a future of hopelessness and dispair. I knew young musicians who dreamed of a career in a symphony orchestra, but those groups were folding one after another. I knew students in the business school, but corporations were dismissing even junior and senior executives. A conversation with a senior in engineering was typical: "What will you be doing next year?" His face told me the answer, but I awaited the words: "I don't have a job. None of us do. Nobody is interviewing." I could tell he wanted to pour out his problems. "You and Sue were planning to get married," I continued. "We don't see how we can," he answered. "We would have to live with her folks or my folks. Neither of us wants to do that. Besides, they are just hanging on."

Those who could move into a family business after graduation were
luckier than most. Even they, however, were probably displacing a
regular employee.

The most wistful stories never surfaced until afterwards. High
school graduates who had long dreamed of college never got to go.
There were the six Sumner children: the oldest three got a college
education, one becoming a lawyer, one a doctor, one the wife of a
corporation executive. Then the family's income collapsed, cutting
off the three younger members with a high-school diploma; of them
one became a policeman, one a mechanic, and one a secretary in an
insurance office.

Nepotism was an ugly word. Employers decreed: No family
should have two breadwinners. Gus and other graduate wives found
it impossible to get steady jobs. Once both of us kept the Underwood going twenty-four consecutive hours, typing a thesis so its
author could meet a deadline. Its 150 pages at 10 cents a page
yielded $15, a magnificent sum. A psychology major needed help
with tedious sorting and counting, part of an experiment on which
his dissertation was based. In weeks of eye-straining work, Gus
earned $20. She insisted I buy a new suit with it, in case I had a
chance for an interview.

Harshbarger, assigned the new radio course, gathered a small
group, including Gus, to broadcast weekly programs for the university station, WSUI. One of the others was a sophomore, Ed Reim-
ers, who became a professional announcer and for many years was
the voice of Allstate Insurance. The group broadcast drama, stories,
poetry, interviews. Gus took part in radio plays, broadcast a weekly
poetry program, interviewed professors on their specialties—one
being with Lee Travis, professor of speech pathology. Three years
later she secured a similar position on KMBC, one of Kansas City's
two large stations. She was doing well and was enjoying her work
immensely when one day the studio director asked her: "Does your
husband have a job?" "Yes, he does," she said. "Well then, we'll
have to let you go. We can't employ a woman whose husband has
employment."

During the depression, unemployment touched 25 percent of the
working force, a tragic figure; doubly so because most of those out of
work had been the sole breadwinners for their families.

I cherished my relationship with Harshbarger and Barnes. We

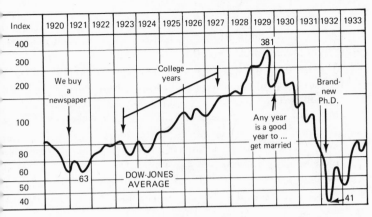

| Index | 1920 | 1921 | 1922 | 1923 | 1924 | 1925 | 1926 | 1927 | 1928 | 1929 | 1930 | 1931 | 1932 | 1933 |

The Dow-Jones Industrial Average is a well-known index to the general prosperity of the stock market and indirectly of the country. In the decades shown it fluctuated between 41 and 381 (sixty years later it touched the 800s and 900s).

The long climb out of the pits that started in 1933 moved sluggishly, taking four years to reach 195. In 1937 it dropped again, touching a low in 1942, the year after Pearl Harbor. Not until 1954, a full quarter-century after that 1929 day, did it again reach 381.

One can plot the major events of one's life alongside this curve and speculate how one's major career decisions might have been affected by the state of the economy.

reminded ourselves that the really important fact was our own good health and that of our loved ones. We told each other that we should be grateful to have a roof over our heads. But it was hard to believe our own words.

Barnes received a letter from the superintendent of nearby Marengo. "We're having our annual declamatory contest next week. We need three judges, but have only $10. Can you persuade three of your seniors to help us out?"

How could anybody pass up a chance to make $10? Barnes proposed that we split the sum three ways, $3 each to Barnes and Reid, and $4 to Harshbarger, who would drive us in his new Plymouth. For $3 one could buy ten cans of pork and beans, ten pounds of hamburger, five loaves of bread, and a pound of butter. The superintendent was amazed to see this top-flight talent appear to judge a mere high-school contest; normally we would command $15 to $25 each. Barnes said easily, "We did not happen to be busy tonight, so we thought we'd come over to judge for you. We're greatly interested in your program." The contestants were de-

lighted. We not only judged but we also spent an hour or mor
giving the contestants individual suggestions. Seldom had $1
brought so much professional time and talent.

In June, Gus and I loaded the Oakland with all our possession
and drove to her home, setting up our summer quarters in the bi
screened-in porch. She got her usual playground job, guiding activi
ties at a park at $100 a month, which would at least see us throug
the summer.

I joined the Des Moines branch of the International Typographi
cal Union to see if I could pick up some linotyping. The secretar
assessed me a reinstatement fee of $25, but was pessimistic abou
chances for finding work. "You can put your name on the board a
the *Register*. They are not hiring, but occasionally some one i
absent and his chair can be filled by a name from the board." At th
Register, the composing-room foreman told me a similar story.
wrote my name on a slip and placed it at the bottom of a waiting lis
of four. "We have been using only one or two substitutes a day," he
said. "But maybe work will pick up, at least in the fall. Come i
every morning before 8:00. If you have been hired for the day, yo
will find your slip opposite a machine number."

Next morning, I decided to walk the forty blocks to the *Register*.
saw no reason for squandering a dime on streetcar fare. I strolle
along the beautiful residential section of Grand Avenue and onto the
Locust Street business district. Stores were just opening: young
men were sweeping sidewalks, washing windows, loading or unload
ing trucks, or, inside, rearranging merchandise. Young women,
nicely dressed, were checking in at office buildings. Was this a
depression? The world seemed busily at work, enjoying the opportunity to be doing something. I reflected how fabulous it would be
to have a steady post. I would be very good at sweeping sidewalks or
washing windows. Fifteen or twenty dollars a week would be a
handsome income for my favorite young married couple.

Eventually I arrived at the imposing *Register and Tribune* building, not so impressive as the Government Printing Office, but considerably more substantial than the Smith-McCarthy Typesetting
Co. I took the elevator, joining the scores of others who were hurrying to work, and found myself inside the composing-room door.
Gathered around twenty machines operators and machinists were
starting their day's labors. I looked at the board; there was my slip,

exactly as I had left it the day before. The name at the head of the list, Jeffers, had been hired, but nobody else. Hagerty, McDonough, and Reid were still at liberty. In another minute I met Hagerty, who explained the customs of the shop. "Jeffers has been on the list a long time. Often he's the only one hired."

I envied Jeffers's lordly position—a substitute who was even now actually at work. I realized that Hagerty and McDonough would be hired before Reid was.

I reintroduced myself to the foreman and, as he was in no mood for extended talk, asked him casually if I could walk around, and took his grunt to mean that he didn't mind. I looked over the shoulders of various operators to see what they were setting. Nothing seemed startling. I located a stylebook and noted that the *Register* capitalized only when absolutely necessary and avoided commas wherever possible. A reporter uses shorter sentences than a senator, a supreme-court judge, or a patent attorney.

I saw no women on the floor. In fact, during my entire linotyping career of thirteen years, I worked alongside only three women, including Mother.

Occasionally I asked an operator a question, hoping he would connect this curious person with the bottom name on the list of substitutes. Jeffers, Hagerty, McDonough, Reid.

Back on the streets, I walked to the State Capitol. By now the sidewalks were crowded. Window washers and sidewalk sweepers had finished their duties and had gone inside, turning into clerks and stock boys. I would love to be a clerk or a stock boy. Inside, people were serving customers and doing the usual shuffling of papers and letters.

At the Capitol I wandered in and around exhibits gathered from early Iowa days: a covered wagon, an ancient buggy, a gown worn by a governor's lady, flags from previous wars. I invested a quarter in luncheon in the basement cafeteria and crossed the wide grounds to the State Historical Library, seeing men in old clothes reading newspapers, or sprawled on the grass, napping, arms folded over eyes to blot out the sunlight.

The library's reading room was crowded; in depression times, men flock to libraries, partly to scan the few "Help Wanted" ads in the newspapers, mainly to relieve their utter boredom. I settled down to an afternoon's reading before starting the long walk home. I decided that my summer game plan would be to report each morning at the *Register*, work if hired, and if not to go to the library to revise the pages of my shattered dissertation.

At the supper table in the Towner household I could get a daily report from Gus's father on the electrical contracting business; it had hit bottom. Contractors bid so fiercely for the limited amount of construction that little margin was left for error or mishap; those who won bids sometimes lost on them. Once her father sold a big pipe wrench off his work bench to get a couple of dollars to meet a few simple needs. Some press nights I went over to the *Booster-Express* in nearby Valley Junction partly to help run a press or a folder but mainly to be around people who were busy and working.

When I reported at the *Register* one morning, I found that I had actually been hired. The first few hours went without incident, but in the afternoon I was given a segment of stock-market reports to set. I lost so much time getting the hang of it that the foreman fussed at me. Next morning when I reported I found my slip had been removed from its slot. When I protested, the foreman said that I had simply not met the required number of lines. When I reminded him that my only difficulty had been with market reports, he reluctantly replaced my slip. On my second day, a good two weeks later, I was whizzing along when he came over and dumped the lines I had already set into the hellbox. "You're working too fast," he muttered. "You're not supposed to go above the required output." The third day came the middle of August, and although no one complained about my being either too slow or too fast, I decided to abandon the field altogether to Jeffers, Hagerty, and McDonough.

I had paid $25 in union dues and had reclaimed only $24—three days at $8 a day. General Sherman said it for all of us: "War is hell." A depression is also hell.

53

Just as I was pondering how to finance another year at Iowa City, the department offered me an instructorship teaching twelve one-hour sections of the beginning speech course, so we returned for another year.

I evolved a plan for revising my dissertation that would not only read like a rhetorical study, but would *look* like a rhetorical study, especially to people outside the area. I gave the opening chapter a conventional title: "Rhetorical Aspects of the Fox Biography." As the body of the study was an analysis of four of Fox's principal speeches, I gave each chapter a plain, unadorned title, such as "The Speech of November 26, 1778." Subheadings through the chapters, such as "Organization of the Speech," "The Speaker's Methods of Persuasion," and "Circumstances under Which the Speech Was Delivered" let the hurried reader know that the study must have been written by someone interested in speech. The subtleties could go by the board; surely no one could say now that the study was not focused. Each chapter ended with "Conclusions" and the final chapter was headed "Summary and Conclusions." Surely any one glancing at it now would "just know" that it was a dissertation. In my mind all of this was a giant step backward, but the plan met the local situation. I could of course use the wide range of original materials I had gathered, the value of which could hardly be questioned. I needed all year to complete the new version, but eventually got the approval of various advisers.

At this point I had a brainstorm: why not take the manuscript home, set it in type, and print it as a book? I could put it on slugs in about the same time I could retype it on a typewriter. The graduate school had long had a rule that candidates must either deposit twenty-five printed copies of their dissertation or post a performance bond, a ploy designed to get dissertations handed in in the form of printer's copy, ready for publication. Nobody, of course, had ever deposited any printed copies, and I doubt whether the requirement of posting a bond was enforced, but printing my study would conform to those lofty rules.

I began the task of setting forty galleys of type. I revised freely as I worked, just as I would have had I been retyping. After the type was set and proofread, I made up the pages, with chapter headings, page numbers, and footnotes, all strictly routine for a printer. I had spent three weeks on what turned out to be a 124-page book.

From a wholesaler I ordered special book and cover paper. From a Des Moines commerical typesetting shop, like the kind I had worked in at Chicago, I selected attractive type for cover and title page. I thought a pressrun of a hundred copies would fill all possible future demands. I took the stack of large, flat, printed sheets to a bindery, which gathered, stitched, and glued them into a book.

A week later I deposited twenty-five copies with the dean. Surely, never before had any candidate printed his dissertation *before* his oral examination. I handed a copy to each professor on my examining committee. No one commented; each acted as if reading a printed dissertation was a daily occurrence.

The dean did not reject this revised version; perhaps he did not even notice it.

The examination was set for the house chamber of the Old Capitol building—Iowa's first legislative hall, the showpiece of the campus—on the afternoon of July 14. The choice of Bastille Day seemed to me appropriate. This prisoner of campus politics now had at least an outside chance to be set free.

I took my place at the long, wide, polished table, facing the six professors charged to represent the graduate faculty. Back in my county courthouse, the case would have been billed as "The State University of Iowa vs. Loren Reid." The odds were formidable. The stale, stagnant air inside seemed twenty degrees hotter than the ninety-degree temperature outside. I settled down for a two-hour session. I had spent the preceding four weeks reviewing every course, everything I could think of.

As chairman, Baird invited me to state the major features of my research. The first questioner, the professor of physics, representing an "outside" department to make sure that humanists and social scientists got away with no shenanigans, suspicious of a study that consisted of paragraphs instead of figures, grumbled: "What's the purpose of all this?" Well, I'm still in deep trouble, I said to myself, but I stressed the value of public discussion and the significance of studying the methods of a man who was preeminently an advocate of such human rights as freedom of speech, freedom of worship, the abolition of the slave trade. He offered no response. After a couple of other questions, I overheard a faint whisper from one member of the committee to another: "It's hot; let's get out of here." Someone mumbled: "Move we approve the candidate." The chairman put the question; there was a murmur of *ayes;* we adjourned.

We had been there twenty minutes.

I found Gus outside and told her I had passed.

"Of course," she said. "I was sure you would." A pause. "You know, we need to get some groceries."

Later I learned that the dean was upset that the examination had been so brief and sent a note around reminding committees to do their duty by future candidates and grill each one a full two hours.

In the years that followed, the twenty-five copies of *Charles James Fox: A Study of an Eighteenth Century Parliamentary Speaker*, deposited in the university library, served a practical classroom purpose. In various seminars, students were required to read and discuss it; the supply of copies made it possible for everybody in the seminar to read it concurrently. Its 124 pages could be read in an evening or two. It became a model, to be equaled or excelled. Both its virtues and its faults could be readily spotted, thus making lively discussion possible. It could serve students as a starting point for their own thinking, still leaving room for modifications, adaptations, and entirely new creations.

One compliment, of cosmic dimensions, I will forever treasure.

To tell it I must leap ahead to a later time. After leaving the Iowa campus I did not return until well after World War II, when I suddenly decided to call on Baird at his office. I walked past three students waiting in the anteroom, opened his door, and said "Hello"; he was advising another student, but greeted me with the cordiality I always cherished: "I'm busy for a while, but if you can come back later, we'll go out to the house and have refreshments." When I agreed, he introduced me to the three who were waiting with these few words: "Students, this is Dr. Reid," and returned to his inner office.

One of the young ladies asked: "Dr. Loren Reid?"

"Yes," I replied, flattered to be readily identified. I looked at her more attentively. She was extremely good-looking: blonde, blue-eyed, well groomed. No jeans those days.

"You're the chairman of the speech department at the University of Missouri?"

"Yes, I am." She had a fine, intelligent way of speaking. I took a step closer.

"And you're the executive secretary of our national association," she went on, using the tones that one reserves for *senator, Nobel Prize winner, quarterback*. Perhaps, also, she was surprised that I was so young looking.

I had to nod my full assent, noting that across her lap she had a mink-dyed muskrat coat. I recognized the breed, as I was making payments on one at the time.

"And," she continued, and there was a breathless pause, "you wrote the dissertation on Charles James Fox."

"Yes, yes I did," I replied, thinking, "Now she is the kind of perceptive, refined student that Baird has always attracted."

"Well," she reflected, drawing a new breath, "I'll be a son of a bitch."

To the best of my knowledge, the graduate dean did not hold up any more dissertations in speech. There were still tensions, frustrations, nervous moments, but the ground had been broken. Over the country, after 1932, departments of speech began to attract bright young men and women candidates by the score. They were to become college presidents, deans of liberal arts colleges, department heads, professors; they held top offices in the profession and won the principal awards; they wrote monographs and text books. They founded, or helped to found, state and regional professional associations. At the end of 1934, there were 48 doctorates in speech; in 1940, 150; in 1944, 319; in 1950, 621. By the eighties, the total had exceeded 8,000. And the number of departments of speech approved to offer the doctorate multiplied tenfold. I can think of no discipline that has had a more rapid growth in so brief a time.

Now I return to the summer of 1932. Commencement was an outdoor, evening ceremony. The heat wave had broken; the sky was clear. With thirty others I stood in rented cap and gown to receive the blue and gold hood of an Iowa Ph.D. We were lined up in pairs, in alphabetical order. Next to me was a speech colleague, Herold Ross, of De Pauw. He had also survived a rumble with the graduate dean.

As we quietly stood, a candidate broke ranks and walked to the head of the file. "What subject are you getting your Ph.D. in?" she asked Number 1.

"Physics."

"Well, I got mine in psychology. I worked harder for my degree than you did."

Before he could retort, she had addressed Number 2. "History." Again she responded: "I worked harder than you did."

Others were from botany, chemistry, engineering, German. The inquirer had obviously been around a long time, had survived much torment, and had died a little in the surviving. To each her answer was positive: "I worked harder than you did."

She came closer and closer to where I was standing. "What did you get your degree in?" She hurled the words at me.

I looked her straight in the eye. I, too, had survived torment and had died a little in the surviving. "Speech."

She reflected, but only a second. "You worked harder than I did," she conceded.

In minutes we heard the stentorian voice of Benjamin Franklin Shambaugh, Professor of Political Science, Introducer of Visiting Lecturers, Grand Marshal of Commencement, head and shoulders well visible above the potted palms with which the temporary platform was decorated. He guided candidates and spectators through the invocation, the address, the awarding of various degrees. Always the Ph.D.'s are conferred last of all, the climax of the program, the tribute to a centuries-old tradition. I can still hear him:

"And now . . . will the candidates . . . for the degree . . . Doc-tor of Phil-os-o-phy . . . please rise."

Seventy-six trombones could not have done it better.

We stood tall and proud, physics and history, botany and chemistry, psychology and speech. As one by one our names were called, we stepped forward to have the hood draped over our shoulders and to receive our diplomas. "With all the rights and privileges thereunto appertaining."

On the printed program, members of the audience could see, if they wished, that one candidate had written about a British orator named Charles James Fox. The Department of Speech and Dramatic Art could now claim to have graduated seven Ph.D.'s thus far. By year's end, nationwide, there would be thirty of us—two for every three states.

The benediction was spoken, and the crowd dissolved. The man was there from the bookstore to recover our caps and gowns. Each of us was congratulated by other students who would some day do what we had done.

I rushed to Gus and we gave each other an enormous hug. Hand in hand we walked to our apartment home. Overhead we could have seen the Big Dipper and the North Star, but we did not trouble to look.

54

The 1932 presidential campaign focused on the nation's sad economy. Since people got little help from the courthouse or the state legislature, they looked to Washington. Hoover was making an active, though plodding, effort to stay in the White House. In their convention, the Democrats passed over an able candidate by the name of Newton D. Baker to select a New York governor by the name of Franklin D. Roosevelt. The country knew little about him; he seemed to be a pleasant-enough fellow. In the 1920 Republican landslide he had been defeated as the vice-presidential candidate; later he had been stricken with paralytic polio. Now he was as fully recovered as he would ever be.

Roosevelt had listened to the convention proceedings in Chicago by radio, and when he heard that he had been nominated, telephoned the delegates that he would accept the nomination in person. That was the first of the many innovations he was to make. Previously the candidate had awaited a formal visit by a committee to tell him what he already knew. Roosevelt's acceptance speech was the first in a series of memorable speeches. He pledged a "new deal" for the American people. He also, incidentally, promised to bring back beer. That must have been good news for the printers at the *Iowan.*

I said that the campaign focused on the economy. There was, however, a more subtle, yet more significant, feature of the campaign: the widespread use of radio communication. We not only had a well-defined issue, but a striking and dramatic way of discussing it. The art had come a long ways since Al Smith's "raddio" four years previously. Roosevelt was to show the country how to use the medium forcefully, dramatically; his masterful speaking set a standard that was not to be surpassed. Gus and I must have heard every major speech of the campaign. Along with many other young couples we could not afford a radio, but whenever an important speech was scheduled, we went with others to a home that could.

Even Hoover, ordinarily as dull a speaker as ever sat in the White House, profited by the medium when he appealed for the farm vote in perhaps the best speech he ever delivered. Speaking in Des Moines, he declared that the country had come within a hair's breadth of going off the gold standard, but he had prevented it. The packed hall roared with approval. Go off the gold standard? might as well level the Capitol. The speech was broadcast from coast to coast.

The national Democratic party chiefs were so shaken by Hoover's speech that they said to the Iowa chiefs: "Tell us whom you want to reply to Hoover, and you can have him." "Send us Jim Reed," said the Iowa group; and the next week the Missouri senator, the most eloquent man in the country when a rebuttal speech was needed, came to Des Moines to answer the president. In Iowa City a roomful of us gathered around a radio in the Harshbarger home to hear the reply. Reed had spoken hardly ten minutes when anyone could see that Hoover's argument was demolished beyond recovery, laid low by this master of censure and ridicule.

Iowa's Democratic county committees, fully aroused, lifted their hopes and urged Democrats to file for offices even in the strongest Republican areas. Iowa, which with an exception or two had gone Republican since the founding of the party, now had a chance to go Democratic.

When the vote was tallied in November, Roosevelt had carried not only Republican strongholds like Iowa but every other state in the nation except Maine and Vermont. The slogan, "As Maine goes, so goes the nation" was altered to "As Maine goes, so goes Vermont." At the New Hampshire–Vermont state line a wag erected a sign: "Leaving the United States." The following summer, the beginning of the dust-bowl years, Iowans erected their own sign, addressed to the new president: "You gave us beer, now give us rain."

At Valley Junction, Father, once a Missouri postmaster, now saw a chance of becoming an Iowa postmaster. Eventually he put a Roosevelt commission alongside the one that Wilson had signed decades before.

Once in the post office, Father gradually relinquished newspaper responsibilities to Mother, and later, to Don, and turned to his first love, writing. As he had often entertained us with yarns about his northwest Missouri days, I suggested that he weave them and his later Iowa experiences into a book. "Write them as weekly installments for the *Booster-Express*," I urged. "Set them two columns wide and save the type. When you get enough type, print a thirty-two-page signature. Keep printing thirty-two-page batches and soon you'll have your book."

This plan suited a newspaper editor's habits of writing, and he set to work. He wrote scores of letters to get the information he needed to make his story accurate. Eventually the book appeared as *Ups and Downs;* copies still survive in family collections and state historical libraries. All in all he reported for, edited, or published seven different Missouri and Iowa newspapers, and in his book described the people he knew and the events of those years.

55

That fall a permanent job seemed unlikely. If I had known what I know now, I would have written speech departments all over the country—there still weren't many—and to English departments that offered speech courses. Even so, I might have landed an appointment that paid not real money, but scrip.

In December, I learned of a second-semester opening at Westport High School, in Kansas City. The salary mentioned was $2,000, but the superintendent wrote that in view of a scheduled 10 percent cut the successful applicant would get only $1,800 the following year—a move that seemed eminently reasonable considering the state of the Union.

I did not want to return to high-school teaching after having spent three years preparing myself for a university post. Yet my professors could only advise me to apply. I saw young Ph.D.'s in other fields, also unable to find positions, stay on at Iowa in research assistantships at poverty-level stipends.

I wrote an application letter, eventually receiving a reply from Superintendent George Melcher to come to Kansas City for an interview. At my own expense.

After an all-day train ride, I arrived late and got a room at the Pickwick. When I awoke, I saw the management had pushed a copy of the *Kansas City Times* under my door. I read the giant headlines: MASSACRE ON UNION STATION PLAZA. Federal officers, taking a gangster to prison, had been attacked by his pals. Machine-gun fire had raked the station platform. It was an early form of terrorism. I had crossed that platform only a few hours before. Gangster warfare, born during Prohibition, was another face of the depression. I wondered what kind of city I had come to.

I met Superintendent Melcher in his downtown office. Slightly stout, with a neat mustache, pointed beard, and twinkly eyes, he reminded me of Santa Claus—maybe that was a good sign. His questions indicated a genuine interest in my credentials.

The proposed teaching schedule included two classes a day of sophomore English, two classes of what was called Expression, and one in Public Speaking. The word *expression* had a nineteenth-century ring about it, recalling Delsarte, Cumnock, Emerson, and other renowned elocutionists. One of my high-school English teachers had been a pupil of the Cumnock system, and my interpretation teacher at Iowa had reflected the elocution tradition. So my education had bridged the gap between the revered, old field, and the new critical, scientific, historical approach that was part of the expanding, exploding concern with communication everywhere around us.

Just as he seemed ready to close the deal, he observed: "Of course you can also direct a play." I thought of my one course with Barnes, of the hours watching directors like Morton and Payne. I also thought of the men selling apples in the streets, the soup lines, the "No Employment" signs on factory gates. "Of course," I said.

Melcher closed the interview with a few kind words, encouraging but noncommittal. At Westport I talked to Principal Holloway and Vice-Principal Miller. I discovered that the enrollment was fifteen hundred, four times that at Vermillion. I inspected the auditorium where I would direct my first play; it had no facilities for spotlights or floodlights. I took the streetcar back to the Pickwick, collected my suitcase, and doubled back to the Union Station, keeping an eye out for federal officers and gangsters, and returned to Iowa City.

I narrated the interview to Gus and to my colleagues. I talked to Arnold Gillette and Hunton Sellman, on the theater staff, about play directing. They drew sketches and recommended books. I would have to light and set the stage as well as direct the actors.

When a letter came offering me the position, Gus and I had already decided to accept. Three years ago we had dreamed of a university position at $3,500. Now we were going to a high school for only a little more than I had received in South Dakota, despite the arduous years of getting a graduate degree. Even so, the new job might have some permanence. And in March, the new president in the White House might actually usher in the New Deal that he had promised. Happy days are here again, the band had trumpeted. After the bad news, good news might be just around the bend.

Right now I would report for duty in Kansas City and rent an apartment; Gus would remain behind, pack our goods, including our new Anglo-Persian, in boxes and barrels for shipment by freight, and join me. I did not realize then that I would be the first Ph.D. in speech to teach in Missouri.

The evening before my departure, the Harshbargers invited us to supper. We had just finished when the Bairds arrived. "How nice," I thought, "that the Bairds should happen to drop in." In a few moments, couple by couple, just about everybody in the department showed up for the evening. It was a cheering farewell party. I felt doubly sorry about leaving. Iowa City seemed to be the center of all things vital.

Next afternoon I stood on the rear platform of the Rock Island when it pulled out of the station, waving at Gus as long as she was in sight. I saw Iowa City get smaller and smaller and finally disappear altogether, gradually being replaced by acres of snow-covered fields. When the train stopped at Grinnell, I looked at the nearly empty platform but I could visualize the times when it was crowded with undergraduates, starting home for the holidays. At Des Moines I transferred to the southbound branch and several hours later crossed the border into my native state.

I had been away twelve years, long enough to get a high-school diploma, three college degrees, and a bride. It was time to come back to Missouri.

Acknowledgments

The main thread of this semiautobiographical report is, of course, my recollection of the events. My parents preserved the letters I wrote during the years I was away from home, so this correspondence supplies details that otherwise might have been blurred.

I have also consulted periodical sources such as *The Osceola Tribune*, *The Osceola Sentinel*, *The Des Moines Capital*, *The Des Moines Register and Tribune*, *The Washington Post*, *The Iowa City Press-Citizen*, *Grinnell and You*, and, occasionally, *The New York Times*, and *The Kansas City Star*. Annuals such as *The Cyclone* (Grinnell) and *The Hawkeye* (University of Iowa) have also been useful.

The public-relations offices of the Burlington and the Rock Island have answered inquiries about routes and timetables. The State Highway Commissions of Iowa and Missouri have provided road maps of Missouri and Iowa for the twenties. The *Des Moines Register* frequently printed highway maps so that its readers could be alerted to new construction and the accompanying detours.

Directors of special collections and services at The State Historical Society of Missouri, the University of Missouri, the Iowa State Historical Society, the University of Iowa, and Grinnell College have helped supply answers to a wide variety of questions. The University of Iowa, Grinnell College, and the Government Printing Office furnished photographs. I have consulted pertinent parts of the Shambaugh, Seashore, Mabie, and Department of Speech and Dramatic Art papers at the University of Iowa, and sections of the minutes of the trustees' meetings at Grinnell College.

H. Clay Harshbarger, *Some Highlights of the Department of Speech and Dramatic Art* (Iowa City: The University of Iowa, 1976), comments on problems incurred in the development of graduate study in speech. David G. Barnes, *The Contributions of William Norwood Brigance to the Field of Speech* (Ann Arbor: University

288 **Finally It's Friday**

Microfilms, 1970), describes difficulties in earning a doctorate in speech during the early period.

Cecil F. Lavell told the story of his amnesia most fascinatingly in "The Man Who Lost Himself," *Atlantic Monthly*, November 1917.

The Sioux Falls Argus-Leader printed a feature by Leone Hart Koster about Anne Vaith's boardinghouse in its 2 May 1977 issue. George Deklotz, then coach, and Orville Westlund, secretary to the superintendent, supplied information about Vermillion High School teachers, students, and events.

Don Reid, for thirty-five years managing director of the Iowa Press Association, shared pictures of Osceola days from his collection and bolstered my memory of various incidents.

Collier's Weekly for 11 January 1928 carried an interview of Grantland Rice with E. C. Quigley. Quigley died in 1960, at the age of eighty-one; around the country metropolitan newspapers also carried stories (for example, *Kansas City Star*, 11 December 1960).

Once more I express my deep appreciation to the University of Missouri Press for the interest its director and staff have shown in all phases of the publication of this book.

Index